Buddhist and Taoist Practice in Medieval Chinese Society

Ascetic Śākyamuni. White stone sculpture with traces of black and greenish pigment on hair curls. Yüan dynasty. Courtesy of the Royal Ontario Museum, Toronto, Canada.

Asian Studies at Hawaii, No. 34

Buddhist and Taoist Practice in Medieval Chinese Society

Buddhist and Taoist Studies II

Edited by David W. Chappell

Asian Studies at Hawaii
University of Hawaii
UNIVERSITY OF HAWAII PRESS

© 1987 University of Hawaii Press
Manufactured in the United States of America

Library of Congress Cataloging-in-Publication Data

Buddhist and Taoist practice in medieval Chinese society.

  (Buddhist and Taoist studies ; 2) (Asian studies at
Hawaii ; no. 34)
  Includes bibliographies and index.
    1. Buddhism—China—History. 2. Taoism—History.
3. Buddhism—Relations—Taoism. 4. Taoism—Relations—
Buddhism. I. Chappell, David W., 1940-   .
II. Series. III. Series: Asian studies at Hawaii ;
no. 34)
DS3.A2A82   no. 34 [BQ120]   950 s [294.3'0951] 86–30808
ISBN 0–8248–0957–2 (pbk.)

Contents

v

BUDDHISM AND TAOISM IN CHINESE SOCIETY

Abbreviations

HTC *Hsü Tsang-ching* (Supplement to the Tripiṭaka). Hong Kong: Fo-ching liu-t'ung ch'u, 1967. 150 vols. This is a reprint of the *Dai-Nihon Zoku-zōkyō*. Kyoto, 1905–1912. 150 boxes.

T *Taishō shinshū daizōkyō*. Tokyo: Daizō Shuppan Kabushiki Kaisha, 1924–1932. 100 vols.

TT *Tao tsang*. Taipei: I-wen, 1977 reprint edition. 61 vols.

ZZ *Dai-Nihon Zoku-zōkyō* (Supplement to the Manji edition of the Tripiṭaka). Kyoto: Zōkyō Shoin, 1905–1912. 150 boxes.

Introduction

DAVID W. CHAPPELL

A pressing need in the recent study of Chinese religion is to connect Buddhist and Taoist doctrine with the actual activities of practitioners. In the past there have been some excellent institutional studies of Buddhism in China (by Ch'en, Gernet, Welch, and others), and there is a growing body of translations and doctrinal studies. What has been lacking has been a way to integrate the depth of Buddhist insights and doctrines with our knowledge of the actual practice and experience of Chinese Buddhism historically. In examining pivotal figures and movements in Chinese Buddhism from the fifth to the twelfth centuries this volume attempts to reconnect theory and practice so that we can see how Chinese Buddhism evolved in response to the social and cultural context of China.

After entering China, Buddhism intermingled with the needs and expectations of people in society (chapters by Lai and Corless) before it could develop its own self-sufficiency to rise to its greatest heights in the four major Chinese Buddhist schools (chapters on T'ien-t'ai by Donner, on Pure Land by Pas, on Ch'an by Zeuschner, and on Hua-yen by Shim). Religion and society, church and state, were never separate in China. Although the government used religion for its own support (chapter on Emperor Hsüan-tsung by Benn), eminent Buddhists also used government sponsorship for Buddhist purposes (chapter by Dalia). Usually the interaction was not with the government, however, and the book ends in the Sung dynasty with a study of the development of a new sermon format to meet the needs of laity (chapter by Levering). Accordingly, this volume is arranged roughly in historical sequence into three stages: the influence of Chinese culture upon the early practice of Buddhism in China, the independent development of Chinese Buddhism, and later efforts to apply Buddhism in Chinese society.

The essay by Charles Benn is the only study not focused on Buddhism. Thus this volume complements Volume 1 in this series, which centered on Taoist themes. Nevertheless, Benn's analysis of the way in which Emperor Hsüan-tsung implemented his Taoist ideology provides a fascinating example of the imperial role in Chinese religious life. Since the T'ang dynasty was generally pro-Taoist, it also provides important information on the political context in which Buddhism found itself during its golden era when Pure Land, Hua-yen, and Ch'an became established movements.

The theme of the volume is religious practice. Chapter 1, by Whalen Lai, breaks new ground by creatively reconstructing the context and significance of China's earliest preceptual text *(T'i-wei Po-li Ching)* for guiding Buddhist laity. Lai shows how a Buddhist cultic movement (the *i-i*) grew up in imitation of the behavior of monks and provided an alternative to the traditional family orientation of Chinese society. These lay associations were based on faith in good works as a means to a better rebirth as men or gods *(jen-t'ien);* sociologically they were connected to the "*sangha*-households" for support of the monasteries. Although following Buddhist models of behavior, they lacked understanding of basic Buddhist doctrine and were later classified as pre-Hīnayānic. Nevertheless, Lai shows how these groups won enormous popularity for Buddhism in early China because of their economic and religious benefits and formed a popular Chinese view of Buddhism which is still pervasive among Chinese today.

The evolution of Chinese Buddhism in the midst of Chinese cultural values persisted in the sixth century. For example, Buddhism and Taoism responded to the perennial Chinese concern for long life (or immortality) in a variety of ways which sometimes complemented each other and sometimes challenged each other. The ambiguity between Buddhism and Taoism at this time is neatly illustrated by the spiritual journey of T'an-luan. In Chapter 2 Roger Corless observes that T'an-luan was often known to his contemporaries as a Taoist sage expert in alchemy and practices for longevity. Although he was known in Japan as a Chinese pioneer of Pure Land Buddhist doctrine, many of his texts are filled with visualizations reminiscent of communication with Taoist deities. Thus T'an-luan is a fringe figure who integrated Taoist and Buddhist concerns through the Buddha of Infinite Life, O-mi-t'o-fo (Amitābha).

The four major schools that arose in the Sui-T'ang era (589–906) are considered the high point of Chinese Buddhism. However, it is not quite correct to say that they achieved this reputation by concentrating so fully on Buddhism that they cut themselves off from Chinese culture and functioned independently within the Buddhist tradition. The work of translation, exegesis, and *vinaya* study was actually more specialized and removed from Chinese society than were the T'ien-t'ai, Pure Land, Ch'an, and Hua-yen religious movements. As the essays by Donner, Pas, Zeuschner, and Shim reveal, these four schools are the pinnacle of Chinese Buddhism because they relate the most developed Mahāyāna Buddhist insights and practices to living experience in a way Chinese could understand. Specifically they show Buddhism engaged in the personal arena where the focus is on how individuals can realize calmness and insight, freedom and compassion, in the midst of the struggles and contradictions of their inner and outer lives.

Neal Donner's essay on Chih-i (538–597) illustrates this theme very well. The aim of Mahāyāna Buddhism is not aversion to the world, although aversion may be helpful at times. Rather, Mahāyāna asserts that there is no final separation from the world since we carry it with us and embody its causes and conditions. This Buddhist insight, which grew out of the *nonmonastic* Indian Mahāyāna tradition, agreed with the Chinese affirmation of history and society. Accordingly, as a Buddhist and Chinese, Chih-i did not recommend abandoning the world but affirmed the nonduality of enlightenment and the passions. That is to say, the Buddhist response at its highest level is calmness and insight into the conflicts and pain of ordinary existence and thereby provides a means of liberation in the midst of life. Accordingly, Chih-i devised guidelines for his advanced students showing them how to practice "meditation on evil." Chih-i has been called the Aquinas of Chinese Buddhism; because his thought integrated vast areas of Buddhism, it is complex, comprehensive, and profound. Donner's essay is significant because it penetrates one of the most revolutionary and subtlest developments of Chih-i's thought. As the first study of T'ien-t'ai attempted in North America in more than two decades, Donner's contribution makes an auspicious new beginning and demonstrates the growing sophistication of Buddhology in the west.

Shan-tao (613–681) represents a very different response to this "world in us" dilemma. Struck by the futility of attaining liberation from oneself and by oneself and awed by the power of Pure Land visualizations, he advocated devotion to Amitābha and rebirth in his Pure Land as a means of escaping this world. Although at first glance this philosophy appears to be world-denying, Shan-tao had his own way of affirming mundane existence. His writings strongly oppose the elitist attitudes of religious professionals who felt that the benefits of Amitābha's compas-

sion were available only for those who had considerable religious training. On the contrary, Shan-tao defended the accessibility of the Pure
Land for ordinary people, and he developed liturgical practices, art, and
writings to support their involvement. Indeed, he went so far as to claim
that the filial piety practiced by the laity was as efficacious as devotion to
the Buddha by clergy. In the Japanese tradition Shan-tao has been
cherished almost exclusively for recommending *nembutsu* (invoking the
name of the Buddha) as sufficient for salvation. Because of the fresh
comprehensive research of Pas, however, we see the diversity of Shan-
tao's skills and the wide variety of devotional means that he recommended. Thus we can appreciate Shan-tao's relentless effort to affirm the
value of ordinary virtue and simple devotion as a legitimate means to
make contact with the saving power of Amitābha.

Ch'an Buddhism is considered the crowning conclusion of Chinese
Buddhism, and its literature is the most voluminous of all the schools.
Nevertheless, in its concern to realize immediately one's Buddha-nature
and to speak from the enlightened point of view, it offered few guides for
basic practice. Zeuschner's essay is exceptional for making available for
the first time material from Northern Ch'an which did discuss meditation and expedient aids. Emphasis is given not to lengthy practices, however, but to invocation of basic principles and scriptures (the Five *Upāya*)
to affirm the task of constant mental awareness in action. Through practicing perpetual mindfulness undisturbed and unimpeded by mental conceptualization and attachments, one's mind becomes identical to the
Buddha himself. It is with this orientation that Ch'an cut through the
encumbrances of the Buddhist establishment and focused attention on
immediate experience, the place of enlightenment.

Probably the most sophisticated and inaccessible of Chinese Buddhist
developments is Hua-yen philosophy. Nevertheless, Buddhist doctrine
arose out of practice and was read in order to illuminate personal experience and transformation. When doctrine became too preoccupied with
intellection, there usually was a voice to call it back. Such a person for
Hua-yen was Li T'ung-hsüan (646–740), whose synthesis of doctrine and
practice was the inspiration for Korea's major reformation by Chinul
(1158–1210). Shim's study of Li T'ung-hsüan, the first to appear in
English, provides an important corrective in Hua-yen studies by empha-
sizing the understanding of religious practice in Hua-yen. Specifically
Shim explores the role of faith as understood by Fa-tsang and criticized
by Li T'ung-hsüan. Instead of basing himself on the gradual movement
toward enlightenment through the step-by-step development of "faith,
understanding, practice, and realization" over countless lifetimes, Li
stressed the idea that one is already identical with Buddhahood. Indeed,

this faith in the purity of our Buddha-nature, the *dharmakāya,* is the initial experience of enlightenment and provides the necessary basis for all practice. This conviction was also a crucial element in the Ch'an doctrine of sudden enlightenment, and like Shen-hsiu (d. 706) Li T'ung-hsüan explained away the necessity of practice through "three aeons" or "three rebirths" (see Zeuschner's essay). Using the layman Sudhana as the model of religious practice and attainment, Li proclaimed the possibility of enlightenment for ordinary people in this lifetime and in this body.

What are the achievements which T'ien-t'ai, Pure Land, Ch'an, and Hua-yen share in common? I would suggest that when Buddhism entered China, it offered a means for interpreting and mitigating the suffering of the people during and after the collapse of the Han dynasty. While Buddhism gave many external sources of support (new literature, saviors, rituals, and a new community, the *sangha*), it was often wrongly thought to offer another form of Taoist supernaturalism, ascetic withdrawal, or conventional morality. It is to the credit of the Sui-T'ang schools that they broke the boundaries of conventional religiosity based upon elitism, karmic retribution, rebirth in heaven or hell, and the quest for immortality by their emphasis on transforming ordinary life into "wondrous existence" *(miao-yu)* through faith, insight, and mindfulness. Thus these four schools offered transcendence in the midst of life and broke down the distinctions between sacred and secular activities.

These breakthroughs became the gifts that Chinese Buddhism offered to Korea, to Japan, and now to the west. In Chinese history, however, the weight of the early Buddhist establishments continued in the face of these reformations. Moreover, as Chinese political structures reconstituted themselves in the T'ang and Sung, they worked to exclude Buddhism from conspicuous participation in society. As an illustration of the limits placed on Buddhism by the political context within which it lived, Charles Benn offers a surprising new study of how Emperor Hsüan-tsung vigorously used religious establishments for his own self-glorification.

By instituting a network of temples *(miao)* throughout China for the worship of his ancestor Lao-tzu and of himself as Sage Emperor, Hsüan-tsung developed his own personality cult to consolidate his power. This elevation of Taoism as a means of political legitimation shows the potential for theocracy in China and suggests that Taoism was more suitable for this purpose than Buddhism, which was foreign in its origins and more independent in its ethics and its religious and social organization.

In spite of political efforts to contain Buddhism safely within its monastic walls, some officials tried to involve Buddhists with their regimes because of the prestige of Buddhism in Chinese society. After the

fall of the pro-Taoist T'ang dynasty, the early Sung turned to Buddhism
for political leverage, much as the Sui dynasty (589–618) had done before
them. A notable example of this strategy was the court sponsorship of
the monk Tsan-ning (919–1001). He had developed literary pursuits in
his youth and thereby won the support of influential monks and officials. Although he was made a member of the Han-lin Academy and was
commissioned by the emperor to compile the *Sung Biographies of Eminent Monks* and *An Outline History of the Sangha,* the court never
matched either Sui Wen-ti or Emperor Hsüan-tsung in its use of religion
to consolidate the empire. Dalia, however, gives a vivid picture of how
the government and the *sangha* were interrelated through informal connections. Following Buddhist doctrine, Tsan-ning evolved a comprehensive vision of harmony between Buddhism, Confucianism, and Taoism
and between Buddhism and the state. Accordingly, Tsan-ning served the
new Sung dynasty as a voice for integration and also became a model of
Chinese Buddhist historiography for later scholars. Dalia's essay, the
first study of Tsan-ning to appear in English, analyzes the steps in Tsan-
ning's rise to prominence and examines the rationale he gave for his
political involvement.

While Tsan-ning excelled in writing history, Ta-hui (1089–1163) helped
to develop a better method for Chinese Buddhist masters to instruct lay
society. As Levering carefully demonstrates in Chapter 9, Ta-hui effectively pioneered a new teaching device aimed at the laity: the *p'u-shuo*
sermon. Unlike the *T'i-wei Po-li Ching,* however, Ta-hui did not teach a
doctrine which was only preparatory for enlightenment and liberation.
Rather, he used the provisional truth of karma and morality to lead his
listeners to see the need for an ultimate truth transcending the confines of
karma without negating it—namely, the truth of *śūnyatā.* Thus Ta-hui
showed a way for Ch'an to be involved constructively with the world and
also helped to forge a path of enlightenment in the daily life of laity.

The concerns expressed in Lai's essay (Chapter 1) find resolution at the
end in Levering's study of Ta-hui (Chapter 9). Laity can emulate monks
not only in form but in content. The time frame covered in this volume is
seven hundred years, time enough for Buddhism to move from child-
hood to maturity in China, time enough to change from being a foreign
import and to have fused with Chinese cultural values and patterns.

In spite of historical moments when Chinese Buddhism expressed
enlightenment in the midst of daily life, most Chinese Buddhists perpe-
tuated the model from the fifth century whereby they emulated the
behavior of monks and sought a better rebirth. Perhaps the major permanent change in Chinese religiosity was the almost universal acceptance
of the western Pure Land as the goal of this rebirth and the substitution

of Buddhist saviors in place of folk deities. Otherwise, the heights realized by the Sui-T'ang schools were lived out by only a few.

If the majority of Chinese Buddhists did not adopt all the various innovations traced in this volume, at least these new developments became part of the cumulative tradition. Thus at special times certain individuals, monasteries, or regions were able to embody some of these advances which had become enduring options within China's religious heritage. Our effort has been to note those innovative points in Chinese Buddhist history when religious pioneers planted new seeds. What still remains to be done is to survey regions of China to discover which of these new developments had become widespread and prominent features of Buddhist practice at various periods in medieval Chinese society.

Buddhist and
Taoist Interactions

1

The Earliest Folk Buddhist Religion in China: *T'i-wei Po-li Ching* and Its Historical Significance

WHALEN W. LAI

Buddhism entered China in the first century and found a foothold after the collapse of the Han dynasty in A.D. 220. In the Wei-Chin period (220–420), neo-Taoist interest in the emptiness philosophy of the *Prajñā-pāramitā* sutras led to what is known as Gentry Buddhism in the south, while non-Chinese invaders in the northern dynasties practiced Caesaro-papist State Buddhism. These two traditions are fairly well known in English studies.[1] However, a third and later tradition, the Plebeian Buddhism that took on independent expression late in the fifth century, has escaped general notice. The only survey of this tradition in English is Kenneth Ch'en's short summary in *The Chinese Transformation of Buddhism*. As Ch'en notes, the Chinese-fabricated sutra, the *T'i-wei Po-li Ching* (henceforth abbreviated as *TWPLC*), is the earliest expression of this tradition and represents the first known attempt to align the *pañca-śīla* (the five precepts in Buddhism) with the five Confucian "perma-nents" (virtues) and the five element theories in Taoism. The sutra there-fore signaled a Buddho-Taoist synthesis in early Chinese Buddhist his-tory.[2] The full significance of the sutra's intention and the social movement it created, however, have not been explored. The relationship between this early folk Buddhist faith and the later folk Buddhist reli-gion, as studied by Daniel Overmyer, needs also to be better understood.[3] The present study attempts to put this early tradition in its historical and international perspective in fifth and sixth-century China and to provide pointers for understanding the direction of later popular Buddhism.

In 1942, Tsukamoto Zenryū had called attention to this plebeian tradi-tion within Northern Wei Buddhism and reconstructed fragments of this

lost sutra.[4] More recently Makita Tairyō of Tokyo University has identified a Tun-huang text (Stein no. 2051 in the British Museum) as the second scroll of the *TWPLC*.[5] The availability of the *TWPLC* now permits
a better appreciation of the contents of this faith, and a topical translation of the Tsukamoto fragments and the Stein text is presented later in
the chapter. Makita also reports discovering in the Pelliot manuscripts
what might be remnants of the first scroll of the *TWPLC*.[6] Until the final
critical edition of the texts is compiled, a full translation and analysis
cannot be made.[7] Important as the preceding scholars' work has been, I
believe certain aspects of this faith have been overlooked. The following
historical background pertains to the emergence of this third Buddhist
tradition in China.

HISTORICAL ORIGINS

The plebeian Buddhist faith is known as *Jen-t'ien-chiao,* "Man-Heaven
Teachings," and its social organization is known as *i-i* or *i-hui*.[8] It did not
take form until the gentry Buddhist tradition had secured a general
respect for this foreign faith and perfected the craft of apologetical writings. However, it was the state support of the *saṅgha* fellowship in the
north that enabled the Buddhist establishment to expand in ways unknown to the southerners. By the middle of the fifth century, the temple
establishment had moved beyond the earlier, simpler lifestyle of the
ascetic monasteries to being owners of grand temple estates and temple-
related economic enterprises. Emperor T'ai-wu (r. 424–452) was understandably shocked, in 446, by the discovery of a well-endowed temple in
Ch'ang-an, different from his expectations of "the life of poverty"
proper to monkhood. The temple had gold and silver (donations) and
bows and arrows, perhaps to help defend its holdings in a chaotic period.
Probably through the instigation of the Confucian Tsui Hao, the temple
was shown to be equipped with secret chambers for alleged debaucheries
(possibly only special alcoves for female devotees). What followed was
the Buddhist persecution of 446 and a temporary setback for the *saṅgha*.
The decree was lifted in 452 when T'ai-wu died, and a Buddhist revival
began, led by the monks previously enslaved and brought back from
Liang-chou on the northwestern frontier of China.

Liang-chou had been a vibrant Buddhist center since the fourth century. In touch with the Central Asian outpost of the Chinese empire, Tun-
huang, Liang-chou inherited many more Central Asian Buddhist practices than were available in the Buddhist centers of the central plain of
China. A North Indian, Shih-hsien, was appointed leader of the *śramaṇas* in 452, but the architect of the revival was his successor, the

famous T'an-yao.[9] T'an-yao apparently followed two conscious policies: on the one hand, to appease the *tathāgata*-kings of Northern Wei with grand projects in and near the capitals; on the other hand, to create a new and independent social basis for the dharma. Thus, after having finished sponsoring the carving of Buddha statues, "miraculously" modeled upon the living and dead emperors, T'an-yao sponsored, when the opportunity arose, the creation of *sangha*-households and Buddha-households:

> T'an-yao petitioned and proposed that members of the P'ing-ch'i domain [left without a supervisor at a lord's death] and any peasant who could donate sixty measures of grain to the *sangha*-officials every year should be made members of the *sangha*-household; and that the grain should then be designated *sangha*-grain to be used to help the needy in lean years. He also petitioned that grave offenders and official slaves be constituted into Buddha-households and made servants of the temples as cleaners, sweepers, and transporters of grain. Emperor Kao-tsu consented and soon *sangha*-households, *sangha*-grain, and temple-households spread all over the provinces.[10]

Such a program was not illegitimate since the Buddhist *vinaya* permitted the Buddha and *sangha* to "hold property." T'an-yao was probably also drawing upon practices in Tun-huang or Liang-chou. In this way, a separate monk bureaucracy was set up beside the civil administration with its own economic base among the peasantry. The peasant members were regarded as part of a metaphysical *sangha* and not originally, and never in theory, involuntary hereditary slaves of one particular temple.[11] The mass support for this program meant that the monks must take on the burden of ideologically edifying the plebeians:

> The leader of the *śramaṇas*, T'an-yao, grieved over the previous destruction [in 446–452] and rejoiced over the present revival and prosperity. Thereupon he gathered a group of monks in the Grotto Temple in Pei-t'ai to translate various sutras so that the dharma would be transmitted to later generations and continue unbroken. At that time, there was the monk T'an-ching, who, seeing that the older translations of various sutras were lost in the fire [of persecution] and there was nothing to instruct the common people with during those days of the Buddhist revival, produced thereupon the *T'i-wei Po-li Ching* in two scrolls. The purpose was to lead the people to higher understanding, but there was much that was false in its teachings. Thus it says that the T'ai-shan in the east is called "*t'ai*" in Chinese because, this being where yin and yang alternate, it is called "*t'ai*" or "change." . . . [There were other flaws.] . . . In the old catalogue of sutras, there was a *T'i-wei Po-li Ching* in one scroll, the teaching of which is in keeping with other sutras. But T'an-ching mixed stones into gold and therefore the work is said to be a fabrication. Its whereabouts now are unknown. In the early years of the K'ai-wang period [581–600], the people

around Kuan-nei [the Wei River] still frequently practiced the T'i-wei cult.
Members of this *i-i* would put on robes and hold bowls every fortnight, keeping the precepts and watching over each other. The cult is widespread with
many followers.[12]

The author of this piece is Tao-hsüan (596–667) writing in the *Hsü Kao-
seng-chuan* concerning T'an-yao. Several points are evident: that the
TWPLC was fabricated for the people after the persecution for expedient teaching purposes, that the cult was very popular up to the end of the
sixth century, and that something happened in the seventh such that, by
the time Tao-hsüan was writing, the once popular treatise had been
declared a *wei-ching,* "fabricated sutra," and already was lost.

The *i-i* associations were clearly associated with the *sangha*-household
experiment. In nature they were different from the gentry circle of Hui-
yüan at Lu Shan or the Ching-chu-she association under the Ch'i prince
Wen-hsüan-wang or the Fa-she association of the Liang monk Seng Yu.
The *i-i* was no intellectual, aristocratic, or learned gathering. As a popular movement, it anticipated the Sung Buddhist associations, although in
ideology it was very different from those later Pure Land devotional
communities.[13] From the surviving inscriptions at the various cave sites
where *i-i* members had pooled their resources to build statues, we know
that the society varied in size from as few as ten members to as many as
two hundred. In the T'ang period, there were *i-i* numbering up to a thousand and even two thousand members. Although they constituted a con-
tinuation of the Wei *i-i,* the T'ang associations had already shifted their
loyalties to sutras other than the *TWPLC.* Male members of an *i-i* or
i-hui called themselves the "sons of *i* (village)" and female members were
"mothers and daughters of *i.*" Large T'ang associations would have
grand masters of *i (ta-i-chu)* above the lesser masters *(i-chu)* and divided
their labor in terms of their being responsible for inner or outer, eastern
or western, sides of a cave or in terms of the elements in the sacred site:
path, Buddha-hall, pagoda, pillar, heavenly palace, tablet, bell, flag,
incense table, burner, lamp, this or that Buddha or bodhisattva statue,
and so forth.[14] Even communist scholars, who have denounced the
"blood and tears" that went into building other monumental projects
like the Great Wall, recognize that Buddhism, as a religion, was able to
mobilize people from all classes—without physical coercion—to build
artifacts.

The zeal to build statues and to copy sutras, though absent in the
TWPLC, was characteristic of the *i-i.* This pharisaic show of outward
piety was later displaced by the more evangelical activities of the Sung
dynasty Pure Land *she.* Already by the T'ang dynasty (618–906) the

TWPLC was recognized by scholar-monks to be untrustworthy and was being pushed aside by the rise of the sinitic Mahāyāna schools which formed cults based on Indian sutras and Buddhas other than Śākyamuni of the *TWPLC*. T'ien-t'ai, Hua-yen, and, above all, Pure Land were sponsoring their own associations. More generous monks like Tsung-mi recognized the legitimacy of the Jen-t'ien-chiao,[15] but most Chinese doctrinal classifications in the major schools would not regard it to be "the word of the Buddha." The demise of the organized Jen-t'ien-chiao cult notwithstanding, its basic philosophy—karmic rebirth as humans or as gods *(jen-t'ien)*—survived the centuries and can be found in the sectarian writings uncovered by de Groot in this century.

THE *Jen-t'ien* PHILOSOPHY

The term *"jen-t'ien"* was used by Liu Ch'iu (437–495) in an early doctrinal classification system *(p'an-chiao)*.[16] The Buddha was considered to have taught the Jen-t'ien-chiao during the first twenty-one days after his enlightenment:

> The first period [of instruction] is when the Buddha, soon after his enlightenment, preached to the two merchants, T'i-wei (Trapuṣa) and Po-li (Bhallika), along with their five hundred followers, the five precepts *(pañcaśila)* and the ten good deeds, as well as the law of karmic retribution in samsara. In other words, he taught the *Wu-chieh pen-ch'i-ching* [that is, *TWPLC*]. This was because the recipients of his teaching did not have as yet the necessary roots conducive to the attainment of the trans-samsara path.[17]

The legend of Trapuṣa and Bhallika is scriptural.[18] T'an-ching utilized this fact to produce the lay-oriented scripture, the teaching of which was basically about the performance of good deeds for the sake of better rebirth as humans *(jen)* or in heaven *(t'ien)* as gods. According to Liu Ch'iu, the Buddha then went to the Deer Park at Benares and for the next twelve years taught the Hīnayāna or Triyāna teachings, which are preserved as the Hīnayāna sutras. The Mahāyāna teachings found in the *Prajñā-pāramitā* corpus and the *Vimalakīrti nirdeśa* were revealed by the Buddha in the succeeding thirty years. After that, the Ekayāna (One Vehicle) teaching was taught and that lasted another forty years. Finally, according to the opinions of the time, even the *Lotus Sutra* was superseded at the last moment by the *Mahāparinirvāṇa Sutra* and its "teaching of permanence" (that is, a permanent Buddha-nature). It can be seen, then, that the Jen-t'ien-chiao of the *TWPLC* was the most primitive and the most elementary doctrine, inferior even to the Hīnayāna teachings. I shall use the term "pre-Hīnayāna" to characterize it below.

Although it is often said that Chinese Buddhism was from the start influenced by Mahāyāna, the existence of this popular pre-Hīnayāna faith should alert us to the fact that despite the knowledge of the Mahāyāna ideology, the actual maturation of Mahāyāna consciousness and the sinitic implementation of the bodhisattvic vocation required time. The reason why the *TWPLC* and its related cultus disappeared in the T'ang is that the Chinese Buddhists around the second half of the sixth century finally clearly distinguished Mahāyāna from Hīnayāna and advanced toward a full Mahāyāna faith. The pre-Hīnayānist character of the *i-i* also explains why the *i-i* cannot be seen as an ideological forerunner of the later Sung Buddhist *she*. The Lotus societies *(Lien-she)* in the Sung were monks and lay-bodhisattvic societies in which the leadership passed increasingly to the autonomous laity. They were committed to the Mahāyāna doctrine that nirvana is samsara and to the program of universal salvation. The members consciously took the bodhisattvic vow ("Above to attain nirvana and below to deliver sentient beings") and trusted in faith (in the vow of Amitābha Buddha) or in wisdom (in Ch'anist circles). The more radical elements believed in the imminent arrival of Maitreya, the future Buddha, in the present age of the degenerate dharma.[19] As beings of compassion, members regarded the preachings of the good word more important than the mere building of statues.[20] All these Mahāyāna aspirations and lifestyles were absent in the original Jen-t'ien-chiao (though sometimes present, undigested, in the inscriptions found at the cave sites).

As will be evident in the translation of the *TWPLC*, the Jen-t'ien-chiao generally (with a few exceptions due to the author's poetic license) did not assume to aspire beyond samsara: The primary goal was *jen* and *t'ien*. The Sung ideal of a layman-bodhisattva going to and returning from nirvana to work for others in this world could not be present in the *TWPLC*. Gautama the Buddha remains (in the surviving texts that I know of) the one Buddha mentioned in the *TWPLC*.[21] The Buddha, though compassionate, was not perceived in the Mahāyāna fashion as a savior who can transfer his merits to his children; this bodhisattva motif was absent. Gautama was basically The Teacher, and his basic teaching for the common people was the five precepts: not to kill, steal, be adulterous, drink, or lie. These are objective norms, the performance of which would promote the person's better rebirth. Neither faith (in the sense of Pure Land faith) nor wisdom (in the Ch'an sense) were seen as leading to enlightenment or Buddhahood (virtually a nonissue in this pre-Hīnayāna faith); only *acts* of worship and donation counted.[22]

If, in retrospect, the Jen-t'ien-chiao appears to be so much *du et des* and if, again in retrospect, the merit-grasping zeal to build statues and temples among the *i-i* members appears so pharisaic and presumptuous, it was because at that time there was a strong faith in karmic action.[23] Although it is not completely appropriate to use a Sanskrit term here, I still think *karmamārga* (understood as a general term: the path of works) may describe this naive faith best. Like Luther's condemnation of works, mature sinitic Mahāyānists in T'ang and Sung learned to be critical of "mere karmic works." (Not inappropriately perhaps, the two dominant schools in Sung are Ch'an representing *jñānamārga* and Pure Land, *bhaktimārga*.[24]) From the ideological perspective of these two later schools, Buddhist scholars have passed judgment on the inferior Jen-t'ien-chiao, faulting it for being concerned with "this-worldly benefits."[25]

The worldliness of the *TWPLC* is both necessary and inspired. It is necessary because the *TWPLC* is explicitly not directed at trans-samsaric ends; the search for nirvana is possible beginning only with the next period of teaching (in Liu Ch'iu's scheme) that was reserved for Hīnayāna monks. It is inspired because there is a basic karma-optimism in this teaching—that is, a faith in the efficacy of works and their results. The *TWPLC* was entirely free (except for perhaps one unclear passage) from any doctrine of an imminent age of the degenerate dharma and has no mention of the eschatological Maitreya. Later Pure Land, and often Ch'an, *presupposed* these realities and were karma-pessimistic. Burdened down by a deep sense of karmic sin and disillusioned with the logic of piecemeal actions, they turned to faith or to wisdom—that is, to the dramatic power of the bodhisattvic vow (by Amitābha or by oneself) or to the suddenness of *bodhicitta* intuition.[26] (Neither tradition denied karmic work; but good work was *a posteriori* to faith and wisdom and not *a priori* leading to it.) The pre-Hīnayāna faith of the Jen-t'ien-chiao was indeed naive and outward, but it was also *justly* this-worldly and optimistic. Its obvious limitations notwithstanding, it was also the training ground for the emergence of sinitic Mahāyāna consciousness.

Perhaps more important than the philosophy behind the *TWPLC* is the institutional structure that it espoused. The *TWPLC* was known also as the *Wu-chieh-ching* (*pañcaśīla* sutra) and therefore belongs to the genre known in China as *chieh-ching* (*śīla* sutra). The *TWPLC* was not meant to be a philosophical text dealing with meditation *(samādhi)* or wisdom *(prajñā)*. As a lay-oriented preceptual text, the *TWPLC* does not even belong to the *vinaya* section of the Tripiṭaka (three-basket canon). The *vinaya* or *prātimokṣa* sutra is about monastic precepts for the full-time monk. The *TWPLC* is clearly based on the general ethics taught by the Buddha. Since this genre is not found in the *vinaya* proper, it remains unclear how it was transmitted. Some texts, like the *TWPLC,* are clearly fabricated, but not all could have been native creations. As early as the Later Han period, a *chieh-ching* on *Receiving the Ten Good (Precepts)* was available, and Dharmakṣema translated a number of these precept texts including one directed at the *upāsaka* (laymen).[27] There seems to be a conscious attempt to instill, slowly, the *śīla* prerequisite for entering into the Chinese *sangha,* with *vinaya*-obeying Indian or Central Asian monks acting as the overseer:

Indian/Central Asian *bhikṣu*—250 *śīla*	
Chinese disciples *(śramaṇas)*—10 *śīla;* identifiable with special surnames ("India" and the like)	strict idea of *sangha* membership
Chinese laymen *(upāsaka)*—5 *śīla*	*sangha*-householder or *i-i* "adopted" member

However, based in part on the laymen *chieh-ching* precedence, China eventually produced the Mahāyāna bodhisattva *śīla* sutra, for lay and monk bodhisattvas alike—that is, the *Brahma Net Sutra.* This sutra was later used, especially in Japan after Saichō, to replace the "tedious Hīnayāna rules" of the traditional *bhikṣu* in Indian Buddhist (Hīnayāna as well as Mahāyāna) traditions.[28]

It is usually said that the *vinaya* was introduced late into China (not until Fa-hsien's time at the end of the fourth century) because of a lack of neo-Taoist interest in new rites. Chih Tun had money to buy a mountain retreat and Tao-sheng delighted in eating beyond noon! Perhaps asceticism was indeed difficult. As Lewis Lancaster at Berkeley suggested to me,[29] however, it could also be that the Indian and Central Asian monks were intentionally and conscientiously withholding the full precepts from those they may have regarded as uncouth converts. What was released at first to the Chinese was not the *vinaya* but these lesser *śīla* or *chieh-ching* designed for the laity and novices *(śramaṇas)*—that is, popular literature current in Central Asian communities. One notes that the word *bhikṣu* (the fully ordinated monk) was used sparingly in the records of this period when compared with its liberal use in later times. Shih-hsien and T'an-yao were officially "leaders of the *śramaṇas*" *(sha-men-t'ung)*— that is, leaders of the Chinese monks who had presumably adopted the full ten *śīlas* but not the impossible two hundred and fifty or so *lu.* The *TWPLC* was another *chieh-ching,* but one directed still to a lower rank-

ing in the *sangha* community: the laity. The Stein manuscript of the
TWPLC generally assumes that the leader of the laity (in China) was a
śramaṇa. Only in one place was the term corresponding to *bhikṣu* ever
mentioned and significantly only in the context that "the Buddha and the
bhikṣu are the only persons to whom the reverent 'homage' [*nan-wu*, or
more popular *nan-mo;* J. *namō*] can be paid." Laymen should not
address one another or even their *śramaṇas* with this holy term reserved
for Buddha and *bhikṣu*. For this reason, I would think that the *TWPLC*
(its interesting Buddho-Taoist philosophical synthesis notwithstanding)
should be seen above all as a China-produced preceptual sutra as early
Chinese authors suggest. The *TWPLC* is thus a unique *chieh-ching* with
its roots in Liang-chou and beyond—that is, Central Asia—and is a well-
conceived didactic treatise for Chinese *śramaṇa*-teachers and peasant-
students. This interpretation would also explain why the *TWPLC* incor-
porated so many native Chinese *chieh* or taboos into its own *śīla*.

As a plebeian *prātimokṣa* sutra, the *TWPLC* subscribed to a precep-
tual formalism in order to safeguard the sacred teachings of the Buddha.
The Buddha was the ultimate teacher (rarely a savior, primarily a didactic
Buddha);[30] the *bhikṣu* was the next exemplar of the path tread by the
Enlightened One, and the *śramaṇas* were to be dutiful transmitters.
Extraordinary emphasis is put on the proper transmission of the teachings, the methods and the steps, the sins of a bad teacher, even the personal danger of producing a misguided student. Lay persons are sharply
warned not to administer the five precepts unless a *śramaṇa* cannot possibly be found. The Buddha, the ultimate teacher, is of course more
important than one's parents. Parents see you through one lifetime, but
the Buddha's grace spans lives—as another fabricated sutra then emphasized.[31] Parents cannot help a deviant son, but one's preceptual master
may intercede on one's behalf before the Buddha. (This intercession
should not be understood in terms of a savior role even involving the
Mahāyāna notion of the transference of merits; the *TWPLC* follows the
earlier understanding that karma is entirely the individual's responsibility.) With so much said about the Chinese Buddhist commitment to filial
piety, it is essential to note that the *TWPLC,* the most important plebeian
sutra, did not subscribe to it. Accordingly, there might be a deeper significance to the *i-i* members' appellations as "sons, mothers, and daughters
of *i-i*." (The term *i*, "righteous," may have the meaning of an "adopted"
member of the Buddha family or *sangha*—that is an adopted son and so
forth.)[32] The Jen-t'ien-chiao, initiated by monks trained by Indian or
Central Asian monks, was possibly a daring experiment in founding a
new brotherhood in the same way that the Christian church at one time

undermined primary ties and produced its own *sangha*-household, the Corpus Christi.

Reading the sections in the *TWPLC* dealing with the importance of rules, of formal adherence and perpetual watchfulness, one realizes that this early plebeian movement, in one sense, liberated men from old familial ties and norms only to put them under a new set of rules.[33] In that sense the movement resembles other early medieval cults in which "forms" are important and is unlike the much later protestant cults (like Sung Buddhism) in which individual conscience demands the freedom of personal expression. Piety is structured in the *TWPLC* after the models of the rule-abiding elders, the *bhikṣus*. Only when this fact is recognized can we understand the curious line in Tao-hsüan's description of the *i-i:* "Members would put on robes and hold bowls every fortnight, keeping the precepts and watching over each other." Overlooked by many scholars, what is described here is none other than the confessional *uposatha:* the earliest *prātimokṣa* congregation (under the Buddha) in which monks gather every fourteen days in the forest, recite the rules, and confess their sins to one another. The Chinese peasants in the sixth century, at the urging of *śīla*-conscious Liang-chou monks, were literally putting on coarse clothing and holding begging bowls in imitation of the monks' *uposatha* and confessing their sins against the *pañcaśīla*.

It must have been quite a sight to behold: simple pious souls gathering in the fields at night and confessing their sins against the Buddha's precepts. Theirs was the naive trust in the sacred rules and confidence in one's action to better one's lot in the next life. This phenomenon probably marks the high point of Central Asian influence in North China in matters of authentic Buddhist preceptual behavior. Once sinitic Mahāyāna arose in T'ang, this monkish style of piety was covered over by the more abstract, more universalistic vogue of Mahāyāna faith in the Buddha (*not* in works or in precepts). For clergy and laity alike the liberal bodhisattva precepts of the *Brahma Net Sutra* then ruled supreme. The glory that once belonged to a *bhikṣu*-centered, *śramaṇa*-administered confessional piety (denounced so casually now as pre-Hīnayāna or too Hīnayānistic) faded and, in time, was forgotten and lost.[34] The new Mahāyāna bodhisattvic consciousness then created its own social and ideological forms. And, for one thing, it accepted filial piety![35] Yet even the birth of sinitic Mahāyāna was, in my opinion, from the womb of this pre-Hīnayāna faith. The historical irony in that metamorphosis will be dealt with later in this essay, but first topical acquaintance with the *TWPLC* translated selectively below—with notes and explanations—is necessary before the subtle transformative impact of the work can duly, and perhaps for the first time, become intelligible.[36]

T'i-wei Po-li Ching (Trapuṣa Bhallika Sutra)
Compiled by T'an-ching
(Partial Translation, Arranged Topically)

The Prologue and the Basic Teaching

When the *tathāgata* attained the Tao under the *bodhi* tree, for seven days no one knew that he had so attained the highest mystical state *(samyak-saṃbodhi)* except for the two gentry devotees T'i-wei and Po-li. These two were versed in yin-yang and knew thoroughly the art of tortoise shell divination, the *I-ching* [Book of Change], and fortune-telling.[37] They alone knew that the Buddha had attained enlightenment. Together with the god of the tree, T'i-wei [and Po-li] offered food to the Buddha and so did the four heavenly kings. The Buddha, after eating the food, preached to T'i-wei [and Po-li] the law of rebirth in the various paths of existence.

The Buddha said: Those people who keep the five precepts will be born as humans. Those who complete the ten good deeds will be born in heaven. Those who are ungrateful will be born as animals. Those who are miserly and greedy will become hungry ghosts. These are the laws of karmic rebirth in the five paths.[38]

The Buddha said: The ten good deeds are in tune with the mystical numbers of heaven and earth. Not to kill constitutes humanity *(jen)*. Not to steal constitutes wisdom *(chih)*. Not to tell lies, not to flatter, and not to deceive constitute trust *(hsin:* faith, trustworthiness). These five pertain to heaven. Not to be greedy, not to be lazy, not to be licentious, and not to speak lewdly constitute righteousness *(i)*. Not to drink [alcohol] constitutes propriety *(li)*. These five pertain to earth. Thus there are three pertaining to body, four to speech, and three to thought. These are the five precepts and the ten good deeds. The ten good deeds are included within the five precepts.[39]

The Magnificence of the Five Precepts

The five precepts are the greatest prohibitions under heaven. If one violates the five precepts, one violates the five constellations in heaven, the five mountains on earth, the five rulers in space [the cardinal points plus the center], the five organs of the body.

The five precepts are the mother of the various Buddhas. If you want to follow the path of the Buddha, read this sutra. If you want to become an arhat, read this sutra.

The five precepts are the roots of heaven and earth, the fountainhead of the various luminous spirits. Heaven depends on them to harmonize yin and yang. Earth depends on them to give birth to the myriad things. They are the mother of all things, the father of all spirits, the origin of the great Tao, the root of nirvana itself. They are the basis of the four matters, the five heaps, and the six faculties. The four matters refer to the four great elements [earth, water, fire, wind]. The four great elements are originally pure. The five heaps are originally pure. The six faculties are originally pure.[40]

> Note: The five precepts are made the ontological foundations of the Chinese universe; they are put on a par with prajñā (wisdom, the mother of Buddhas and bodhisattvas) and are said to lead—in this instance—beyond samsaric rebirth to arhatship.

Correlations with the Chinese Five Elements

The elder asked the Buddha: Why is it that there are five and not four or six? The Buddha said: Five is the root of heaven and earth. . . . Five is the major number of the universe. There are five constellations in heaven, five mountains on earth, five organs in man, five elements in yin-yang, five rulers in space's lordship, five virtues in the world, five colors . . . and, in the Buddha-dharma, the five precepts. Not to kill is paired with the east, the direction of wood, because wood represents humanity and humanity nurtures life. Not to steal is aligned with the north, to water, because water means wisdom and the wise one does not steal. Not to commit adultery is assigned to the west, to metal, for metal is righteousness and the righteous one would not be licentious. Not to drink is associated with the south, to fire, for fire reflects propriety and propriety prevents loss [of self-control]. Not to lie pertains to the center, the locus of earth, and the principle of earth is trust. Men of deceptive words look to both sides, unable to abide in a central position; the center is that which would not incline toward the false sides.[41]

> Note: This alignment of the pañcaśīla with native Chinese schemes of the five elements is the earliest but not the definitive one in Chinese Buddhist thought.[42]

Not to kill is humanity. . . . During the yang spring, the myriad things are alive and growing. In the first and second months, lesser yang dominates and nurtures all things. Therefore one should love life and loathe killing because to kill [in spring] is against humanity. Not to be adulterous is righteousness. . . . In the seventh and eighth months, lesser yin dominates. Avoid jealousy and envy in your actions, for they endanger your body. Retain and preserve life within and avoid excesses without that might deplete your essence [semen]. Refrain from selfish desires and licentiousness. Not to drink is propriety. . . . In the fourth and fifth months, the greater yang dominates. Alcohol brings about intoxication and the mind runs wild and the mouth speaks untruths, harming thereby the body and its allotted lifespan. Avoid drinking, for the drunkard is without a sense of propriety. Not to steal is wisdom. . . . In the tenth and eleventh months, the greater yin dominates. Things withdraw. The thief fails to model himself after heaven—he still grabs after things and hoards them. Therefore theft is prohibited, for to steal is to be lacking in wisdom. Proper words spoken mean trust. . . . The months pertaining to this are the third, the sixth, the ninth, and the twelfth. When the center dominates, it controls the four realms. However, evil words [deviating from the center] harm people; their root cause lies in the mouth. As words fly forth, harm follows. The ether *(ch'i)* extends outward; the body is harmed. The body being harmed, life is shortened. Therefore the tongue should be restrained, for the talkative person lacks trustworthiness.[43]

Note: A basic religious Taoist concern for the physical well-being of the body and the prolongation of life is found in the preceding passage, where the rationalized correlations are extended to the Chinese calendar.

Buddho-Taoist Fasts, Crisis Days, Gods, and Karmic Justice

In one year, there are three long fasts. In one month, there are six fasting days. Three times the lamps are lit as bright as the sun and moon. Various taboos should be observed on the day of the Eight Kings, otherwise known as the eight festive days.

The elder Trapuṣa asked the Buddha: World-Honored One, why the three long fasts in a year? Why the first, the fifth, and the ninth months? Why are the eighth, fourteenth, fifteenth, twenty-third, twenty-ninth, and thirtieth days chosen as the six fasting days in a month?

The Buddha said: In the first month, the lesser yang dominates. The ten thousand spirits are changing their locations. Yin and yang are in intercourse and the myriad things are growing as the ether of the Tao nurtures them. The crown prince fasts on the first day of the first month and practices quietude to aid the spirit of harmony and the germination of myriad things. He does so until the fifteenth day. In the fifth month, the greater yang dominates. The myriad things change their position. The grass and trees have finished budding, but the ten thousand things are not yet fully manifested in full growth. Even the matured ones are not in their peak. They are following the way of the living ether. Therefore one should fast on the first day of the fifth month until the fifteenth day to aid the ether in completing the growth of myriad things. In the ninth month, the lesser yin dominates. *Ch'ien* and *k'un* [heaven and earth] change. The myriad things come to an end. They wither and are set free again. Living things hibernate and the spirited ether returns to its roots. The Tao is calm and a fast should be kept from the first to the fifteenth of the ninth month. . . . Things live and die according to the Tao. There is a great prohibition in heaven and earth. Therefore I instruct my disciples and those who delight in the good to keep the various taboos and fast in order to safeguard the spirit.[44]

> *Note:* The primitive asceticism of fasting on tabooed days according to the seasons is found in the *Yüeh-ling* (Monthly Ordinances) designed for the Chinese emperor;[45] it is aligned here with Buddhist taboos (Skt., *śīla;* Ch., *chieh*) and ascetic self-control (yoga).

There are three reasons for preaching and receiving the precepts: to neutralize the cold and yin elements in the four seasons; to avoid violating the moon, the sun, and the open sky; and to gain a good harvest in the year.[46]

> *Note:* The agrarian world view of the Chinese peasant is most evident here.

By the year's end, there would have been three reviews and eight verifications. Every month, there are six reports. The three realms are bright and clear. In the five directions are recorded the deeds and misdeeds of sentient beings. The five officials receive their order to verify the records for reward or punishment. The grades are many. The heavenly host, the king, the prince, the messengers, the sun and moon, the ghosts and spirits, Yama of hell and the hundred gods, and so forth will go about on the first, the fifth, and the ninth month to report on humans. The deeds of kings, ministers, eight barbaric tribes, birds and beasts, ghosts and nagas, will be reported to the four heavenly kings. On the eighth, fifteenth, and thirtieth days of the month, the reports are shown to be consistent and without discrepancies. There is no undeserved punishment under heaven as the accounts of good and evil in the three realms are constantly reviewed. Doers of good will be born in heaven. The rulers of the four directions, the five spirits, the king, and the ministers will prolong their lives. Below, Yama and his five ministers will decide on the fortunes and administer rewards and punishments accordingly. Thus the three long fasts are instituted in light of the three reviews.[47]

> *Note:* Mechanical karmic justice requires no agents to administer it, but the Jen-t'ien-chiao (borrowed probably from the *T'ai-p'ing-ching* tradition) admitted such adjudicators. The three long fasts are supposed to be based on an

Indian tradition expressed by the *Ta-chih-tu-lun:* Indra turns a jeweled mirror on the world, beginning counterclockwise with the south in the first month and again on the fifth and ninth. Tsukamoto finds this tradition to be baseless.[48]

The eight verifications are associated with the days of the eight kings: *(Brahmā)* heaven, Indra, his attendants, the five spirits, the four heavenly kings, Yama, spirits *(asuras),* and gods *(devas).* They review and verify the records, decide on life or death, merits and demerits to be added or subtracted, and whether the person intends to follow the way or not, whether his intention was great or small, whether the person was charitable (or instructive), and whether he had left home to become a monk. The records are reviewed according to the days of the eight kings [the first days of spring, summer, fall, winter, and the equinoxes and solstices], these being the times when the gods of heaven and earth, yin and yang, are changing their positions. Heaven and earth are active on the eighth, fourteenth, fifteenth, twenty-third, twenty-ninth, and thirtieth days of the month. The reports are handed up during the quarter moon, three-quarter moon, and full moon, and on the first and last crescent nights. . . .

The Buddha said: On the eighth day, the messenger is sent; on the fourteenth, the crown prince; on the fifteenth, the four heavenly kings [and repeat for the twenty-third, twenty-ninth, and thirtieth]. They will be on earth recording the good and the evil. . . .[49]

Note: The *TWPLC* uses the crisis days for moral stocktaking and places extraordinary emphasis on universality, impartiality, and impeccable justice. These tabooed days had limited the medieval Chinese legal code regarding the proper days for capital punishment.

New Rites: The First Mantra and Circumambulation

On the eight days of the kings, the person should chant in praise: *Nan-wu-fo,* "Homage to the Buddha." *Nan* is taking refuge; *wu* is body; *fo* is enlightenment. Therefore chant *nan-wu-fo.* ["I take refuge personally in the Buddha."] *Nan* is to be on the side of; *wu* is good; *fo* is wisdom. Therefore chant *nan-wu-fo.* ["I side with the good and wisdom."] *Nan* is reverence; *wu* is to serve; *fo* is enlightenment. Therefore chant *nan-wu-fo.* ["In reverence I serve the Buddha."] *Nan* is taking refuge; *wu* is body; *fo* is enlightenment. Therefore chant *nan-wu-fo. Nan-wu* is fear and awe; *fo* is the essence of enlightenment. Therefore chant *nan-wu-fo. Samyaksaṃbodhi* is the Buddha himself. Therefore call upon him quickly in homage thrice and gain immediate peace.[50]

The elder Trapuṣa said: The showering of flowers, the lighting of incense and lamps, are to show reverence through offerings, but what good can there be in the circumambulation of the statue? The Buddha answered: Circumambulation will produce five rewards: The person will gain a good complexion in his next life; his voice will be fine; he may be reborn in heaven; he may be reborn into families of lords and nobles; he may gain nirvana. What causes the good complexion? It is his rejoicing in seeing the Buddha. What causes the fine voice? It is his reciting the sutra while circumambulating. What causes the rebirth in heaven? It is his will and intentional faithfulness to the precepts while circumambulating. What causes rebirth into aristocratic families? It is his act of honoring the feet of Buddha with bowed head and face. What causes the attainment of nirvana? It is the accumulation of good karma.

The Buddha then said: In circumambulating the statue, three acts should be present. In raising your foot, reflect upon the act of raising your foot. In putting down your foot, be mindful of the act of putting down your foot. Thirdly, you should not look left and right or spit within the temple compound.[51]

> Note: The Chinese peasants were here being taught a simple mantra, the meaning for a hitherto unknown practice (circumambulation), and a simple form of contemplative mindfulness derived from Buddhist meditation.

The Power of the Teachings and the Sutra

The Buddha said: Those who want good fortune in the next life, read this sutra; those who want a long life in the next rebirth . . . who want to follow the way of the Buddha . . . who want to become arhats . . . acquire wisdom . . . desire a good complexion . . . stop evils . . . avoid ills and regrets . . . avoid becoming ghosts, spirits, and nagas . . . be free from birth, old age, sickness, and death . . . and attain nirvana, read this sutra. Follow the teaching and your wishes will be granted and the heavenly gods will protect you from harm.[52]

> Note: The TWPLC goes on to relate how the multitude rejoiced at the teaching, how Trapuṣa received the pañcaśīla, and how the merchants attained purity and various states of meditative excellence including even anupatti-dharmakṣānti for Trapuṣa and others.[53]

On the Sacred Transmission of Śīlas and the Proper Way

Trapuṣa asked: . . . There are people in my country who delight in the good. If there are good men and women who, upon hearing about the five precepts, would like to embrace the faith . . . can a practitioner pass on the teaching? . . . The Buddha answered: The precepts are like the boat and the precept master the captain. . . . The incapable person should not assume the role of the master for he would only drown, unable to save himself or others. If there are people who can keep the five precepts and never deviate from them, being knowledgeable about the ways of deliverance and the proper actions, they may pass on the precepts. . . . The master must help his disciple to erase his past karma by first instructing him in the three-graded confession of past sins up to today. [Confession is to be accompanied by blood from the pores and blood from the eyes, then by sweat from the pores and blood from the eyes, then by heat from the body and tears in the eyes.] Then he must pass on the five precepts according to the way the teaching should be taught [not missing or mistaking anything or reversing the order of importance and so forth]. . . . To foolishly transmit the precepts will imperil both parties. . . . The Buddha and the *bhikṣu* can receive reverence from the people, but the elders should not receive homage or be addressed with *"nan-wu."* . . . If afterward [following the transmission of the precepts of a lay person] there is present a precept-keeping *śramaṇa,* then the task of instruction should be handed to him and the people should receive the precepts again officially from him. . . . In the matter of the five precepts, the master is most important. Keeping the five precepts is like juggling five sharp knives in the air. If you miss catching one, all five will fall and hurt people. To break one precept is to break all five, harming men and gods, and the offender deserves to fall into the three evil paths with no hope of ever leaving them. . . . If a disciple of a precept master becomes a monk and yet cannot fulfill his task, the master himself cannot be delivered. . . . If a master does not keep the rules, he is not a disciple of the Buddha. In that case, both the master and his disciple cannot be relied upon and neither can be delivered. . . . [54]

If there is a man who can serve the Tao and recognize the merit of the teacher . . . [then he is comparable to] a great criminal who recognizes that a certain elder is on good terms with the king. The king respects the elder and listens to his intercession. In his wisdom, the criminal . . . takes refuge in the elder. The elder accepts him and compassionately teaches him, saying that [having received donations from lay people] he would intercede on the man's behalf before the king. . . . [55]

Note: This long passage reveals unquestionably the *śīla* and *vinaya*-consciousness of the *TWPLC* and its utter seriousness about its proper transmission. The importance of the teacher is further demonstrated in the following parable which shows how this lay Buddhist piety put the family second—a trait that is absent in the *chieh (Tao chieh)* tradition of the *T'ai-p'ing-ching.*[56]

A person fails to follow a master in his life and finds himself in hell.
He regrets his mistakes and says: During my life, I did not follow a
teacher's instruction and failed to do good. Foolishly I loved material
things and left them to my wife. How I wish I had been charitable! Now
my possessions, my wife, my wealth, my land, household, and jewels are
left on earth and cannot be brought here. Alone I suffer with no one
knowing my sorrow and no one to save me. The teacher comes to him
and says: You did not believe me in your life and failed to follow my
teachings; now you should know who could have helped you. The man
says: I was foolish and thought only about my parents, wife, siblings, relatives, servants, and possessions. They are in the world and cannot help
me here. When I was alive, I treated you as an outsider. Now I know you
are more intimate to me than my parents or wife by a hundred, a thousand, times. Only three things follow me to hell: . . . my fate, my sin,
and a teacher. . . . I have regret now. My master, you *are* my parent
through the kalpas. . . .[57]

Insights into Human Existence and the Mind

The five hundred merchants rejoiced in hearing the sutra. Everyone kept
it in his heart and all said: The aim of the doings of sentient beings is to
keep themselves in the path of human existence. . . . The Buddha said:
It is as you said: Rebirth in the human realm is rare and as difficult as
this example. There are two persons, one on top of Mount Sumeru dan-
gling a string down and the other at the foot of the mountain holding up
a needle and hoping to thread it. A distance of 3,360,000 *li* [miles] separates them and a strong wind is blowing. Can he succeed in passing the
thread through the needle's eye? . . .

The five hundred merchants said: Highest One, the mind of many flees
in every moment, comes in the next, disappears in a second, is reborn
afterward. Crafty indeed is the mind, its action endless. A hundred
minds, a hundred thoughts *(nien)*, constitute a hundred bodies. The will
of a man is difficult to guard. The mind is the basis of the body, but the
mind cannot be seen, cannot be verified. . . . The Buddha said: Retribu-
tions in the five paths are all based on the mind. If the mind contemplates
(nien) the Buddha, there will be the reward of the Buddha. If the mind
contemplates man, there will be retribution through human rebirth.
Thoughts about animals will produce animal rebirth. Thinking on the
crane will produce rebirth as a crane. Evil thoughts will lead to evil punishment. Good thoughts will lead to good reward.[58]

Note: These scriptural sentiments are similar to the *Dharmapada's* humanistic,
ethical, and often mind-centered teachings.

Dark Clouds on the Horizon

The Buddha took hold of a handful of earth and asked the elder: Is there more earth on the ground or in my hand? The elder answered: There is much more on the ground. . . . The Buddha said: In future generations, those who become my disciples will be as plentiful as the earth on the ground but those who can keep the precepts and attain liberation are as limited as the amount in my hand. . . . In the future, few can take up the ascetic life or keep the precepts. Even if there are, they would be so uncommon that others would criticize them, unable to recognize their merits.[59]

> *Note:* The preceptual formalism of the *TWPLC* leads to this realistic appraisal of the hardship involved—minus the Mahāyāna confidence in ultimate universal salvation.[60] Many are called but few make it.

The Buddha told Trapuṣa: I am now entering into nirvana. After I pass away, there will arise in years to come five kinds of chaos: chaos in the way of kings, chaos among the people, chaos due to ghosts and spirits, chaos due to the rise of ninety-six heresies stifling the way of the Buddha, and chaos disrupting the true teaching *(saddharma)*. At that time, there will be *śramaṇas* who do not keep the precepts, who wander about freely, doing what they please without inhibitions. Even if there were precept-keeping *śramaṇas,* the people would deride them, confusing them with their opposites and accusing these innocent ones of practicing selfish deeds and breaking the rules while pretending to be outwardly pure. Because of these lies, the common people and members of other teachings will believe the false charges. . . .[61]

> *Note:* The five kinds of chaos might well be a retrospective description of the persecutions of A.D. 446 and T'an-ching's defense of the pure *sangha* against the charges of temple abuses. They are also prophetic in anticipating the rise of unregistered, roving monks in the next period. I personally do not think that the eschatological motif of the degenerate dharma is implied in what seems to be a realistic assessment of the times.

Details of Retribution Based on the Pañcaśīla

. . . He who loves to wear long gowns will be reborn as the long-tailed beetle. . . . He who asks others to donate and, when refused, becomes angry will be reborn as a lion. . . .[62]

> *Note:* Toward the end of the second scroll of the *TWPLC* there is a long section on rebirth through sympathetic resemblance. Then there is a long list of rewards and punishments pertaining to the person who fulfills and the person who breaks each *śīla.*

. . . [The person who refrains from taking life will be rewarded with:]
a long life; peace and security in all future lives; freedom from any harm
due to arms in war, tigers or wolves and poisonous insects [or beasts];
rebirth in heaven after death with endless longevity there; and rebirth on
earth after that stay in heaven and long life here. . . . [The person who
takes life without compassion will be punished with:] a short life; a multitude of fears; much resentment and vengeance directed against him;
descent of the soul after death to hell beneath Mount T'ai, where the soul
will undergo torture and examination, branding by iron and boiling of
the flesh, piercing of the body and dismembering of the bones until the
person can neither live nor die as he prefers; his sin in taking life is so
great that he will not leave hell for a long time; and a short life after his
rebirth in the human realm—death in the womb, soon after birth, ten or
a hundred days or more later, a year or more after birth. . . .[63]

> Note: There follows a list of ills accompanying the alcoholic which proves to
> be the longest one, thirty-six items in all.[64] It is based on the list in the *Ta-chih-
> tu-lun.* The extraordinary emphasis on sobriety can only be appreciated in the
> light of the yogic ideal of rational self-control of emotions and in light of the
> fact that historically the Buddhists inculcated the Chinese love for tea (pre-
> viously used only as medicine).[65]

Impact of the TWPLC

The *TWPLC,* selectively translated above, may not be an authentic Buddhist sutra, but then few Mahāyāna sutras are the authentic words of the
historical Buddha—they are the living words of the *transhistorical* Buddha.[66] Despite its accommodation to the Confucian five permanents or
virtues, it remains aloof to the dictates of filial piety. Despite its adapta-
tion to Taoist or yin-yang philosophies, it remains faithful to a karma
doctrine basic to the Buddha-dharma. Above all, it underlies the central-
ity of the *pañcaśīla*—to my mind, still more universalistic, or at least less
cumbersome, than the Chinese ethics of that time.[67] Historically, Northern Wei produced most of the plebeian sutras,[68] unless we take into
account the *pao-chüan* (Precious Scroll) genre in Ming-Ch'ing times during another period of Buddho-Taoist synthesis. The *TWPLC* was not
interested in *wu* (nothingness), *k'ung* (emptiness), *li* (principle), or *hsing*
([Buddha]-nature) that intrigued the gentry Buddhists and promoted the
eventual fabrication of an intellectual sutra like the *Yüan-chüeh-ching
(Perfect Enlightenment Sutra)* in T'ang.

Socially the *TWPLC* was much more important than the armchair
Buddhist speculations produced in the southern dynasties. The *sangha-*
household experiment and the *TWPLC* led, at first, to *śramaṇa-*con-

trolled evangelical activities and then to similar activities by roving, un-registered, and sometimes even rebelling monks from the first decade of the sixth century on. Precept-conscious laymen were passing on the *pañcasīlas*. The pious and the opportunistic were building stupas and temples and claiming ecclesiastical independence. Mahāyāna ideals surfaced to challenge the state, and Maitreya played a role in one or two of the Buddhist "peasant revolts."[69] The imperial government was not free from the abuses either. *Saṅgha*-grain was inappropriately used for building gorgeous temples in the capital or channeled for monks' retreats instead of being stored for welfare purposes. Clergy working for the state, lower monks siding with the people, and pure monks critical of the secularization were divided on the aim of the *saṅgha*-household experiment. It is not possible to map out in detail here the inner contradictions that finally led to the thorough Buddhist persecution in 574–576, but there are two mysteries in the history of Northern Wei that may, I think, be solved by an insight into the *TWPLC*.

It is said that a turncoat monk, Wei Yüan-sung, was in part responsible for the Buddhist persecution. This monk, toward whom Buddhist historians were very ambivalent, petitioned Emperor Wu of Northern Chou to abolish the *saṅgha* on the basis of a Mahāyāna program that would totally secularize the Buddhist fellowship.[70] If indeed samsara is nirvana and if the bodhisattva should work in the world, why still keep a separate institution and an otherworldly path? Why not turn the state into the *saṅgha* and make the king the truthful caesaropapist ruler that he was supposed to be? Kamata Shigeo, following the positive evaluation of Wei Yüan-sung begun by Tao-hsüan, suggested that the Buddhist persecution itself was motivated by reform-minded Buddhists.[71] However, supposing Wei Yüan-sung was a lower cleric sympathetic with the people and critical of temple abuses, it would not be difficult to see an ironic legacy of the *TWPLC* in Wei's petition to the king. Wei wanted to secularize or Confucianize the *saṅgha,* turning cities into temples and men of Confucian virtue into Buddhist leaders. The precedence already existed in the *TWPLC*. If the *pañcasīla* are the five Confucian virtues, what prevents Wei from drawing the conclusion that, indeed, the fulfillment of the Confucian duties would be the proper goal of the *pañcasīla?* The sinicization of the Buddha-dharma implied in the *TWPLC* points then to the petition of Wei and the persecution of separate Buddhist establishments.

Of course, the persecution involved a complex set of factors besides the ideological link I have described. Emperor Wu simply had to trim the excesses of a *saṅgha,* a state within a state, that had grown to disproportions. Supposedly the number of monks *(seng)* defrocked in the persecution numbered three million in 574 in the north alone. There is no way that this number can be authentic and no way that we are dealing with genuine monks or even *śramaṇas*. The impossible count cannot, however, be passed off simply as an exaggeration. Statistical exaggeration also existed in the second peak Buddhist period in Chinese history, around A.D. 700 in the reign of Empress Wu. Yet even in that most prosperous era, the exaggeration does not go beyond eight hundred thousand monks. The only way to account for this large figure of *seng* in 574 is to realize that, perhaps for the only time in Chinese Buddhist history, the word *seng* does not denote "monk" but any member of the *sangha* (Ch., *seng-chia*) according to the liberal understanding of *sangha* as all the followers of Buddha.[72] If this hypothesis is correct, then the members of the *sangha*-household were regarded as *seng,* along with the *śramaṇas* and the *bhikṣus*. Perhaps then the term *"i-i"* or *"i-hui"* meant more than just the righteous or the pious of an association or a village but also included the adopted *(i)* members of the *sangha*[73] who were given—to the exasperation of the court—the privileges given then to monks (exemption from secular tax and corvée). Northern China in the sixth century was, quantitatively speaking, heavily Buddhist with three million "monks"! The credit goes to T'an-yao, the *sangha*-household, and the then-popular *TWPLC.* It was the very success of the sutra which led to its political demise.

The *TWPLC* also led to the rise of sinitic Mahāyāna. The 574–576 persecution forced the Chinese Buddhists to rethink their identity. The founders of the sinitic Mahāyāna schools in Sui and T'ang rejected the unilateral reduction of Buddhist nirvana into Confucian samsara attempted by Wei Yüan-sung, the "Mahāyānist" rebel. The founders also rejected the *TWPLC;* they recognized the dangers it posed. The correlations of the *pañcaśīla* with native schemata led to a popularization of Buddhism, true, but also to the dilution of the dharma. In a creative and almost charismatic breakthrough to higher Mahāyāna understanding of the true bodhisattvic vocation, eminent Chinese monks and founders turned away from the *TWPLC,* questioned the limitations of its pre-Hīnayānist teachings, and, one by one, mapped a new program for the future of Chinese Buddhist consciousness. The story of the formation of sinitic Mahāyāna belongs to another study and lies outside our concerns here.[74] What we have seen is the courageous innovation of sixth-century China, the creation of the Jen-t'ien-chiao, the contents of its key scripture, the *TWPLC,* and, finally, that natural and perhaps gracious demise of this sinicized faith as, having laid the foundation of the future of the Buddha-dharma, it bowed and faded out from center stage.

Notes

The author is grateful for a faculty research grant from the University of California, Davis, for the preparation of this essay.

1. See Kenneth Ch'en, *Buddhism in China* (Princeton: Princeton University Press, 1964), pp. 121–183.

2. Kenneth Ch'en, *The Chinese Transformation of Buddhism* (Princeton: Princeton University Press, 1973), pp. 56–58.

3. Daniel Overmyer, *Folk Buddhist Religion* (Cambridge: Harvard University Press, 1976). This important English study hardly mentions the *i-i* groups that formed in connection with the *TWPLC*.

4. See Tsukamoto Zenryū, *Shina Bukkyō no kenkyū: Hokugi hen* (Tokyo: Kōbuntō, 1942), pp. 293–354; this is the first significant study on the subject.

5. Makita Tairyō, "*Tonkohon Daii-kyō* no kenkyū," *Bukkyō Daigaku daigakuin kenkyū kiyō* I (1968); pp. 137–185, and II (1971); pp. 165–197 (hereafter cited as *BDDKK* I and II).

6. The first scroll contains the Chinese-sounding fragments that Tsukamoto discovered earlier but were not found in the Stein manuscript. I shall not include this recent discovery in this study.

7. My preliminary translation of the extant fragments was done for the Center of Asian Studies, University of Illinois at Urbana-Champaign, and supported by the National Endowment for the Humanities.

8. Interpretations of Northern Wei, attempted here, are based on my study of the religious situation in "The Awakening of Faith in Mahayana: A Study of the Unfolding of Sinitic Motifs" (Ph.D. dissertation, Harvard, 1975). The facts are available in the *Wei-shu;* see Tsukamoto Zenryū and Leon Hurvitz, *Wei Shou on Buddhism and Taoism* (Kyoto: Kyoto University, 1956).

9. On T'an-yao, see Tsukamoto, *Hokugi hen,* pp. 133–164.

10. My translation is based on the edited text and notes in Tsukamoto and Hurvitz, *Wei Shou,* and on Hurvitz's renditions of this passage.

11. See Tsukamoto, *Hokugi hen,* pp. 165–214.

12. *T* 50. 428a.7–21.

13. See my "Tales of Rebirths *(Wang-sheng-chuan)* and the Later Pure Land Tradition in China" in the forthcoming volume on Pure Land in the Berkeley Buddhist Studies Series, edited by Lewis Lancaster and James Foard.

14. See Yamazaki Hiroshi, *Shina chūsei Bukkyō no tenkai* (Tokyo, 1942), pp. 765–831; Ch'en, *Chinese Transformation,* pp. 282–286.

15. Tsung-mi, *Yüan-jen-lun,* translated as *Essay on Man* in T. W. de Bary, ed., *The Buddhist Tradition* (New York: Random House, 1969), pp. 179–196.

16. By a coincidence, the phrase *t'ien-jen* is also employed in Han thought in a similar system of "correspondence between the five elements," but there is no proof that the *TWPLC* intends *jen-t'ien* to be read in that way.

17. Cited by Makita, *BDDKK* I, p. 139, from Kuei-chi's *Ta-ch'eng fa-i chu-lin.*

18. For early sources see Ch'en, *Chinese Transformation,* p. 56f, n. 90.

19. Suzuki Chūsei noted some of the differences in his "Sodai Bukkyō kessha no kenkyū," *Shigaku zasshi* 52 (1941): 65–98, 205–241, 303–333.

20. The popular press in Sung-Ming replaced the need to build monuments; preaching became more important than lavishing the temples with gold.

21. Other Buddhas as objects of devotion were present in the caves and statues sponsored by the *i-i*.

22. Donation or charity, however, is not explicitly mentioned in the *TWPLC*.

23. These practices are not explicitly encouraged in the *TWPLC* either, and it should be noted that Trapuṣa and Bhallika were seldom found in the surviving sculptures of this period. Alexander Soper identified apparently only two incidences. I am grateful to Nancy Price for pointing this out.

24. Again I apologize for relying on these Hindu terms; the Christian "ladders of merits" (spiritual stages achieved through work, speculation, and contemplation) seems no better.

25. Japanese: *gensei rieki*.

26. The paradoxical hope/despair syndrome in sinitic Mahāyāna thought cannot be analyzed in full here. Although T'ang Buddhism is often said to be optimistic and world-affirming, it was based on a transcendence of despair after the 574–576 persecution. In one sense, T'ang Pure Land thought is much more inward, private, sober, and somber in color than the public and festive Wei Buddhism.

27. See Makita, *BDDKK* I, p. 183.

28. There is no evidence that Indian Mahāyāna monks followed a Mahāyāna *vinaya* different from the traditional (Hīnayāna) *vinaya*. Mahāyāna and Hīnayāna monks were able to live in one monastery in India and Central Asia because the general *vinaya* rules were shared. In China, and especially in Japan, however, the *Brahma Net Sutra* was said to supersede the old rules. Opinions expressed in this section are mine and contrary to tradition.

29. In private conversation.

30. The predominance of the perception of the Buddha as a didactic Buddha and as a historical Buddha (preceding Maitreya to come) had been shown by Tsukamoto; transmundane and savior Buddhas like Amitābha and Avalokiteśvara became prominent in the surviving cave sculptures after about A.D. 700. I hope to refine Tsukamoto's analysis in a future study on "Didactic, Cosmic, Savior, and Patriarch Buddhas" in Chinese Buddhist history.

31. "Your parents can only nurture you through birth, old age, sickness, and death in this one lifetime, but the Buddha is delivering people [from samsara] endlessly in ten thousand years," says the *Fo-shuo fen-pieh shan-o so-ch'i-ching* as cited by Makita, *BDDKK* II, pp. 192–193.

32. *I* is the Mencian term for righteousness. The Chinese monks already regarded themselves as sons of the Buddha *(shi-tzu)* when, after Tao-an, the surname *Shih* for monks became standard.

33. When Christianity pushed aside the Jewish laws, it set up its own code and Christian monasticism was just as structured as the Buddhist variety. Early medieval piety does *not* produce post-Reformation or post-Sung individualism.

34. Generally speaking, Theravāda society is more *saṇgha*-centered. Mahāyāna, however, proclaimed the Buddha to be the crowning jewel and focus of faith. According to Trevor Ling, this is supposed to explain the greater political role of Buddhism in Theravāda countries, but I think that opinion overgeneralizes; see Ling's *The Buddha* (New York: Scribner's, 1973).

35. The *Brahma Net Sutra* makes filial piety the basic *śīla*.

36. The present translation is abbreviated from an earlier version.

37. Omenological texts of the Han period were still popular in Wei.

38. The traditional six paths of rebirth need not have been truncated to fit the fivefold Chinese pattern since the Sarvāstivādins allegedly already had the five-path theory.

39. From Tsukamoto fragments 1, 3, and 7; see Tsukamoto, *Hokugi hen,* included in Makita, *BDDKK* I, pp. 151ff., with the same numbers.

40. Tsukamoto fragments 4, 5, and 6, *Hokugi hen.*

41. Tsukamoto fragments 7 and 8, ibid.

42. See Ch'en, *Chinese Transformation,* pp. 58–59.

43. Tsukamoto fragment 12, *Hokugi hen.*

44. Tsukamoto fragments 16 and 17, ibid., and (overlapping) Stein text in Makita, *Tonkoho Daii-kyō, BDDKK* I, p. 146.

45. See the chapter on *Yüeh-ling* in the *Book of Rites, Li Chi.*

46. Tsukamoto fragment 12, *Hokugi hen.*

47. Tsukamoto fragment 17, ibid.; Makita, *BDDKK* I, p. 146f.

48. Tsukamoto fragment 17, *Hokugi hen.*

49. Tsukamoto fragments 17 and 19, ibid.; Makita, *BDDKK* I, p. 147f.

50. Makita, *BDDKK* I, p. 148. This mantra probably anticipated the popular use of a similar one directed to Amitābha Buddha.

51. Tsukamoto fragment 15, *Hokugi hen.*

52. Makita, *BDDKK* I, pp. 149–150. Repetitions have been omitted in the translation.

53. See Tsukamoto fragment 13, *Hokugi hen.*

54. Makita, *BDDKK* I, pp. 150–156; translation much abbreviated. The three-graded confession was traditionally associated with Shan-tao's Pure Land piety prior to the rediscovery of the *TWPLC.* See Makita, *BDDKK* II, pp. 186–187.

55. Makita, *BDDKK* II, pp. 168–171.

56. According to Taoist scholars, the *chieh* seems to pertain to filial piety; see Max Kaltenmark, *Lao Tzu and Taoism* (Stanford: Stanford University Press, 1969). Taoism was still committed to the family.

57. Makita, *BDDKK* I, pp. 168–171.

58. Tsukamoto fragment 2, *Hokugi hen;* Makita, *BDDKK* I, pp. 163–164, then 166; translation slightly rearranged.

59. Makita, *BDDKK* I, p. 171.

60. On Mahāyāna's victory over its defamers, the *icchāntika,* see the *Mahāparinirvāṇa Sutra.*

61. Makita, *BDDKK* I, p. 156.

62. Ibid., pp. 159–160.

63. Ibid., pp. 173, 176–177.

64. See Makita, *BDDKK* I, pp. 181–185.

65. On Buddhism and alcohol, see chap. 7 in Ōchō Ēnichi, *Chūgoku Bukkyōshi no kenkyū* (Kyoto: Hōzōkan, 1958), pp. 214–344.

66. If Mahāyāna sutras have Hindu influence, why not sinitic influence?

67. Confucian *li* (rites), in practice, excluded the uncultured.

68. A source illuminating the living Buddhist tradition in China and a source being tapped by Makita in several essays on this topic.

69. See Tsukamoto, *Hokugi hen,* pp. 241–292.

70. Komura Yōshō, *Shubu honan no kenkyū* (Tokyo: Azuma, 1968).

71. Kamata, *Chūgoku Kegon shisōshi kenkyū* (Tokyo: Tokyo University Press, 1965), pp. 262, 281–287.

72. The term *saṇgha* can be used narrowly to designate the monastic order or liberally to signify the Buddhist fellowship as a whole.

73. Compare the development of lay brethren attached to Christian monasteries.

74. See Whalen Lai, "The Emergence of Sinitic Mahayana: T'ien-t'ai," a paper delivered to the annual conference of the Association for Asian Studies, Toronto, 1976.

2

T'an-luan: Taoist Sage
and Buddhist Bodhisattva

ROGER J. CORLESS

*Our first teacher T'an-luan was customarily honored by
Emperor Liang as a bodhisattva: When he received the Pure
Land teaching from the Tripiṭaka master Bodhiruci, he burned
his texts on immortality and took refuge in the Buddha of
Sukhāvatī.*[1]

T'an-luan, who probably lived from 488 to 554,[2] wrote the first systematic treatise on Chinese Pure Land Buddhism which has come down to
us: the *Wu-liang-shou Ching Yu-p'o-t'i-she Yüan-sheng Chi Chu* (*T*
40.826–844), "Annotations to the *Gāthā* (Buddhist Verses) on the *Praṇidhāna* (Resolution) to be Born (in Sukhāvatī) with the *Upadeśa* (Dialogue) on the Sutras of Amitāyus," known for short as the *Wang-sheng-
lun Chu* or simply *Lun Chu*. The *upadeśa* is an autocommentary on a
gāthā summarizing the virtues of Sukhāvatī, purporting to be by Vasu-
bandhu. The *gāthaupadeśa,* taken by itself, is practically unintelligible,
but in T'an-luan's extensive notes *(chu)* it becomes an elaborate and precise defense of Sukhāvatī Buddhism, such that Shinran could call T'an-
luan "the first teacher" *(honji).*[3] According to the traditional, and only
complete, biography in the *Hsü Kao-seng Chuan* (*T* 50.470), T'an-luan
became a *śramaṇa* (novice), perhaps at about fourteen years of age, and
assayed a commentary on the voluminous Mahāsaṃnipāta *(Ta Chi
Ching).* Understandably his health broke down before he could get very
far with it, and nothing of the work has survived. He wandered south in
search of a cure, recovered after a vision of the gate of heaven opening,
and continued wandering in order to find a recipe for longevity or earthly
immortality. He is said to have met the famous Taoist master T'ao Hung-
ching (455–536) and received from him ten volumes of immortality
texts.[4] Returning home, he stopped off to see Bodhiruci I at Lo-yang and
ask him whether the Buddhists had anything as good as his recently
acquired Taoist texts. He got a straight answer: Bodhiruci "spat on the
ground" and told him that even if he could obtain "youth in old age and

never die," he would still be within samsara; but if he were to study the *Kuan Ching* he would obtain liberation *(vimokṣa).*[5] Accordingly, it is reported that T'an-luan burnt his immortality texts and devoted himself to the *Kuan Ching:* the sutra on Amitāyus and his land of Sukhāvatī.[6]

It is remarkable that, after such a dramatic beginning, T'an-luan's work should have been ignored until Shinran rediscovered him in twelfth-century Japan. The first commentaries are Japanese and belong to the Edo period. This essay will question the historicity of T'an-luan's conversion from Taoism to Buddhism and suggest that its reality is rather to be found in the confessional *Heilsgeschichte* of Pure Land Buddhism. The idea of a "conversion" from Taoism to Buddhism is in any case rather odd, and it will be argued that there are many Taoist elements remaining in T'an-luan's Buddhism; that he can be, and perhaps in fact was, regarded as a Taoist master *(Tao Shih)* to the end of his life; and that his fame as a Buddhist opponent of Taoism is posthumous, although, as we shall see, not undeserved.

TAOIST ELEMENTS IN T'AN-LUAN'S BUDDHISM

Immortality

A Taoist might seek either longevity, extending his life on earth, or immortality, "dropping the body" and going off to live forever in the mysterious regions. In general, the former end was accomplished by concentrating the breath *(ch'i)* and the latter by practices designed to curry the favor of the deities who, if they so pleased, could remove one's name from the Book of Death and enter it into the Book of Life, after which one was accorded the ultimate Chinese happiness of a post in the heavenly bureaucracy ("promotion to higher glory," as they say in the Salvation Army), and having such an assurance, one then took the (physically poisonous) elixir of immortality.[7] T'an-luan's interest seems to have been with the former goal: He wished to live long enough to complete his commentary on the Mahāsaṃnipāta, and he was famous at the capital for his practice of medicine; in fact the emperor honored him because "whenever he came across an illness, he could diagnose it."[8] It was this search for earthly longevity which led T'an-luan to Buddhism, and the rebuff attributed to Bodhiruci is precisely to the point:

> There is no comparison! Where on this earth can you find a method *(fa)* for longevity *(ch'ang-sheng)?* Suppose you could obtain youth in your old age and never die: Even having done that, you would still be rolling round in the phenomenal realms *(san-yu;* Skt., *trailokadhātavaḥ).* [T. 50.470b.27–28]

The Buddhist texts that were then said to be presented as superior to the Taoist ones are called "the prescriptions of the Greatest Immortal" *(Ta-hsien fang)* which would lead to release from samsara *(chieh-t'uo sheng-ssu)* (*T* 50.470b.29 and c.1). This remark represents an authentically Buddhist viewpoint that even admission to the ranks of the deities does not liberate from death. The greatest immortal is the Buddha whose name is Amitāyus, "He of Limitless Life" (Wu-liang-shou Fo), an alias of Amitābha,[9] "whose lifespan is so long," says T'an-luan later, "that its limits are inconceivable" (*T* 40.826c.3–4).

In the *Lun Chu,* T'an-luan repeatedly stresses the extrasamsaric nature of Sukhāvatī and the immortality of all its inhabitants. Each time an excellence of Sukhāvatī, Amitābha, or his bodhisattvas (that is, all Amitābha's faithful followers post-mortem, led by Avalokiteśvara and Mahāsthāmaprāpta) is mentioned, it is set off from a deficiency in samsara—for example, Sukhāvatī is flat because samsara is full of rough terrain which causes suffering (*T* 40.829b.27–c.7). Samsara, he reminds us, consists of the triple world *(trailokadhātavaḥ):* the realm of desire *(kāma-dhātu),* the realm of form *(rūpa-dhātu),* and the realm of formlessness *(ārūpya-dhātu).* Sukhāvatī is outside these three:

> The Mahāprajñāpāramitā Śāstra says: "This Pure Land is not included in the triple world" [*T* 25.340a.20–21]. How can we say this? Since it is without desire, it is not in the realm of desire. Since there is ground to stand on *(ti chü),* it is not in the world of form. Since it has form, it is not in the world of formlessness. . . . Its existence is extraphenomenal *(ch'u yu, erh yu),* and we call it "subtle" *(wei).* [*T* 40.830a.17–20]

That is, Sukhāvatī is free from passion *(virāga),* it has form, and it is firm; therefore it fulfills none of the conditions for any of the phenomenal realms, which are characterized by sensuality *(kāma),* insubstantial shapes and colors *(rūpa),* and abstract states *(arūpa).* A gloss in the text spells it out clearly:

> Extraphenomenal *(ch'u-yu)* means "outside the triple world." Existence *(yu)* means "the Pure Land exists." [*T* 40.830a.21]

Thus, although it is extraphenomenal, it is not a phantasm like, say, a fairy castle *(gandharvanagaram).* It is, in fact, quite simply, "the Pure Land," pure of any kind of defilement (*T* 40.828a.5–b.1) and in every respect inconceivable *(pu-k'o ssu-i; acintya)*—that is, pure of all discursive thought *(vikalpa)* (*T* 40.836c.18–838c.1, passim). Immortality in such a place is, obviously, "without comparison" to the maintenance of youth during old age, as Bodhiruci is reported to have said.

Meditation

T'an-luan divides the Pure Land praxis into five *nien-men,* gates or methods (*men* is used explicitly in both senses) of recollection *(smṛti):* bodily worship; vocal praise; mental contemplation; resolution *(praṇidhāna)* to be born in Sukhāvatī; and "turning toward" *(hui-hsiang)* beings both by distributing merit to them before one's birth and returning from Sukhāvatī to help them after one's birth.

Meditation/contemplation *(kuan-ch'a)* is dealt with at considerable length: Its discussion takes up well over half the text.[10] The meditation is entirely concerned with the visualization of Sukhāvatī and its inhabitants in minute detail. It is remarkable that although both Buddhists and Taoists of the time were fascinated by breathing techniques in meditation, T'an-luan mentions breathing only once, in a laconic reference to the *Abhidharmakośa,*[11] and then dismisses it as irrelevant for his purposes. This concentration on visualization, its doctrinal roots and salvific effects, rather than on discourse or any other of the traditional meditation techniques, seems to be without precedent in Chinese Buddhism. It can, of course, be traced to the sutras. But T'an-luan does not, as we might expect, focus on the thirteen tableaux and nine *in extremis* visualizations given to Queen Vaidehī in the so-called *Amitāyurdhyāna Sutra:* He plunges straight into the tedious lists of jeweled trees, pearly lotuses, talking streams, and whatnot which spread across the pages of the *Larger Sukhāvatīvyūha* like the syrup of an Indian sweetmeat, divides them up in a way quite his own (insecurely suspended from the *gāthaupadeśa*), and ascribes each to a special resolution *(praṇidhāna)* of Amitābha while in his "causal stage" *(in-yüan ti)* as Dharmākara Bodhisattva.[12]

It is difficult to account for this interest in the precise features of the landscape and the appearance of the Buddha and bodhisattvas, except on the basis of T'an-luan's Taoism, wherein he would have learned that accurate visualizations of the immortals and their palaces were essential for ultimate transference to the mysterious regions and union with the Tao.[13] Occasionally he deliberately alludes to Lao Tzu, Chuang Tzu, and other unquestionably Taoist texts in recounting the excellences of Sukhāvatī (as in *T* 40.828c.26–829a.6), and it is tempting to connect his description of Amitābha, the Buddha of the West, as a compassionate mother who leads to the yin state of rest beyond samsara, with the Taoist goddess Hsi Wang Mu, who is yin.[14]

The visualizations, although they may be Taoist in inspiration, are entirely Buddhist in content. T'an-luan divides them first into visualizations of the land *(kuo-t'u),* which he calls the "furnishings" or "container" *(ch'i),* and visualizations of the beings *(chung-sheng; sattva),*[15]

and then he further divides the beings into the Buddha and the bodhisattvas. This is the standard classification into what La Vallée Poussin has
called "le monde des êtres et le monde réceptacle."[16] For T'an-luan these
"two worlds"[17] are mutually interdependent in every way,[18] and the
description of them follows the sutras precisely.

Invocation

T'an-luan's second gate of recollection is that of vocal praise *(k'ou-yeh
tsan-t'an)* in which he advocates invocation of Buddha *(nien-fo)*. His discussion of this topic is quite short (*T* 40.835b.11–c.17), as is his exegesis
elsewhere (*T* 40.833c.20–834c.27) of the recommendation in the sutra to
invoke Amitābha ten times with the formula *nan-mo wu-liang-shou fo*
(see *Sacred Books of the East* 49:2, pp. 197–199), although, of course,
invocation evolved into the most typical of all Pure Land practices.

What interests us here is T'an-luan's explicit comparison of Buddha
invocation with the casting of Taoist spells. After telling us that the name
Amitābha (He of Infinite Light) signifies the Buddha's essence of *ami-
tābhā* (infinite light), which in turn signifies infinite wisdom *(wu-liang
chih)*, such that the vocal pronunciation of Amitābha affects the opera-
tion of infinite wisdom in the mind, he allows an objection that a name is
only a label and cannot affect what it signifies. T'an-luan replies that
names are of two sorts:[19] (1) names which are other than things *(ming i
fa)*, arbitrary labels, "like a finger pointing at the moon," and (2) names
which are the same as things *(ming chi fa)*, such as "the names of Buddhas and bodhisattvas, the *Prajñāpāramitādhāraṇī*,[20] spells *(chin-chou)*,
and suchlike spoken phrases *(in ts'u)*."[21] To convince the *adversus diabo-
lus* that "name-things" exist and work, T'an-luan mentions a spell to
cure edema and one to protect soldiers from injury, which he claims are
in the *Pao P'u-tzu*.[22] Then he mentions the use of quince moxibustion to
cure a sprain,[23] but says everybody knows *(shih-chien kung chih)* that
simply by calling out "quince" one can also be cured. Now, he continues,
the *Śūraṅgamasamādhi Sutra* speaks of a poison-dispelling drum *(vipra-
vāsa-dundubhi)* whose sound causes weapons to drop out and wounds to
heal,[24] and which symbolizes the passion-dispelling voice of Buddha.
This last functions in the inconceivable realm *(pu-k'o ssu-i ching-chieh;
acintyadhātu)* and thus, although it is similar to a Taoist spell, it is far
more powerful: Indeed, it does not merely bring physical health but initi-
ates one into enlightenment (*T* 40.836c.1–4). The name Amitābha is,
then, a name-thing functioning in the inconceivable realm.[25]

Omnilocation

After physical death, according to T'an-luan, the successful Pure Land
exercitant is born *(wang-sheng)* in Sukhāvatī, where he is said to *te fa-*

shen or, more elaborately, *te ch'ing-ching p'ing-teng wu-wei fa-shen.*[26] He enters a *samādhi* called *pao-sheng san-mei (vipākaja-samādhi),* the *samādhi* which is produced *(ja)* as the fruit or recompense *(vipāka)* of his and the Buddha's combined efforts.[27] As a result of this *samādhi,* he manifests anywhere and everywhere as needed, without, however, moving from Sukhāvatī or having notions of going and returning, just as the sun manifests in hundreds of rivers but does not leave the sky (see *T* 40.833a.24–25).

Fa-shen is, of course, *dharmakāya,* and the longer term may be *pariśuddhisamatāsaṃskṛtadharmakāya,* the *dharmakāya* which is unconditioned, nonarisen, and pure. The problem is with the character *te.* It presumably cannot mean that the bodhisattva obtains "a" *dharmakāya,* for this would involve the absurdity of a plurality of *dharmakāyas.* There does not seem to be any satisfactory way of reconstructing a Sanskrit original for the term. In Taoism, however, the phrase *te Tao* (attain/ obtain/possess the Tao) is quite commonly applied to the "arrived man" *(chih-jen).*[28] Such a perfected Taoist manifests everywhere and is in fact no different from the Tao itself. For T'an-luan, once one has attained or obtained or come into possession of the *dharmakāya,* he manifests everywhere and, though in fact different from a Buddha, he is functionally indistinguishable from a Buddha.[29] Thus does T'an-luan appropriate the esoteric dream of the highest and most elusive Taoist adepts and dispense it to the simplest peasant in the formula of the *nien-fo.*

T'AN-LUAN AS A TAOIST MASTER[30]

We have seen that some of the principal features of T'an-luan's Buddhism are controlled by his interest in Taoism. Yet he always realizes the Buddhist objection that Taoism is not effectively transcendent, that it is just an extension of ordinary, samsaric, modes of being.[31] There are indications, however, that his contemporaries regarded him as a Taoist master *(Tao Shih)* who dabbled in Buddhism.

The *Tao Tsang* regards him as a "Buddhistically Taoist master"[32] who wrote on "nourishment of the breath" *(fu ch'i).* The eleventh-century Taoist encyclopedia, *Yün-chi Ch'i-ch'ien,* "Seven Leaves from the Cloud Satchel" (*TT* 684), mentions a text called *T'an-luan Fa-shih Fu-ch'i Fa,* "The Dharmācārya T'an-luan on the Method of Nourishment of the Breath," but the text itself has been lost.[33] T'an-luan was known as "the great adept of Wei who investigated the mysteries" *(Wei Hsüan-chieh Ta-shih),* and he lived in the "monastery of he who was among the mysteries" *(Hsüan-chung Ssu).*[34] *Hsüan* is equivalent to *Tao,* and *Hsüan-chung Fa-shih* is a title given to Lao Tzu.[35]

"Taoism" is an umbrella term covering anything from calisthenics through augury to immortality. *Fu-ch'i* is a comparatively elementary activity which is preliminary to the serious quest for immortality but need on no account lead to it. There is no evidence which suggests that T'an-luan ever broke with society, went into retreat, and practiced the complicated and exquisitely vexatious rules that might earn him the recognition of worthiness for entry into the Book of Life:[36] He was traveling around looking for prescriptions. Whatever he eventually found, now known to us cryptically as *hsien ching,* was apparently effective enough for the emperor to set him up in a monastery which, although it had a Taoist name, was close enough to civilization for a large congregation of laypeople to be present at the time of his edifying birth into Sukhāvatī[37] and for him to be dubbed "Divine Phoenix" *(Shen Luan)* because of his excellence as a diagnostician.[38]

If this interpretation is correct, it would explain the absence of Chinese Buddhist commentaries on T'an-luan. By the time he had been picked up, dusted off, and enthroned as the first teacher of Sukhāvatī Buddhism by Shinran Shōnin, his Taoist therapies had been forgotten and his patients were long dead; his status as a thoroughly well-read and creative Buddhist thinker had come to be recognized; and it was therefore assumed, as the *Shōshinge* says, that T'an-luan had been honored by the emperor because he was regarded as a bodhisattva. It is unlikely that the *hsien ching,* whatever it was or they were, was actually burnt, and the whole account of the meeting with Bodhiruci smacks too much of "that's the way it must have been" to be credible as history. But if one wished to express mythologically the superiority of Sukhāvatī Buddhism over Taoism and to show how T'an-luan came to believe in this superiority, one could not do better than write the story the way it appears in the *Hsü Kao-seng Chuan.*[39]

NOTES

1. From Shinran's Shōshinge (*Kyōgyōshinshō,* 2); see *Shinshū Seikyō Zensho* (Kyoto, Shōwa 15), vol. 2 (Shūshi-bu), p. 45, lines 4a–5a. "Emperor Liang" is apparently Emperor Wu of Liang (r. 502–549). The *Ching-t'u Lun* of Chia-ts'ai, which is more a *Gesta Sanctorum* of Pure Land notables than a collection of biographies, states that "Emperor Hsiao-wang of Liang *(Liang-kuo T'ien-tzu Hsiao-wang)* . . . worshiped T'an-luan as bodhisattva" (*T* 45.97c.11). The *Hsü-seng Chuan,* however, which is earlier and perhaps to be preferred, seems to indicate Emperor Hsiao-ching of Eastern Wei (r. 534–550) (*T* 50.470c.2) as T'an-luan's admiring sovereign but says nothing about his being regarded as a bodhisattva. This, as we shall see, is a significant omission.

2. See Hsiao Ching-fen, "The Life and Teachings of T'an-luan" (Ph.D. dissertation, Princeton Theological Seminary, 1967), pp. 23–31.

3. Two other works on Sukhāvatī purporting to be by T'an-luan are extant: an

apparently liturgical work, *Tsan A-mi-t'o Fo Chi* (*T* 47.420–424), and a short expository piece, *Lüeh-lun An-lo Ching-t'u I* (*T* 47.1–4). Leo Pruden has translated the latter piece as "A Short Essay on the Pure Land by Dharma Master T'an-luan," *Eastern Buddhist,* new series, 8:1(May 1975):74–95. Pruden uncritically accepts T'an-luan's authorship and argues that it is a supplement to the *Lun Chu,* but according to Ishida Mitsuyuki in *Jōdokyō Kyōrishi* (Kyoto: Heirakuji Shoten,1962), p. 62, n. 1, and references given there, its authenticity is no longer accepted by Japanese scholars. I have prepared a translation of the *Tsan A-mi-t'o Fo Chi* into English sprung rhythm suitable for chanting, under the title "Canticles to Amita Buddha," together with some notes on how the text differs from a Japanese work of Shinran bearing the same title *(San Amida Butsu Ge)* (forthcoming from the journal *The Pure Land*).

4. *T* 50.470b.16: *hsien ching* (or *fang*) *shih chüan.* It is usual to translate this as "the *Hsien Ching* in ten volumes," but no such text is otherwise known, despite the desperate advocacy of various Taoist texts which happen to be ten volumes long. Thus "ten volumes of immortality texts" (or "prescriptions") seems to me on many grounds to be a far more likely interpretation.

5. *T* 50.470b.25–c.2.

6. By the term *Kuan Ching* I understand the following group of four texts considered as a unit: (1) three sutras, that is, the *Larger Sukhāvatīvyūha,* the *Smaller Sukhāvatīvyūha,* and the so-called *Amitāyurdhyāna Sutra;* (2) one *śāstra,* the *Wang-sheng Lun.* It is on this unitary group of texts that T'an-luan writes a *chu.* It seems to me quite implausible to identify, as is often done, the phrase *Kuan Ching* with the so-called *Amitāyurdhyāna Sutra* simply because it is also sometimes referred to as *Kuan Ching,* and I claim to find internal evidence in the *Lun Chu* which explicitly prohibits this identification. See my Ph.D. dissertation, "T'an-luan's Commentary on the Pure Land Discourse" (University of Wisconsin, 1973), p. 8f.

7. For an example of the latter quest, see William C. Doub II, "A Taoist Adept's Quest for Immortality" (Ph.D. dissertation, University of Washington, 1971). Dr. Wolfgang Bauer, in a lecture delivered at the University of California, Berkeley, on 3 October 1977, emphasized what he saw as a distinction between post-mortem transference to the paradises and to heaven: The former were happy places located at the fringes of the world, and much sought after, whereas the latter was a forbidding apotheosis of the earthly bureaucracy, to be avoided if at all possible. This distinction, however, is not evident in the text translated by Doub, wherein the practitioner is only too anxious to take off for the heavenly court and deploy his official seal for all eternity. One may wonder if perhaps the distinction should not be drawn between "Taoistic Taoists" (who wanted to flee the bureaucracy) and "Confucianistic Taoists" (who wished to aggrandize the bureaucracy).

8. *Tui ping, shih yüan* (*T* 50.470c.11).

9. The Tibetan tradition distinguishes Amitābha from Amitāyus as Dharmakāya and Sambhogakāya; iconographically, the latter is adorned, the former is not. T'an-luan uses a number of titles as aliases of the Buddha of Sukhāvatī: His general name is Amita, and the forms Amitābha and Amitāyus are frequently used as special names; in the *Tsan A-mi-t'o Fo Chi* (see note 3 above) Amita is addressed under eleven titles all having the broad meaning of "unhindered light." The Sino-Japanese tradition has followed T'an-luan in these identifications.

10. The text is about fifty-four columns long in the Taishō edition. Contempla-

tion is discussed in slightly more than thirty-two of the columns: *T* 40.827c.29–833c.13; 836a.5–19; 836a.28–841b.3.

11. *T* 40.835c.21–22. See also *Kośa,* chap. 6 (Lamotte's revised translation, *Mélanges chinois,* 16:4, p. 155).

12. The connection between these resolutions and the forty-eight of the *Larger Sukhāvatīvyūha* (*T* 12.267c.17–269b.6), of which T'an-luan shows himself well aware, is never discussed.

13. See Henri Maspéro, *Le Taoïsme* (Paris: Gallimard, 1971), pp. 303–317.

14. *T* 40.830a.27–29; see related passages at 838a.27 and 838b.8–9; see also Maspéro, *Le Taoïsme,* p. 312.

15. Passim, but especially *T* 40.836a.28–29. T'an-luan defends his use of *sattva* for Buddhas and bodhisattvas at *T* 40.831b.17–28; the Mahāyānists use *sattva* even for those outside of samsara in order to avoid falling into nihilism *(ucchedavāda).*

16. *Bouddhisme: Études et matériaux: Cosmologie,* Académie Royale de Belgique, Classe des Lettres et des Sciences morales et politiques et Classe des Beaux-Arts, Mémoires, 2nd series, vol. 6, fasc. 2 (Brussels, 1913).

17. *Erh shih-chien* (*T* 40.829a.27; 841c.6–7).

18. *T* 40.841c.11–19.

19. *T* 40.835c.2–17.

20. Of the many candidates which have been proposed for the honor of being identified with this *dhāraṇī,* my vote at present goes to the *Aparamitāyur-jñānahṛdayadhāraṇī* (Mochizuki, *Bukkyō Daijiten* 1:65); by reciting it six times daily for ten days one obtains a vision of Amitābha.

21. *T* 40.835c.6–8.

22. The battle spell is similar to a passage in the *Nei-p'ien,* 15, but is by no means an exact quote (see the English version by James R. Ware, *Alchemy, Medicine, Religion in the China of A.D. 320,* Cambridge: M.I.T. Press, 1966, p. 249f.); the edema spell is unidentified. Michibata (see note 30 below) simply calls them folk beliefs (p. 1005) and claims that the *Pao P'u-tzu* was handed down orally, so that T'an-luan may not have known it directly.

23. *Mu-kua tui huo yun:* "Quince *(Pyrus japonica)* is applied with a fiery iron." See Ilza Veith, *The Yellow Emperor's Classic of Internal Medicine* (Berkeley: University of California Press, 1972), p. 210 and n. 3, for an apparently related technique.

24. *T* 40.835c.15–16, which refers back to 834c.1–9 and *T* 25.633b (see Lamotte's translation, *Mélanges chinois,* 13, p. 151).

25. Although he does not use the term, T'an-luan's explanation of "name-things" illuminates the meaning of *chen-yen* as a translation of *mantra:* It is not merely a true word but "a word which is Truth," an effective or efficient sound which may or may not be a label as well. Peter Crossley-Holland has called *mantra* "a sonorous embodiment of the truth"; see "The Ritual Music of Tibet," *Tibet Journal* 1 (3–4) (Autumn 1976): 50.

26. *T* 40.828c.9 et passim.

27. *T* 40.840a.23; see also Mochizuki, *Bukkyō Daijiten* 2:1790a. A great deal of confusion has arisen from attempts to fit the standard Trikāya system onto the *Lun Chu.* But there seem to be two *kāya* systems: an economic system belonging to Amitābha (an indivisibly double unmanifest/manifest *dharmakāya: dharma-tādharmakāya/upāyadharmakāya)* and a soteriological system belonging to the bodhisattvas (an apparently preexistent and unarisen *pariśuddhisamatāsaṃskṛta-*

dharmakāya which, when attained or obtained, begins producing *nirmita* forms). The term *sambhogakāya* nowhere occurs. See my dissertation, pp. 62–65.

28. Maspéro, *Le Taoïsme,* p. 315.

29. The problem of imputed perfection, which to my mind T'an-luan never quite solves, is dealt with at *T* 40.840b.8–c.9 et passim. T'an-luan's argument depends in part upon an interpretation of the *Larger Sukhāvatīvyūha* which would have been impossible had he read the Sanskrit text as we now have it. See my dissertation, pp. 282–284, 287–290. The idea was ultimately crystallized by Shinran as lateral transference (*ōchō,* rendered by D. T. Suzuki by the acrobatic term "crosswise leap") in his Division of Teachings system (*Kyōgyōshinshō,* 3) according to which the *nembutsu*-exercitant is "transferred," suddenly and without progressing through the bodhisattva levels, "laterally"—that is, he does not move up since he is already at the pinnacle of perfection.

30. Much of the material in this section is taken from Michibata Ryōshū, "Donran to Dōkyō tono Kankei," in *Tōyō Bunka Ronshū* (Tokyo: Waseda University Press, 1969), pp. 1001–1020. I am indebted to Dr. Michel Strickman, an American scholar hidden at the time in mysterious quarters in Kyoto, for bringing this article to my attention.

31. This is perhaps the principal feature of Buddhist polemics: Śākyamuni is said to have rejected his two teachers on these grounds, and the states he reached under them are relegated to the "formless attainments" *(ārūpya samāpatti)* which, though exalted, are not liberation.

32. Michibata, "Donran to Dōkyō," p. 1002: *bukkyō-teki na dōshi.*

33. Ibid., p. 1006.

34. *T* 50.470c.5 and 16.

35. Michibata, "Donran to Dōkyō," p. 1018.

36. Doub, *A Taoist Adept's Quest,* p. 36, has the adept reprimanded by the immortals because he does not stow his shoes neatly. For the grades of Taoists, see Michael R. Saso, *Taoism and the Rite of Cosmic Renewal* (Pullman: Washington State University Press, 1972), chap. 5.

37. *T* 47.97c.21–22.

38. *T* 50.470c.2 and 11–12.

39. Pruden, "A Short Essay," pp. 76–79, arrives at a similar conclusion but, as it seems to me, more precipitously and less securely.

Buddhist Practice

3
Chih-i's Meditation on Evil

NEAL DONNER

T'ien-t'ai Chih-i (538–597) is best known as the founder of the T'ien-t'ai school. He is also famous for his classification of Buddhist doctrines in order of profundity and manner of exposition—a method for bringing order into the vast collection of Buddhist scriptures which had been translated into Chinese in the previous four hundred years. Aside from his enormously influential doctrinal works, however, he was the first Chinese to produce extensive treatises on meditation, thus ending the Chinese dependence on translations of Indian meditation manuals. The Indian manuals were all from the Hīnayāna branch of Buddhism, with the result that their theoretical foundations were not in agreement with Chinese (or any) Mahāyāna. Chih-i's meditation treatises broke new ground by providing the Buddhist community in his own culture with expositions of meditative techniques that were firmly grounded in Mahāyāna thought. He also structured and organized the different methods far more comprehensively than had yet been done, so that in the realms of both theory and practice he became the great systematizer of Chinese Buddhism, a role which has been compared to that of Aristotle in Greek philosophy or Aquinas in Christian thought.

The meditation on evil is one of several types of meditation expounded in the *Mo-ho Chih-kuan* (Great Calming and Contemplation),[1] which is the greatest work of Chih-i and his definitive statement on Mahāyāna "perfect and sudden" meditation. Though the great majority of the meditation methods in this work are founded on Chinese versions of Indian Buddhist scriptures (Hīnayāna meditation manuals, the *Great Treatise on the Perfection of Wisdom*,[2] the Mahāyāna *Mahāparinirvāṇa Sutra*, and others), the systematization and interpretation of them according to Mahāyāna principles of wisdom was Chih-i's own creative contribution to the development of Buddhism. As a consequence, this text became the standard meditation treatise for the T'ien-T'ai school of Buddhism in China as well as the Tendai school in Japan.

From the Mahāyāna point of view, Hīnayāna and Mahāyāna differ in their approach to meditation because the Hīnayānists drew an ontological distinction between (1) the realm of suffering, or ordinary phenomenal life (samsara), and (2) the realm of enlightenment, mystical realization, or absolute reality (nirvana); whereas Mahāyāna understood the two as ontologically identical, teaching that absolute reality is present and attainable in every aspect of one's daily existence. Hence Mahāyānists refer to Hīnayāna as dualistic (but not in the sense of the mind-body dualism of Sānkhya or Cartesian philosophy) and consider themselves to be monistic. The consequence for meditation is that while the Hīnayāna response to the impure factors of the world—sensuality, sickness, death, impermanence—is to cultivate aversion to them, Mahāyāna meditation attempts to "see through" the evil and the impure to discern its inherent (though mind-obscured) perfection.

The *Mo-ho Chih-kuan* is theoretically made up of ten chapters, but actually it contains only seven.[3] The first chapter is presented as an abbreviated version of the projected ten chapters. The systematization of meditation methods which it employs differs from the plan of the later chapters, however, as it is based on the four bodily positions to be assumed during meditation: (1) sitting, (2) standing or walking, (3) alternating between the two, and (4) ad libitum. By comparison, the main body of the text is not based on these four *samādhis* but on ten mental states or attitudes ("modes") as counterposed to ten objects of contemplation (making one hundred subject-object relationships, the majority of which are discussed in detail).[4]

The meditation on evil is not found in the later chapters but only in the opening synopsis. Specifically, it is included in the fourth or ad libitum *samādhi,* along with meditation on the good and meditation on what is neither good nor evil. The fourth *samādhi* or program of religious practice is usually called the "neither-walking-nor-sitting *samādhi*" to distinguish it from the first three: the "constantly sitting *samādhi,*" the "constantly walking *samādhi,*" and the "half-walking-half-sitting *samādhi*" (that is, alternating between walking and sitting). It goes by two other names: the "*samādhi* of following one's own thought" (*sui tzu-i san-mei,* also understood as meaning "optional," "discretionary," or "ad libitum") and the "*samādhi* of awakening to the nature of thought" *(chüeh-i san-mei).* Unlike the other three methods, this *samādhi* is practicable even outside the meditation chamber, for the only essential prop for the meditation is one's own mind. Though the meditation on one's evil thoughts is formally only a third of the practice, it epitomizes Mahāyāna doctrine. The meditations on the other two aspects of mind, the good and the morally neutral, may be understood by reference to this Mahāyāna perspective on evil.

It will be clear by now that the evil which is the object of the meditation is that evil which resides in the self, not that in the external world. Chih-i always presupposes that the mind is fundamentally enlightened; the defilements of the mind *(kleśas)* are relatively adventitious and in their basic nature are simply misperceived factors of enlightenment. He is here in agreement with the view general to Chinese Buddhism (a view which he helped to define) that enlightenment is the natural state of humanity. It is in the meditation on evil that the Mahāyāna approach to meditation taken by Chih-i is revealed most clearly, for the task set before the practitioner is to confront his own impure nature in its every manifestation and transmute it directly into purity (implying a change in his own awareness, not in any hypothetical realm of "fact" or "reality," except insofar as the change in his awareness leads to a different way of his being in the world).

Entering into evil thoughts and impulses in order to understand them and thereby become liberated from them carries with it, however, the danger of becoming contaminated by them instead, a problem to which Chih-i devotes a great deal of attention. In what follows I examine the specific method which Chih-i advances for the meditation on one's own evil thoughts and the caveats he appends to guard against the descent into immorality.

The Four Phases of Thought

Underlying Chih-i's work is the assumption that thought should try to view thought in an act of pure introspection—not to impose control directly but to reach an intuitive understanding of its own nature. The understanding to be attained is defined in terms of realizing the merely provisional validity of the linguistic category "thought," a negative noetic act which produces, or is identical to, the positive insight into the ground upon which this figure, this category of "thought," is projected. This ground, Ultimate Truth or Reality, suffuses the figure until they are one, as the monistic philosophy of Mahāyāna Buddhism must teach.

Each thought appears in four phases or times: This notion is similar but not identical to the traditional Abhidharma analysis of the four stages in the existence of an individual dharma (arising, persisting, changing, perishing). In Chih-i's analysis a thought first does "not yet exist" and finally is "finished existing." One may say from the subjective viewpoint that this is "not-yet-thinking, about-to-think, thinking-proper, and thinking-completed." Chan-jan, the T'ang commentator to the *Mo-ho Chih-kuan,* notes that to contemplate only the first and the fourth phases is the method of certain practitioners of *dhyāna,* those who negate the intellectual faculty altogether. He may be referring to certain Ch'an practitioners. Chih-i argues (in a time before the appearance of the Ch'an school in China) that although thoughts are nonexistent in these two phases, yet there is a sense in which thoughts (or mind)[5] both exist and do not exist. The relationship between the two senses of *hsin* is the same as that between a person and his actions. Mind *must* exist in some sense for religious practice to have any point. Chih-i therefore opposes explicitly both those who uphold the unchangeability (eternality) of mind as well as those who uphold the simple nonexistence of mind. Change, and therefore enlightenment, would be impossible if mind were either absolutely existent or absolutely nonexistent.

MEDITATION ON GOOD THOUGHTS

Evil thoughts are defined in relation to good thoughts, so it is best to digress here with an explanation of what the latter are considered to be and how they are to be meditated upon. The category of the Six Perfections (giving, morality, forbearance, exertion, meditation, wisdom) provides the framework. Any thought whose essence is primarily one of these six qualities is a "good" thought. In contemplating such an act of mind one associates it with any of the six senses (the five plus mind itself as the organizer of sense data) and any of the six actions (standing, walking, sitting, lying down, speaking, being silent). Since these twelve (called the Twelve Items) are all applicable to any of the perfections, one derives 12 times 6 or 72 possible meditations to be applied where appropriate. Chih-i gives details for only some of these meditations, since the others may be understood by reference to them. In the perfection of giving, for example, one internally renounces vision and the object of vision, perceiving that the visual consciousness that derives from them is neither external, internal (because caused), eternal, nor absolutely nonexistent. Moreover each of the four phases of an act of visual consciousness (not yet seeing, about to see, seeing proper, and seeing completed) is incapable of being apprehended. Introducing the four phases into the meditation multiplies the units of meditation to 4 times 72 or 288. The true perfection of giving is to realize the emptiness of giver, recipient, and gift. Thus one gives (while being visually aware of the giving) knowing that all three are empty; otherwise it would not be the *perfection* of giving. Yet "emptiness" also involves avoidance of the attribution of absolute *nonexistence* to any of these three elements.

At the level of the Perfect Teaching (most profound of Chih-i's series of four levels of interpretation of Buddhist doctrine, the others being the Tripiṭaka or Hīnayāna, the Shared, and the Separate teachings), one understands that the attribution of existence and the attribution of nonexistence, as well as their simultaneous assertion and their simultaneous denial, are all efforts to describe the same (ultimately indescribable) ultimate reality, whether of individual phenomena or of the collectivity of phenomena (the "world"). Not to dwell in any of these interpretations while giving is the "featureless giving," the highest form of meditation. When the Three Truths of Chih-i (empty, provisionally existent, and the mean encompassing these) are applied to the meditation in this way the units of meditation multiply to 288 times 3 or 864. These may be practiced in any of the traditional Ten Destinies (from hell-dwellers to Buddhas—modes of reincarnation or degrees of spiritual development), yielding 8,640 units. And finally each perfection has six aspects, according to which of the other perfections (including itself) combines with it, for the Six Perfections, at the level of the Perfect Teaching, perfectly suffuse each other—each is inseparable from the others just as a single variety of incense which has been mashed into a ball with five other kinds is inseparable from them. Thus the meditation includes 51,840 units, from which the practitioner may select according to his need and opportunity. The complexity of Chih-i's thought may be seen by the fact that in order to represent graphically the whole array of possibilities (perfections × perfections × items × destinies × phases × truths) a six-dimensional space would be required.

What Is Evil?

Evil is defined as the opposite of the Six Perfections: avarice, immorality, anger, laziness, mental distraction, and stupidity. These vices may be conveniently styled the Six Antiperfections, the first five coinciding to a remarkable degree with five within the Christian category of the Seven Deadly Sins: avarice, lust, ire, sloth, and intemperance. (Stupidity on the Buddhist side, and pride and envy on the Christian side, do not correspond, however.)

Chih-i's T'ang-dynasty commentator Chan-jan identifies two levels of evil in the Perfect Teaching. At the relative level, evil is whatever is not in accord with the Perfect Teaching; at the absolute level, evil is being attached to the Perfect Teaching itself. The latter is the most rarefied form of evil; Chih-i does not concern himself with it in detail except to say:

> To achieve the realization that evil things are not evil, that everything is Ultimate Reality, is to achieve the Way of the Buddha through practicing the Non-Way—but to develop an attachment to the Way turns the Way into the Non-Way. [*T* 46.17b]

The exposition focuses in fact on desire (immorality), first of the Six Antiperfections, as the paradigm for all forms of evil.

Chih-i must next show that there is no contradiction between evil and the Way. Even if evil is constantly present in one's mind, good will always be found somewhere within it, for every element of existence is present in every other: There are Buddhas in hell and there is evil in Buddhas, for the Ten Destinies perfectly interpenetrate. (This dictum became the basis for the controversial theory of Evil in the Buddha-nature developed in the T'ien-t'ai school in later Sung times.) In fact for laypeople who live constantly amid evil phenomena there may be no opportunity at all to meditate upon the Six Perfections, and it is therefore that selfsame evil which they employ as an object of meditation. As Chih-i puts it, "Evil does not obstruct the Way." He gives a series of examples from scripture to illustrate this idea, including (1) Angulimāla, a murderous bandit who killed 999 people in moral obedience to his teacher's command; (2) a prince who employed wine (contrary to Buddhist rules for laypeople) to make his guests happy; (3) a queen who appeared perfumed and adorned (also contrary to proper modes of conduct) before her king to please him, and also secretly and mendaciously countermanded the king's order to kill his cook (knowing as she did that he would regret his command later); (4) a prostitute who enticed men to herself in order to expound the dharma to them; and (5) the case of Devadatta, the Buddhist Judas, who (as the *Lotus Sutra* states clearly) will also attain enlightenment eventually. To sum up the principle:

> If amid evils there were nothing but evil, the practice of the Way would be impossible and people would remain forever unenlightened. But because the Way *is* present even amid evil it is possible to attain saintliness even though one may engage in the Antiperfections [for example, even Buddhist monks can be angry]. [*T* 46.17b]

Moreover the Way does not obstruct evil, although this is not so relevant for the present meditation. The relationship between the two is analogous to the relationship between light and dark in empty space. A material substratum is necessary in order for either to become manifest; without this substratum their interpenetration is unimpeded, and even with a substratum both are fully present, at least at the level of potentiality.

THE METHOD

The general approach for meditating on evil is described by Chih-i as follows:

> If a person has by nature a great number of desires and is seething with contamination, so that despite his efforts to counter and suppress them they continue to increase by leaps and bounds—then he should simply direct his attention wherever he wishes. Why? Because without the arising of the antiperfections, he would have no chance to practice contemplation. [*T* 46.17c]

He goes on to give a pregnant simile for this process:

> It is like going fishing. If the fish is strong and the fishing line weak, the fish cannot be forcibly pulled in. Instead, one simply lets the baited hook enter and get caught in the fish's mouth, and depending on how close the creature approaches, allows it to dive and surface freely. Then before long it can be harvested from the water.
>
> The practice of the contemplation of the antiperfections is the same. The antiperfections are represented by an evil fish, and contemplation is represented by the baited hook. If there were no fish, there would be no need for hook or bait: The more numerous and large the fish are, the better. They will all follow after the baited hook without rejecting it. These antiperfections will similarly not for long withstand the attempt to bring them under control. [*T* 46.17c]

The meditation on evil thoughts is as multidimensional as the meditation on good thoughts, but it is presented with somewhat greater complexity. The first stage is to realize the emptiness of each thought, and the meditation is focused on this exercise. Both the provisionality and its conformity to the Three Truths must also be realized thereafter, however.

In order to realize the emptiness of each evil thought ("thought of desire"), the emptiness of each of the four phases of desire must be apprehended; and for that to take place one meditates upon the transition from each phase to the next. Chih-i goes into detail only for the transition between the first and the second phases, leaving the others to be understood by analogy.

Assuming that the second phase arises ("about to desire"), then what is the status of the first phase ("not yet desiring")? There are four possibilities: the first phase perishes (is nonexistent), does not perish (is existent, not nonexistent), both, or neither.

Let us take the first case, in which the first phase *perishes* in order for the second phase to arise. Do these two events coincide or not? For them to coincide would involve the contradiction of arising and perishing occurring at the same time. The commentator Chan-jan indicates this could be equivalent to saying that in order for light to come into being the lamp which produces it would have to be destroyed, a clear absurdity. What if the two phases do not coincide? This would involve supposing that events come into existence without a cause; in this case, as Chan-jan comments, flames could come into being spontaneously without originating from something like a lamp, and we could have cheese without milk. This too is absurd.

Secondly, we consider that perhaps in order for the second phase to arise, the first phase does *not* perish (exists). Again, do these two phases, both of them "existing," coincide or not? If they coincide, they are both in existence at the same time and "there would be no limit to the origination [of new entities],"[6] for there would then have to be a "nonexistent not-yet-desiring" which preceded the "existent not-yet-desiring," and this would by the same logic not yet have perished at the moment of the arising of the "existent not-yet-desiring." With such an infinite regression there could never have been a time when the desire was completely nonexistent. Thus they cannot coincide. What if they do not coincide? Then, as in the cheese-and-milk case mentioned above, there would be no cause for the arising of the second phase and entities could arise anywhere, anytime, causelessly. Thus they cannot *not* coincide.

Thirdly, perhaps in order for the second phase to arise, the first phase both perishes and does not perish. But Chih-i says:

> If the second phase arises from the *nonperishing* of the first, there would be no need for the simultaneous perishing of the first. How could such an indeterminate cause produce a determinate effect? Even if the perishing and the nonperishing of the first phase were the same in substance they would differ in their fundamental nature; while if they were different in substance there could be no relationship between them. [*T* 46.18a]

Chan-jan adds:

> If the first phase is both existent and nonexistent by the time the second arises, we have opposite causes producing the same effect. These opposites could not even coexist, much less work together to produce a common effect. [*T* 46.206c]

Finally, what if in order for the second phase to arise the first phase neither perishes nor does not perish? To consider this question, Chih-i introduces the idea of the locus of the event:

Is the locus of this double-negated first phase existent or nonexistent? If existent, then how can we say it is doubly negated? If nonexistent, how could nonexistence be capable of producing anything? [T 46.18a]

This completes the contemplation on one aspect of the transition from the first to the second phase, in which the second phase was held constant ("arising") and the first phase was run through its four alternatives according to the tetralemma. The arising of the phase of about-to-desire is therefore incapable of being apprehended, and as a phenomenon it has been emptied.

In considering the transition from the first to the second phase, it remains for us to analyze the possibilities with the second phase held constant at "not arising" and the first phase run through four alternatives, then with the second phase held constant at "both arising and not arising," and finally with the second phase held constant at "neither arising nor not arising." This yields sixteen possibilities in the transition between the first and the second phase of the moment of desire. In every case it is a matter of seeking the later phase in the earlier and being unable to find it. The other three transitions—from the second to the third phase of desire, from the third to the fourth, and from the fourth to the first phase (of a new moment of desire)—may be considered in similar fashion. Thus in all there are sixty-four transitions, all of which are shown to be empty—that is, unthinkable *(acintya)*.

If this all seems senseless or needlessly complex, one must keep in mind that it is a model of the false, not of the true, and also that, according to Chan-jan, it is specifically intended for those of dull mentality.[7] Bright individuals should be able to realize at a single glance that the development of a desire is incapable of being apprehended by discursive thought. It is the foolish who find this kind of exercise necessary (but "foolish" here means those lacking intuition, not those of meager intellect). The result of this mind-wracking cogitation on the origin of desire is not that the practitioner reaches a rational solution but that, intellectually exhausted, he is forced to admit the impotence of his rational processes to give a coherent account of what he knows through common sense is obviously taking place: the arising of desire in the mind. Once he has reached this realization, the desire is completely emptied of substantiality for him and loses its power to affect him. This is what Chih-i calls the "baited hook."

One may also contemplate which sense-object gives rise to the moment of desire, as well as which mode of activity it is associated with (these are the Twelve Items referred to above). Thus if it arose in association with the seeing of form, then with which of the four phases of seeing of form (not yet seeing, about to see, seeing proper, seeing completed) was it associated? Likewise for the other eleven items.

One may further contemplate what the purpose of the desire is. Desire is broken down into the traditional Ten Destinies: The desire may have been to break the moral code, to acquire dependents, on up to the most exalted desire (which is still a desire and hence an antiperfection): the desire for the Buddha's dharma.

One understands therefore that while the desire is unthinkable, and there can be neither desirer nor desired, yet the desire takes place in a mysterious way (corresponding to the second of the Three Truths, provisionality), and its ultimate nature, its dharma-nature, is between the two (the third truth).

None of the Three Truths can obstruct the others, contradictory though they may appear to be. If the antiperfections (the provisionally existent) could obstruct the dharma-nature (and thereby prevent beings from attaining enlightenment), for example, the dharma-nature would be destroyed—but it is by definition eternal and incapable of being destroyed. Conversely, the dharma-nature or Ultimate Reality cannot obstruct the antiperfections, for we see all about us antiperfections appearing in their provisional aspects:

> Know therefore that the antiperfections are identical with the dharma-nature. When an antiperfection arises, then the dharma-nature arises with it; and when the antiperfection ceases to be, the dharma-nature also ceases. [T 46.18a]

Chan-jan comments here:

> The dharma-nature itself neither comes into being nor ceases to be, but [at the level of relative truth] varies its aspect with the object being contemplated. At the level of Ultimate Truth, however, neither antiperfection nor dharma-nature exists, and a fortiori neither of these comes into being nor ceases to be. Whoever has understood this can view desire as identical with the dharma-nature. [T 46.208b]

This brings us to the central theoretical claim made by Chih-i, expressed in a statement for which he is justifiably famous: "Mental defilements are identical to enlightenment." That is, kleśas are identical to bodhi. There has been some doubt among modern scholars whether Chih-i had adequate scriptural foundation for such a sweeping dictum. Does it not represent an original departure in Chinese Buddhism and a modification of the Indian tradition? But Chih-i supplies the sutra text on which he bases his statement:

> Desire is identical to the Way, and the same is true for anger and stupidity. Thus the whole of the Buddha's dharma is contained in these three dharmas.

But if one should seek enlightenment apart from desire, one would be as far from it as earth is from heaven. [*T* 46.18b]

Translating directly from the sutra (which is the *Chu-fa-wu-hsing-ching,* the *Sarva-dharma-pravrtti-nirdesa,* in the Chinese translation of Kumā-rajīva), the text reads:

> Desire is nirvana, and the same is true for anger and stupidity. Thus there are countless dharmas of the Buddha in these three. Whoever distinguishes desire, anger, and stupidity (from nirvana or the Buddha's dharma) is as far from the Buddha as earth is from heaven. [*T* 15.759c]

Desire, anger, and stupidity are the category known as the Three Poisons, the most basic defilements *(kleśas),* which subsume all of the other varieties. Chih-i's scriptural foundation would thus seem to be adequate, and the text on which he bases his dictum had been current in China for nearly two centuries by the time he gave the lectures from which the written form of his treatise, the *Mo-ho Chih-kuan,* was derived. The modern scholar Ando Toshio includes the foregoing sutra with the *Sūrangama-samādhi Sutra* and the *Vimalakīrti* (both frequently quoted by Chih-i) as one of the scriptures that explicitly declared, before the time of Chih-i, the identity between antipodal categories like the defilements and enlightenment or sexual misconduct and the Buddhist Way.[8] Ando explains that these texts thereby invited misinterpretation and misuse to the extent that many Buddhists understood their doctrines as a simple eulogy of evil ways and thus exposed the *sangha* to anti-Buddhist persecution and morality campaigns. Fully aware of the dangers this doctrine presented, however, Chih-i includes moral discipline and purification as essential preliminaries to the contemplation of evil;[9] he also goes on in his present discourse upon the meditation on evil to present caveats for the practice of this meditation. We shall deal with these caveats below.

That desire (and all *kleśas*) and enlightenment are ontologically identical is a commonplace in the scriptures of Vajrayāna Buddhism. (In the *Sarva-ranasya-nāma-tantra-rāja,* for example, translated in the Sung dynasty, it says: "The Three Poisons of worldly desire, anger, and stupidity are identical to the realm of the *tathāgata.*")[10] As can be seen, however, this is not a new theoretical departure; it is in complete agreement with the monism of the *prajñā-pāramitā* sutras and has, moreover, been stated explicitly by various nontantric texts. Chih-i supplies a series of quotations from the *Vimalakīrti* as well which buttress the assertion: "By following the Non-Way, a bodhisattva achieves the Buddha's Way."[11] Chih-i next quotes: "All animate beings are already identical to the features of enlightenment, so they cannot further attain it; they are already identical to the features of nirvana, so they cannot further attain extinction [nirvana]." This sentence is based on a passage from the *Vimalakīrti* which reads in Kumārajīva's version as follows:

> If Maitreya attains supreme, perfect enlightenment, then all animate beings should likewise attain it. Why is this? Because all animate beings are marked by enlightenment. If Maitreya [bodhisattva] attains extinction, then all animate beings should likewise attain it. Why is this? Because the Buddhas all know that every animate being is ultimately quiescent and extinct; being marked by nirvana, they do not further attain extinction." [*T* 14.542b]

We may concede that Chih-i's quotation represents the sense of the *Vimalakīrti* here. Two further *Vimalakīrti* quotations are given by Chih-i at this point:

> To those who are haughty, the Buddha preaches that separation from carnality, anger, and stupidity is what is called liberation. But to those who lack haughtiness, he preaches that the nature of carnality, anger, and stupidity is the same as liberation. [*T* 14.548a]

and

> All the defilements are the seeds of the *tathāgata*. [*T* 14.549b]

The "haughty ones" clearly refer to the Hīnayāna, which makes a radical distinction between defilements and enlightenment.

CAVEATS

Following his discourse on each of the preceding three *samādhis,* Chih-i appends an "exhortation" in which he waxes eloquent on the benefits of the meditational practice he has described, encouraging the practitioner to engage diligently in it. After this fourth of the Four *Samādhis,* however, an essay of cautionary advice and warnings takes the place of the usual exhortation to practice. Although the "neither-walking-nor-sitting" *samādhi* contains sections on the contemplation of good and of neutral thoughts, it is clearly the contemplation on evil thoughts which requires an admonition to replace the usual call to action.

The problem is this: How can this ultimate teaching of the absolute identity of opposites, a doctrine which in effect teaches that evil and good (let "good" be interpreted as nirvana) are the same, be reconciled with the self-evident need for moral behavior in the world? How can this doctrine be prevented from degenerating into a perverse and antinomian affirmation of evil? Indeed, it is clear that Chih-i feels it *has* been so misinterpreted in the past. In every age (for this dharma is held to be eternal) there have been those who understood such a teaching as a simple eulogy of evil ways. In the relatively recent past (for Chih-i) there were the monkish libertines of North China who called down upon their heads the Northern Chou persecution of Buddhism (A.D. 574–577). Chih-i unquestionably is advancing the view that it was immorality among the Buddhist community which brought on the persecution (whereas many modern scholars emphasize the foreign origin of the religion as the major factor which made it vulnerable).[12] There may have been, he says, some monks who, in practicing and teaching the abandonment of moral restraints,

did succeed to a small extent in concentrating their minds and in gaining a weak understanding of emptiness. But they take no cognizance of their listeners' faculties nor life circumstances and do not penetrate to the sense of the Buddha's teaching. They simply take this one dharma and teach it indiscriminately to others. Now once they have taught it to others for a long time, it may happen that one or two [of their disciples] gain some benefit; but this is like insects accidentally producing legible characters by their random gnawing on a tree. They then take this as proof and say their evil doctrine has been verified. They call other contrary teachings lies and laugh at those who observe moral prohibitions and who cultivate the morally good, saying the teachings of such people are not the Way. Expounding nothing but this pernicious doctrine to others, they cause a host of evils to be committed everywhere.

Now when blind and sightless disciples, who are unable to tell right from wrong and are dull of mind and heavily burdened with defilements, hear such preachings, they act out their lusts. Submitting faithfully and obediently to this teaching, they all discard moral prohibitions. There is nothing wrong that they fail to do, and their sins accumulate as high as mountains. At length the common people are brought to hold the moral precepts in as low esteem as so many weeds. As a result, the king of the land and his ministers exterminate the Buddha's dharma. This noxious tendency has penetrated deeply, and even now has yet to be rectified. [*T* 46.18c–19a]

As if there were still any doubt about his opinion of such interpretations and such behavior, Chih-i attributes the fall of the ancient Chou dynasty (1122–256 B.C.) as well as the Western Chin dynasty (A.D. 265–316) to the rise of immorality, buttressing the assertion with quotes respectively from the *Shih-chi* and the *Chin-shu* official histories. In the latter case it was Juan Chi (A.D. 210–263), one of the famous Seven Sages of the Bamboo Grove, who led the immoralists:

[He] was a gifted person who wore disheveled hair and let his belt hang loose. In later times the children and grandchildren of the nobility imitated him, held that only by engaging in mutually shameful conduct with servants could one achieve naturalness *(tzu-jan),* and called those who vied to uphold the rules of conduct "country bumpkins." [*T* 46.18c–19a]

The misapplication of an essentially true doctrine is further illustrated in the *Mo-ho Chih-kuan* by this amusing story taken from Chuang-tzu:

Take for example [the story of the famous beauty] Hsi Shih. Once she was stricken with a mental illness and took such delight in grimacing and groaning that even the hundred hairs of her eyebrows all grew contorted. Yet it served only to enhance her beauty. The other women in the neighborhood, being ugly from birth, imitated her grimaces and groans but only grew so loathsome in appearance that the poor moved far away and the rich closed their gates, the fishes who dwelt in grottoes dove deeper yet, and flying things escaped into the heights. [*T* 46.18c–19a][13]

The fact is that such people have seriously misunderstood a fundamentally true doctrine. As long as we continue to make distinctions, we are barred from Buddhahood; but if we fail to make distinctions, we are incapable of decent behavior and plummet further from Buddhahood than ever. Clearly there is a paradox here—but as the nature of Ultimate Truth is by necessity paradoxical, this should not be a crippling difficulty. Part of the answer may be found in Chih-i's distinctive doctrine of the Three Truths, already referred to here, in which the fact that things (and thoughts) are empty does not prevent them from being provisionally real. Hīnayānists penetrate to the unreality of things (by analyzing them into their component dharmas), bodhisattvas push further to realize their provisional validity (for they act in the world for the salvation of all beings), and Buddhas fully reconcile the two poles, seeing (as we might put it) that the two viewpoints are as opposite sides of the same diamond, or, one is tempted to add, like the particle and wave theories of light in modern quantum physics, each being valid in the proper context.

The doctrine of the Three Truths means among other things that the need to recognize the oneness of things does not abrogate the need to recognize the distinctions which obtain within this oneness. The solution which Chih-i applies to the problem of immoralist interpretations of Mahāyāna monism can be regarded as one of many possible applications of his doctrine. The point is that it is incumbent upon the teachers of the dharma to make careful distinctions in the capacities of their listeners, just as the Buddha himself did (according to Chih-i's famous system of doctrinal classification known as the Four Dharmas of Conversion or the Four Teachings: Tripiṭaka, Shared, Separate, and Perfect). The Buddha promulgated the teaching that evil and good, desire and the Way, are identical both because it is the ultimate truth and because beings who are immersed in evil have nothing but evil at hand to elevate themselves above evil. (It must be borne in mind that in these contexts desire is understood as the prototype of all other forms of evil.) But the Buddha does not expound this doctrine to those who are unable to understand that it does not exclude the equally valid doctrine that evil and good are quite separate. It is above all to those of keen intellectual faculties who are yet burdened with mental defilements that the Buddha expounds such a doctrine, while the foolish who are relatively pure receive only the teaching of the avoidance of evil and the affirmation of good, as if these were truly separate from each other.

The text makes clear that it is nothing short of criminal to ignore the differences in the capacities of listeners, teaching but a single doctrine to all. (For a modern example of the results of such a practice one might recall the foolish distortions to which the teachings of Marx and Locke have been subjected in the twentieth century.) Chih-i, living in a time before even the printing press existed, much less the electronic media, could assume that if only the will were there, it was possible to prevent the foolish from hearing this powerful, but by the same token dangerous, doctrine of the identity of evil and good, desire and enlightenment.

The aim of the Buddha, and thus of every teacher who transmits his dharma, is to save beings from suffering, and there are cases when he must use the strongest medicine available. It is, says Chih-i, as in the case of a seriously ill child whose parents give it the traditional yellow dragon potion (derived from human excrement) in a desperate attempt to save his life:

> Though it scores the teeth and makes him vomit, if the child takes it, it will cure his sickness. [*T* 46.19b]

But if such a potion is used, it must be with great care:

> One ought to provide oneself with plain hot water to supplement and neutralize it. [*T* 46.19c]

In this case, the "plain hot water" is the caveat which has followed upon the prescriptions for the meditation on evil. Similar caveats should by implication accompany the ultimate teaching whenever it is expounded to listeners whose capacity for understanding it properly is doubtful. Otherwise it is better not to say anything at all.

NOTES

1. *Mo-ho Chih-kuan, T* 46.1–140.
2. *Ta-chih-tu-lun, T* 25.57–756.
3. Scholars disagree on why the last three chapters (and part of chap. 7 as well) were never expounded to conform to the outline of the whole work. The traditional explanation, still accepted by many, is that Chih-i simply lacked time to complete the series of lectures upon which his scribe and major disciple Kuan-

ting based later written versions of the work. This was because the summer *varsa* period (of A.D. 594) had drawn to a close and the monks had to resume their normal duties. The Japanese scholar Sekiguchi Shindai holds to the contrary that since the projected final chapters deal with especially exalted stages of spiritual development, Chih-i, who did not feel that he had himself attained such heights, chose to concentrate instead on the lower stages of the path. See Sekiguchi Shindai, *Tendai Shikan no Kenkyū* (Tokyo: Iwanami, 1969), pp. 54–63.

4. Leon Hurvitz outlines both the system of four (the Four *Samādhis*) of chap. 1 and the system of 10 times 10 from the rest of the work, but here we shall deal only with part of the fourth variety of meditation found in the synopsis: the ad libitum *samādhi*. See Leon Hurvitz, *Chih-i (538–597), Melanges chinois et bouddhiques* 12 (1960–1962): 318–331.

5. Chih-i must use the same character, *hsin,* both in the sense of "thoughts" (or "thought") and in the sense of "the receptacle of thoughts," that is, mind.

6. *T* 46.18a.

7. *T* 46.207c.25.

8. Ando Toshio, *Tendaigaku-ronshū* (Kyoto: Heirakuji shoten, 1975), p. 276.

9. See, for example, the twenty-five preliminary "expedients" of chap. 6 of the treatise, as given in Hurvitz, *Chih-i,* pp. 320–321, or in Dwight Goddard, ed., *A Buddhist Bible* (Boston: Beacon Press, 1970), pp. 441–463, as part of a translation of Chih-i's *Lesser Calming and Contemplation (Hsiao Chih-kuan).*

10. *T* 18.537c.28.

11. *T* 14.549a.

12. See, for example, Kenneth Ch'en, *Buddhism in China* (Princeton: Princeton University Press, 1972), pp. 186–192.

13. Pieced together from *Chuang-tzu,* chaps. 2 and 14.

4
Dimensions in the Life and Thought of Shan-tao (613–681)

JULIAN PAS

Shan-tao, a Pure Land evangelist in the T'ang dynasty (618–906), is generally recognized as the most important contributor to the development of Pure Land doctrine in China.[1] Since the references to him in western literature are brief and often wrong, I shall try to reconstruct his life from the few details which are reliable. Moreover, because the reputation of Shan-tao, even among Buddhist scholars, has become narrowly perceived due to his role as a patriarch of Japanese Pure Land denominations, I shall review a number of his most outstanding achievements seen within his Chinese context.

THE LIFE OF SHAN-TAO

The primary sources on Shan-tao's life are rather limited, often legendary, and occasionally contradictory. The Sung biographical notices are especially questionable. The legend about Shan-tao's suicide by jumping off a willow tree is false, for example, but was later rationalized by splitting Shan-tao into two different persons.[2]

Shan-tao was born toward the end of the Sui dynasty in 613. This date is calculated backward from the year of his death at the age of sixty-eight in 681. His birthplace has been a matter of disagreement: The earliest sources either do not mention it or explicitly state that it is not known. The *JYSC,* however, mentions that his family name was Chu and that he was from Szu-chou in Anhui, but modern scholars such as Iwai Hirosato generally argue that his place of origin is Lin-tzu in Shantung.

When Shan-tao entered Buddhist monastic life sometime between 618 and 627, he was still very young: perhaps only ten. Shan-tao's first teacher is said to be Ming-sheng, from Mi-chou in Shantung. He had been a disciple of the San-lun (Mādhyamika) master Fa-lang, who was a codisciple of Chi-tsang (549–623). Whether Shan-tao had been exposed to any training in the Confucian classics is nowhere mentioned. From his works it appears that he was not very familiar with the Confucian tradition, whereas he shows a broad knowledge of Buddhist texts. His inclination was apparently not toward speculative philosophy (as was emphasized in the San-lun school) but rather toward mystical experience. One senses that the young Shan-tao suffered a great deal of frustration during the early years of his monastic training. Later in his commentary to the *KWLSC* he states:

> Among the 84,000 methods, whether gradual or sudden, everyone chooses the one most suitable to himself. All those who follow a proper course will eventually become emancipated. However, since the obstacles for sentient beings are heavy, those who choose enlightenment through understanding will find it hard to understand.[3]

This statement probably reflects his own experience of intellectual pursuit through the San-lun philosophy: However deep he tried to plunge into the abyss of speculation, he could never reach the end. Confronted with his own powerlessness, he must have looked for an alternative way. There are two traditions about his conversion to Pure Land devotionalism. One relates his chance encounter with a Pure Land image which impressed him so deeply that he went to see Master Tao-ch'o (562–645) to study Amitābha meditation with him.[4] A later Sung biographer holds that he divined the scriptures, that is, opened the Buddhist texts at random for guidance, and so found the *KWLSC*. Thereupon he practiced the sixteen meditations by himself and only much later went to visit Tao-ch'o.[5]

It is not impossible that Shan-tao's casual contact with the *KWLSC* may have triggered a kind of conversion in his spiritual outlook. But the first version written in A.D. 805 seems to be closer to the truth, not only because it appears to be an older tradition, but on account of its inner meaning: Shan-tao, in later life, attached great importance to Sukhāvatī paintings, and this admiration can easily be explained if such a painting had occasioned a great change in his life. He himself had an artistic propensity and the first time he came face to face with the supernatural splendor of Amitābha's land as depicted in a paradise painting, he could have experienced something like a rapture to another world. Thereupon, in his quest to know more about the method of meditation on the Pure Land, he discovered the *KWLSC*, which became for him a manual of daily concentrations.

After his discovery, Shan-tao abandoned the San-lun philosophical quest and spent considerable time traveling to see famous masters. About this period, however, roughly between 633 and 649,[6] the sources are rather confused and it is only possible to estimate his movements. What is reasonably certain are the following points: his visit to Tao-ch'o and subsequent discipleship in Shansi province, his stay on Chung-nan mountain, and his strenuous efforts in Amitābha contemplation and the ascetic life.

The *HKSC* says that Shan-tao "wandered throughout the whole country in search of advice on the Way."[7] Four centuries later, the *WSC* and *HWSC-A* repeat the same information. In the *HWSC-B* more details are provided in an attempt to make a connection with Hui-yüan (334–416) while omitting any reference to Tao-ch'o.[8]

If one tries to reconstruct a coherent chronology of Shan-tao's activities, it appears that after his first awakening to the Pure Land ideal through contact with a Sukhāvatī painting, he found, by mere chance or more likely through a conscious search, a copy of the *KWLSC*. Together with the *vinaya* master Miao-k'ai, he studied this book and practiced the sixteen meditations.[9] Feeling that his lack of experience prevented him from full absorption, however, he looked for guidance and set out on a round-the-country journey. Whether he visited Lu-shan is hard to know. The tradition is late (only attested in *HWSC-B*) and can be satisfactorily explained through Hui-yüan's revived reputation in the Sung dynasty. Thus by Sung times the connection of Shan-tao with Tao-ch'o in the north was being obliterated and was replaced by inventing a link with the eminent master Hui-yüan in the south.

There is, however, a firm base for historical evidence in the records about Shan-tao's discipleship under Tao-ch'o. Although here too some records are overgrown with legend, the bare fact that he went to study under Tao-ch'o for some time is beyond dispute. Tao-ch'o, at that time, lived in the Hsüan-chung monastery at Hsi-ho, which is situated in Shansi province.

A final episode in Shan-tao's formative years is his stay at the Wu-chen monastery, located in Shensi province on Chung-nan mountain. It is not clear from the sources whether he went there before going to see Tao-ch'o or afterward. It seems more probable that he went there after he stayed with Tao-ch'o. The author of the *HKSC*, who omits both his name and place of origin, calls Shan-tao *shan-seng* (mountain-monk). Not only does *shan* (mountain) here refer to Chung-nan mountain, but it shows that later, in the capital, Shan-tao was known as having come from that place rather than from Hsi-ho, residence of Tao-ch'o. Thus it seems that Chung-nan mountain was his last residence before he settled in Ch'ang-an. After Shan-tao left Tao-ch'o, or left Shansi after Tao-ch'o's death in 645, where did he go next? He arrived in Ch'ang-an only about 649, four years after his masters's demise. Moreover, in 645 Shan-tao was about thirty-two years old and needed more personal experience in the Buddhist way of life before he could venture into a life of active teaching. These reasons, which are not strict arguments, seem to indicate that Shan-tao, after being instructed in the meaning and methods of the *KWLSC* by Tao-ch'o, finally withdrew to the solitude of the mountain to practice with even more dedication and self-denial than before.

The *HWSC-B* (written in A.D. 1084) is the only source to report explicitly Shan-tao's stay in the Wu-chen monastery; however, it says that it was before his visit to Tao-ch'o.[10] No direct information is given about the time when Shan-tao left his mountain seclusion and went to settle in Ch'ang-an, the great T'ang capital. The *HWSC-A* indirectly gives some information about his stay in Ch'ang-an: "For over thirty years he did not have his own separate living quarters. . . ."[11] This statement may be explained in two ways: Shan-tao either moved frequently from one temple to another, or, more likely, he was happy to live in a common dormitory. This interpretation would agree very well with his spirit of extreme asceticism. But since this detail, in the context of the *HWSC-A,* refers to his stay in the capital, it seems therefore reasonable to believe that he was in Ch'ang-an for more than thirty years. If we further accept 681 as the year of his death (as will be shown later), we may conclude that he arrived in Ch'ang-an around 645 or later.

If we accept 648 or 649 as the most reasonable date of his entry into a teaching career, Shan-tao was about thirty-five or thirty-six years old. The capital was full of Buddhist activity. A few years before, in the spring of 645, Hsüan-tsang had returned from his long "journey to the west" (India). In 648 the newly built Tz'u-en monastery was solemnly inaugurated and within its compounds an institute for the translation of Buddhist scriptures was organized and directed by Hsüan-tsang. This temple too held significance for Shan-tao: It was erected by the crown prince, the future emperor Kao-tsung, in commemoration of his mother, Empress Wen-te, who had been a personal disciple of Tao-ch'o. In fact, the temple was intended to be an expression of gratitude toward Tao-ch'o, through whose prayers the empress's health had once been restored.[12] At the inauguration of the new temple, fifty monks "of great virtue" were invited, and it seems probable that Shan-tao, once a famous disciple of Tao-ch'o, was among their number, especially because an inscription was found in Ch'ang-an which says "pagoda-tablet of the T'ang Ch'an master Shan-tao from the Tz'u-en temple."[13] This inscription further indicates that Shan-tao at one time lived at that temple. A further guess, but there is no proof for it, would be that this great celebration in 648 was the occasion for Shan-tao to take up residence in Ch'ang-an. The biographical sources are more explicit when pointing to the Kuang-ming temple in Ch'ang-an as the center of Shan-tao's energetic teaching activities, since it is mentioned in a contemporary source, the *HKSC*.[14]

There is one more monastery in Ch'ang-an with which Shan-tao was affiliated: the Shih-chi temple. It is nowhere mentioned in the biographical sources but is known only from an inscription in the Lung-men caves which says that Emperor Kao-tsung of the great T'ang ordered that a sculptured image be made of Vairocana Buddha, eighty-five feet high, together with statues of two bodhisattvas, each seventy feet high, and so forth. This order was issued in 673 and the whole work was completed in 675. The text explicitly states that the execution was to be supervised by a "monk from the western capital: Ch'an master Shan-tao from the Shih-chi temple" and two others.[15] Discussion of Shan-tao's artistic activities will be resumed later; the only conclusion made here is that at some later time in his career, around 673, he belonged to the Shih-chi temple in Ch'ang-an.

From all the foregoing evidence Iwai concludes that Shan-tao, as far as is recorded, lived in four different monasteries: In the Wu-chen temple he practiced meditation; in the Kuang-ming and Tz'u-en temples he preached while at the same time cultivating his own monastic ideals; and finally in the Shih-chi temple he died. This conclusion has a certain degree of probability, but from other vague references in the biographical material one has the impression that Shan-tao lived in quite a few more monasteries, probably within Ch'ang-an. But thus far there is no way to cite definite dates and places.

Next we have to delve into Shan-tao's evangelical activities while he resided in the T'ang capital. First of all the *HKSC* records that after his arrival in Ch'ang-an "he extensively converted the people [to this practice of *nien-fo*]. . . . Numberless men and women respected him [as their teacher]."[16] Sung writers liberally expand on this comment by adding new details: "Thereupon he went to the capital where he vigorously spread his teaching among the four classes of believers,[17] without distinction of higher or lower class. Under his great impact, butchers and wine sellers realized some religious awareness."[18] In the *HWSC-A* the story grows:

Sometimes people would pay him a sudden call and listen to the explanation of some doctrine, or even obtained the satisfaction of joining him in the sanctuary and receiving his personal instruction. If they did not have any previous experience, they would open their minds and ask him to explain; or, having their minds changed, he would transmit to them the methods of the Pure

Land. . . . In the capital and all the districts, among monks and nuns, laymen and laywomen, some threw themselves from a high mountain range; some took their lives by jumping into a deep well; some piled up wood and set themselves on fire as an offering. One generally hears that within the four directions over one hundred persons all cultivated the *brahmācārya* and renounced wife and children.[19]

In his *HWSC-B,* Wang Ku only writes that "Shan-tao equally instructed the various classes of people in the capital: the monks and laymen who submitted to him in their minds were as numerous as those going to market."[20] A later chronicle, the *Lung-shu Ching-t'u Wen* by Wang Jih-hsiu, records that "after three years the whole city of Ch'ang-an practiced *nien-fo.*"[21]

Although religious suicides were not exceptional in Buddhist circles,[22] it is questionable whether laymen engaged in this supreme self-denial. It seems that the foregoing report from the *HWSC-A* is rather colored by legend and is likely an amplification of one historic fact of suicide committed by a follower of Shan-tao and recorded in the *HKSC.* Having made this reservation, it seems beyond doubt that Shan-tao had an enormous impact on the population of the city. Almost all the sources emphasize this aspect of his career. Since Shan-tao from the moment of his conversion to the Pure Land method combined name invocation not only with a rigorous asceticism but with the practice of *kuan-fo* (Amitābha visualization-inspection), it seems beyond doubt that he also tried to communicate these ideals of a higher spirituality to his followers, laypeople as well as monks. If the biographer's statement about one hundred laymen renouncing their families is reliable, it cannot be based on the mere practice of calling the name of a Buddha. Moreover, whereas Tao-ch'o's biographer Chieh-chu in his *WSC* narrates how the master advised his followers to record the number of their invocations with the help of beans, grains of hemp, or wheat, a similar anecdote is not found in any of Shan-tao's biographies. Only in *HWSC-A* do we find a reference to numbers: "Every day they pronounced the name of Amitābha Buddha between fifteen thousand and a hundred thousand times and attained the *nien-fo-samādhi.*"[23] Because of the final section of the phrase—"they attained the *nien-fo-samādhi*"—it seems that for Shan-tao *nien-fo* was more than purely mechanical or magical vocal chanting of the name; it also involved an inner meditative development.

At the age of sixty-eight (in 681), Shan-tao passed away peacefully. Although the common view is that he committed suicide, the story is apocryphal and based on the confusion of various traditions. Leading a life of strict renunciation and self-denial combined with an energetic devotion to the salvation of others, he was considered a Buddhist saint, perhaps closer to the Indian (and Christian) ideal than the Chinese, humanistic model. However that may be, he has been very much respected in China and later on in Japan, where he was even called the reincarnation of Amitābha Buddha.

CONTRIBUTIONS OF SHAN-TAO

Pure Land Writings

Shan-tao wrote at least five works in nine scrolls (volumes), of which his commentary on the *KWLSC* is certainly the most influential. In one short treatise (*T* No. 1959) there is a mixture with another work, which is sometimes mentioned as a sixth. Three works (*T* No. 1979, 1980, 1981) are essentially liturgical, used for ceremonies of Amitābha worship, showing how much importance Shan-tao attached to aesthetically and emotionally impressive rituals.

His commentary on the *KWLSC* is the most mature product of his mental and spiritual development. Some themes were already discussed in his earlier works but appear in this commentary in a more thorough and systematic manner. Historically speaking, Shan-tao's *Commentary* is one among a series of many on the same sutra: Hui-yüan (523–591), Chih-i, and Chi-tsang had written commentaries before him, and after him there were commentaries by Chih-li and Yuan-chao. Tao-ch'o's *An-lo-chi* should also be considered as a partial commentary on the *KWLSC*. Modern research has discovered other commentaries, some of them partially lost. But at least nine different commentaries dating from the Sui-T'ang era have been recognized, which shows the great esteem and popularity of the text. This sutra, besides presenting a now practically lost method of Buddhist meditation,[24] is furthermore a fascinating case of sutra development; if subjected to serious literary criticism, it yields useful information about the development of the Amitābha cult in Central Asia and China.[25]

The abundance of Pure Land writings dating from the Sui and early T'ang period prove that this devotional school was gaining prestige among the Buddhists. In fact, various ideas were being expressed which tried to limit the influence of the new movement. Shan-tao protested against these assertions, sometimes quite vehemently, and established the Pure Land movement as a suitable path for monks and laymen. In that respect also, Shan-tao's commentary on the *KWLSC* is of major significance. The first part is a vindication of what he considers to be the correct interpretation of the sutra. Against those teachers who insist that it was intended for monk-meditators, Shan-tao argues that Sākyamuni offered his discourse for the benefit of Queen Vaidehi and all ordinary beings of the future. Against those who interpret the highest and intermediate grades of rebirth as bodhisattvas (highest grade) and arhats (intermediate grade), Shan-tao vehemently claims that this is not so. In fact, he argues, the spiritual achievements of these saints are infinitely higher and do not at all correspond to the rather easy requirements expressed in the chapters of the *KWLSC* dealing with the three grades of rebirth. Moreover, how can one say that those saints would have to rely on Vaidehi's intercession in order to learn the path to rebirth? Finally, Shan-tao invokes textual evidence from the sutra to remove all further doubt.

The teachers against whom Shan-tao reacts so strongly belong to various Buddhist traditions: Ching-ying Hui-yüan of the She-lun school; Chih-i, the founder of T'ien-t'ai; and Chi-tsang of the San-lun or Mādhyamika school. They believed that meditation, as explained in the *KWLSC,* was not within the power of ordinary laymen. Besides, was not Vaidehi granted the special favor of *anutpattikadharmakṣānti,* which is a fruit of bodhisattva training? Indeed, the *KWLSC* presents a rather simplified method of meditative vision. Compared to other texts of meditation, such as the *Visuddhimagga,* it is far less technical and, having dropped most of the monastic jargon, is more easily understood by an educated layman.

Against the view of those who claimed that Amitābha's land was too transcendent to be within the reach of ordinary mortals, he asserts the positive vows of Amitābha. He becomes very emotional on this point. Against those who said that Sukhāvatī is only a Buddha-realm of inferior quality (a *nirmāṇa*-land), he states that the land of Amitābha Buddha is a *saṃbhoga*-land. In other words, Sukhāvatī is a superior Buddha-realm but still within the reach of common mortals, not in a far distant future but immediately after death. Otherwise, the promises of the Buddha would deceive mortals and this cannot be accepted.

Once these prejudices against the Pure Land faith are removed, Shan-tao goes on to explain his views on meditation (third part of his commentary) and on ethical-spiritual requirements (fourth part). There are other aspects of Shan-tao's teaching that are usually overlooked—probably since they were less controversial and also less important for Japanese Buddhism—but must be considered if one is to understand his total impact on Chinese Buddhism. Four aspects deserve our attention: Shan-tao's treatment of filial piety, his liturgical endeavors, his contribution to Buddhist iconography, and his understanding of *nien-fo.* Although each topic deserves careful study, only the points of major importance will be developed here.

Support of Filial Piety

One of the most serious accusations against the Buddhists in China was their apparent lack of filial piety. As early as the third century Buddhist monks were accused of being unfilial to their ancestors by shaving their heads. During the Northern Dynasties period, Buddhism was persecuted on two occasions by the government; although the circumstances in the two cases were quite different, on both occasions one of the complaints against Buddhism was its lack of filial piety. In 446, the Northern Wei Emperor Wu took extreme measures against Buddhism, which "taught the equality and unity of all classes, withdrawal from society, exemption from taxation, and celibacy."[26] The second suppression took place in the years 574–577 under Emperor Wu of the Northern Chou, who declared in one of his edicts that "Buddhism must be suppressed because it practiced unfilial conduct, wasted wealth, and instigated rebellion."[27]

The Buddhists had become more and more conscious of these accusations, however, and tried to counteract them. Inscriptions in the Lung-men and other caves made during the Northern Wei have frequent references to filial piety.[28] Moreover, several sutras were translated (or composed) which emphasized filial piety as the supreme virtue.[29] On the other hand, several Buddhist authors developed this point in their writings. According to Michibata, eight Chinese Buddhists have to be mentioned: Fa-lin, Tao-hsüan, Shan-tao, Tao-shih, Tsung-mi, Ch'i-sung, Chang Shang-ying, and Tzu-ch'eng.[30]

Shan-tao's teaching on filial piety has to be studied in its historical and literary setting if we are to discover the sources from which he drew his ideas and to compare his doctrine with the traditional Confucian insistence on filiality. A priori it would appear that Shan-tao's insistence on filial behavior shows that he was truly Chinese and suggests the possibility that he had been trained in the tradition of Confucianism. There is no evidence in his biography that he was schooled in the Confucian classics, however. In recapitulating Shan-tao's teaching on the subject, it should be borne in mind that his starting point is the text of the *KWLSC:* The sutra lists filial piety as one of the requirements for rebirth in Sukhāvatī. Shan-tao's comments on this point may thus be summarized:

1. He cites the importance of the parents' function in the reproduction of life and their pains (especially the mother's) in rearing the child.

2. He says that parents are the supreme "field of merits" in worldly life (comparable to offerings to the Buddha in the otherworldly life of a monk or nun). An example is quoted from the Buddha's life story: A monk offered him food during a period of famine, but the Buddha sent him to offer it to his own parents.

3. He cites the Buddha's example of preaching the dharma to his mother in the *Trāyastriṃśā* heaven.[31]

With regard to the first of Shan-tao's arguments, it seems that he was inspired or even directly influenced by a small Buddhist treatise formerly lost but rediscovered among the Tun-huang manuscripts: *Fu-mu en-chung ching.*[32] Some of Shan-tao's ideas are more broadly developed in this sutra, and two of his main themes are very likely derived from this text: the function of both parents with respect to birth (and the mother's function after birth) and the ungratefulness of grown-up children toward their aging parents. Although Shan-tao summarizes these two themes, it would be hard to deny that he used this text or a similar one (now lost) as a direct source of inspiration.

The literary source of Shan-tao's second argument, in which he relates an event from the Buddha's life story, is more difficult to identify but is without doubt of purely Buddhist origin. So is the third argument, the story of the Buddha's ascension to heaven to preach the dharma to his mother Māyā in gratitude for her having been his mother. Although Shan-tao again draws from a purely Buddhist source, it seems that he summarizes the main lines of the *Fo-sheng T'ao-li-t'ien wei mu shuo-fa ching.*[33]

Recapitulating Shan-tao's views on filial piety, it is easy to see his merits as well as his limitations. His merits consist in the fact that he was conscious of the necessity of stressing the importance of filiality. In this respect, he is one among the few Buddhist authors of his time to do so and thus provide his readers with sound Buddhist principles to practice a virtue that was fundamental to Chinese society. His limitation, however, exists precisely in this meritorious contribution itself, for he considers the practice of filial behavior purely from Buddhist grounds. He does not fully use the given opportunity either to build a bridge between Buddhism and Confucianism or to refute the accusations from Confucian circles against Buddhism with reference to filial piety.

This examination of Shan-tao's literary sources has shown that Shan-tao is rather eclectic and misses originality with regard to filial piety. He draws on several Buddhist sources and combines them into one long argument. However, nothing shows that he was familiar with the great Confucian classic: the *Hsiao-ching* (Classic of Filial Piety). This short treatise was probably "written sometime between the time of Mencius and the establishment of the Han dynasty, or roughly between 350 and 200 B.C."[34] It became one of the Thirteen Classics during the T'ang dynasty, which shows that in Shan-tao's own time it must have enjoyed great popularity. It would be normal to expect that Shan-tao would allude to the book or even utilize some of its expressions—for example, from Chapter Nine: "Parents give one life; no bond could be stronger. They watch over their child with utmost care; no love could be greater."[35] That Shan-tao neglects this opportunity implies that he was probably too convinced of the sacredness and sufficiency of the Buddhist view of life to bother with non-Buddhist (or heterodox) principles. In the Buddhist scriptures he found the necessary arguments to establish a truly Buddhist rationale for moral behavior.

This lack of a broad perspective aside, it was his merit to have realized the necessity of commenting upon a virtue which was cardinal for his Chinese audience. To realize better the limitation of Shan-tao with regard to this missed opportunity, a comparison with Tsung-mi would be significant. Tsung-mi had received a classical education before he entered monastic life and was thus far better equipped to harmonize Buddhist and Confucian teachings.[36]

Liturgical Preoccupation

Shan-tao was a man who fully realized the importance of impressive ritual worship, not only for community service but for individuals as well. Although he acknowledges that they are of secondary importance, he sees them as effective means to arouse and increase faith in Amitābha. Anticipating already his view on the five "right practices" *(cheng-hsing)* based on the Pure Land sutras, he lists three kinds of practice which are liturgical in nature and have to do with individual or collective rituals. Although he calls these three "auxiliary actions" *(chu-yeh),* their importance should not be underestimated, for, as well as the "right and determining actions" *(cheng-ting-chih-yeh),* they assure that "the mind is always intimate and close [to the Buddha] and that mindfulness is without interruption: this is called 'continuous action' *(wu-chien)*."[37]

Two main points of interest appear to be present in Shan-tao's liturgical endeavors: first, his recommendations with regard to individual worship, seen as a preparation for meditation; second, his contribution to group worship, for which he actually composed manuals. The first aspect has been dealt with elsewhere,[38] but it needs further clarification since one of his works, the *Kuan-nien Fa-men* (*T* No. 1959), gives richer details than the *KWLSC*. The third section of the *KNFM* outlines the ritual prescriptions to be followed when entering into the sanctuary in order to practice the *nien-fo-samādhi:*

> When about to enter the sanctuary to practice *samādhi,* the devotee must accord with Buddhist practices and first of all put the sanctuary in order, arrange the holy images, and sprinkle the image(s) with perfumed water. If there is no Buddha-hall, a clean house will also do. When it has been duly

sprinkled, one should bring in a Buddha image and set it up against the western wall. A devotee may start off in any month, from the first till the eighth day, or from the eighth till the fifteenth, or from the fifteenth till the twenty-third, or from the twenty-third till the thirtieth. These four periods of each month are all suitable; each devotee takes into account the amount of work at home. [After choosing a suitable time] he purifies himself and starts his exercises from one to seven days. It is extremely important to wear clean clothes; socks and shoes also must be spotless. During these seven days, he should always keep to vegetarian food: soft cakes and coarse rice, pickled vegetables, according to the season but always in great simplicity and with limitation of the quantity.

While staying day and night in the sanctuary, he should continuously control his mind and with single-minded attention perform the *Amitābha-Bud-dhānusmṛti* while mind and voice are in mutual correspondence. He may only sit down or stand up and should abstain from sleep during these seven days. It is not required to worship the Buddha and recite the sutras according to the normal schedule,[39] nor is it necessary to count the beads on a rosary. What only counts is to fold hands and practice *Buddhānusmṛti* while moment after moment imagining the Buddha in order to see him. The Buddha says: "If you imagine and keep the *anusmṛti* of Buddha Amitābha, the incomparable radiance of his truly golden *rūpakāya* sitting in the right position will shine penetratingly in front of your mental eyes." When making the right *anusmṛti* of the Buddha, if the devotee is standing, he should repeat his name ten or twenty thousand times, remaining in that position; if he is seated, he should repeat his name ten or twenty thousand times remaining seated. While in the sanctuary, he should not nod his head and fluster. At either the three periods or the six periods of day and night, he should address himself to all the Buddhas, to all the sages and saints, to all the officials in the netherworld, all the officers of the earth, and all the spirits who watch the deeds of men, and make a confession of all his past transgressions committed by actions, words, or thought. When thus a truthful confession has been made, he should return to the *Buddhānusmṛti* according to the method explained above.

About the objects of his visions, he should not talk irreverently with others. The good he has done, he knows himself; the evil he has committed, he should confess.

He should make a solemn vow neither to touch nor to consume wine, meat, and the five forbidden roots;[40] if he violates this vow, he truly wishes to contract malignant boils all over his body and in his mouth.

Some devotees wish to recite the *Amitāyus Sutra* [*SSVS*] a full hundred thousand times or to invoke [*nien*] the Buddha's name ten thousand times a day, or to recite the sutra fifteen times a day. Others want to recite the sutra twenty or thirty times daily, according to their strength: In this way they wish to be reborn in the Pure Land and to be received by the Buddha.[41]

This quotation is significant as an example of the ambiguity with which the key term *nien* is used by Shan-tao. He does not define its meaning and content but uses the term as ambiguous—that is, including both meditation on Amitābha and invocation of his name. In not a single instance does he use the compound *nien-fo-ming* (*nien* the Buddha's name), although he had ample opportunity to do so. By using the term in its ambiguity, he seems to stress the fact that for him *nien-fo* is both meditative and recitative and should not be separated. In other words, meditation, aiming at the vision of Amitābha here and now, is always accompanied by worship, chanting the sutras, and reciting the name of Amitābha. The title of the section indicates this double feature quite eloquently: Regarding *nien-fo-samādhi, nien-fo* has a double meaning but leads ultimately to the state of *samādhi*. Thus the inference can be made that oral recitation of Amitābha's name, as well as chanting of the sutras, are both performed in view of the higher aim: meditative trance.

The second aspect of Shan-tao's liturgical contribution is with reference to group worship expressed in three works: the *Fa-shih tsan (FST),* the *Pan-chou san-mei tsan (PCST),* and the *Wang-sheng li-tsan (WSLT).*[42] It is hard to decide the chronological order of these writings, but it seems that the *FST* at least was written for the monastic community. Confession and repentance of sins is of primary importance. A description of the Buddhist hells is added perhaps to give weight to the necessity of confession. In one respect, the *WSLT* is the most interesting of these liturgical texts: The main body consists of six hymns of praise selected for use during the six daily periods of worship: sunset, early night, midnight, dawn, morning, and noon. Although in Buddhist literature there are frequent references to these six periods of day and night, this seems to be one of the very first instances that a liturgical usage is made of them, except for the case of Hui-yüan, who is said to have practiced *samādhi* at the six times, and Hsin-hsing who had a ritual of vows following the same schedule.

Shan-tao's liturgical works show his deep concern with worship and meditation. Convinced of the sacredness of time, he tried to inculcate the same feelings into his followers. Finally, by means of artistic representations he appealed to the aesthetic-emotional side of human nature, which in the end is perhaps more persuasive than philosophical analysis.

Artistic Creativity

Shan-tao is famous for his literary and artistic activities: He copied sutras for distribution, painted Pure Land frescoes, and repaired temples and pagodas.[43] His Pure Land paintings may have involved the new style of mandalas in which not only the Sukhāvatī with the presiding Buddha and bodhisattvas are represented but also, in a series of side pictures, the whole text of the *KWLSC*. Examples of such mandalas are still found in

Japan—for example, the Taima mandala. Waley contends that these paintings do not illustrate the sutra itself but rather Shan-tao's commentary on the sutra.[44] In his final years (672–675), Shan-tao, by imperial request, supervised the sculpture of the huge Vairocana group in the Lung-men caves near Lo-yang. His involvement is clearly stated in the inscription on the statues. The only doubt is about the identity of this Buddha. The Vairocana cult was not yet so prevalent in China, and it seems quite possible that Shan-tao, who then was most famous for his efforts to spread the Amitābha cult, was asked to supervise the creation of an Amitābha group which in later years was renamed.[45]

Shan-tao's biographies, although very scanty and brief, never fail to mention his work as an artist: He is said to have painted more than two hundred Pure Land frescoes or scrolls. Their exact nature is hard to know, but, as mentioned above, they seem to have been Sukhāvatī paintings with side scenes illustrating the *KWLSC* and, in some cases, Shan-tao's own commentary on the sutra. A further reference says that his paintings were both frescoes and scrolls.

That Shan-tao attached great importance to these visual aids becomes understandable when one remembers that his own conversion to Pure Land Buddhism was effected when he first saw one such paradise painting. (At least this seems the most likely version.) He therefore regards liturgical and artistic beauty as powerful means to elevate the mind to the heights of contemplation and Amitābha vision.

An indication of his influence may be seen in the artistic activity that went on in the Lung-men caves near Lo-yang. Tsukamoto examined the dated inscriptions of statues and found that, between A.D. 500 and 540, there were 43 of Śākyamuni, 35 of Maitreya, 8 of Amitābha Buddha, and 22 of Kuan-yin (Avalokiteśvara). Between A.D. 650 and 690 there is a drastic change in the proportions; only 8 statues are of Śākyamuni and 11 of Maitreya, whereas 103 are of Amitābha Buddha and 44 of Kuan-yin (Avalokiteśvara). The years from 660 to 680 were the most productive: 76 statues of Amitābha and 30 of Kuan-yin are counted.[46] These years coincide with the peak years of Shan-tao's influence and fame.

One aspect never mentioned in this context is the great popularity of Buddhist hell representations, and one may wonder when this theme came up for the first time in Chinese art. One can only guess about Shan-tao's own contribution, but one thing is certain: He realized the psychological value which descriptions of the tortures of hell might have on people. In one of his early works, the *FST*,[47] he included a vivid image of the many hells where sinners are punished: It was part of a great repentance and confession ceremony. One may wonder whether he also contributed to the popularization of hell paintings.

Shan-tao's List of Right Practices

The three main Pure Land sutras and related texts contain a rich variety of methodological approaches with regard to Amitābha worship. At least four different aspects of *nien-fo* can be distinguished:

1. *Buddhānusmṛti,* or recollection, attentiveness, which occupies a place in the general Buddhist tradition
2. Hearing the name of the Buddha
3. Meditating on the Buddha or, more correctly, visualizing-inspecting, which is already anticipated in the *LSVS* but is more fully explained in the *KWLSC*
4. Calling, or praising the name of the Buddha, as recommended in the interpolated passages of the *KWLSC*

These various aspects are not mutually exclusive; on the contrary, they support and strengthen each other. In Japan, however, a development took place that consisted in a gradual narrowing of the meanings of *nien-fo,* so that with Hōnen there is practically exclusive emphasis on oral invocation.

In sharp contrast to Hōnen's claim,[48] however, it is beyond doubt that Shan-tao praises the practice of meditative vision as the superior one. Shan-tao is quite orthodox in holding the view that meditation leads to a vision of Amitābha and his Sukhāvatī in this present life. Although it does not necessarily include rebirth, rebirth still is the natural consequence and the ultimate reward for those who meditate.

Some confusion has arisen from the various possible meanings of *nien-fo,* as well as from Shan-tao's controversial passage on right practices *(cheng-hsing).* It is necessary to quote the passage at length:

> Practices are of two kinds: first, right practices; second miscellaneous practices. Right practices consist in acting solely according to the practices recommended in the sutras of rebirth. These are called right practices. Of what do they consist?
>
> [i] With single-minded attention recite this *Kuan Sutra,* the *Amitābha Sutra,* and the *Sukhāvatī-vyūha Sutra.*[49]
>
> [ii] With single-minded attention mentally visualize, inspect, and keep in mind the twofold reward of the land.
>
> [iii] With single-minded attention worship Amita Buddha.
>
> [iv] With single-minded attention invoke Amita Buddha through oral invocations *(k'ou-ch'eng).*
>
> [v] With single-minded attention praise and offer to the Buddha. These are called right practices.
>
> In these right practices two kinds are contained: right and determining

actions *(cheng-ting-chih-yeh)* and auxiliary actions *(chu-yeh)*. The former is with single-minded attention to *nien* the name of Amita, whether walking or standing, sitting or lying, without concern for the length of time, at every single moment without desisting. This is called the right and determining action because it is in accordance with the vows of Amita Buddha. Worship and recitation and the like are called auxiliary actions.

Besides these two kinds of action, right and auxiliary, all the other kinds of goodness are called miscellaneous actions *(tsa-hsing)*.

If one cultivates the former two practices, right and auxiliary, the mind is always intimate and close [to the Buddha] and mindfulness is without interruption: This is called continuous action *(wu-chien)*. If on the other hand one cultivates the latter, miscellaneous actions, the mind is often interrupted. Although one can also direct oneself toward rebirth and obtain it, these are called interrupted and miscellaneous actions.[50]

This passage is extremely important if we are to understand Shan-tao's viewpoint correctly. Citing this text, most, if not all, interpreters have concluded that Shan-tao recommends five different activities as most significant and divides them into two categories: primary (calling the Buddha's name) and secondary (the four remaining actions).[51] The fallacy inherent in this division is obvious: Shan-tao clearly says that "worship and recitation and the like" are auxiliary actions. The primary action is *nien-fo* with its twofold meaning of meditation *and* recitation. To reduce *nien-fo* to only one aspect is to do an injustice to the text.

Another passage from his commentary substantiates this exegesis: In the discussion of the very lowest group of persons who will be reborn, Shan-tao comments that when the pains of agony oppress the evil-doer, a compassionate teacher consoles him and teaches him to perform *nien-fo (Buddhānusmṛti)*. In his condition, however, it is impossible to practice *nien-fo-ming;* then the teacher changes his method and urges him to recite orally the name of Amitābha *(k'ou-ch'eng Mi-t'o ming-hao)*. If the invocations, whatever their number, are uninterrupted, the guilt of many kalpas will be erased and a golden flower, symbolizing Amitābha Buddha, will appear in welcome.[52] Here Shan-tao clearly distinguishes between two practices: The better one is *nien-fo,* also called *nien-fo-ming;* the other, less recommendable but still efficacious, is to recite the name of the Buddha orally *(k'ou-ch'eng . . . ming-hao)*. This is the passage in which the distinction is made most clearly; all other passages which are not so clear should be interpreted in this light.

To conclude, then, when Shan-tao enumerates the five right practices he affirms that they are all based on the three Pure Land sutras. Whereas worship and chanting are auxiliary practices, however, only *nien-fo* is the right and determining practice infallibly leading to rebirth and the state of nonretrogression. The *nien-fo* practice comprehends various aspects: hearing and calling the name, meditating on Amitābha. Each of these actions leads to rebirth if the one condition is fulfilled: single-minded attentiveness, which Shan-tao in another context explains as performed from within the three mental dispositions of absolute sincerity, deep faith, and true desire to be reborn in the Pure Land.

SHAN-TAO'S INFLUENCE

Shan-tao's writings and his life show him as a man of moderation, without exclusiveness of approach, without extremes: There is a method of rebirth suitable to everyone. This is an aspect that may be relevant to religious seekers of all times. Although Shan-tao himself followed the arduous path of meditation and self-denial, he allowed for the weakness of others and extended to them the compassion and the infallible promises of the Buddha. Even simple invocation of the Buddha's name was an authentic way to emancipation if the mental states of deep faith, sincerity, and true longing were at least realized.

Shan-tao's total influence on Chinese Pure Land Buddhism must be seen as penetrating and comprehensive. Both from the biographical information and from his writings, one becomes convinced that his impact was not limited to the masses and to the propagation of an easy way to salvation; he also offered monks and serious lay-disciples a practical method of aspiring to the Buddhist ideals. Here meditative Amitābha vision and spiritual-ethical discipline are recommended as the two essential gates through which one may enter into Sukhāvatī.

NOTES

This essay was first read at the conference of the International Association for the History of Religion, Lancaster, August 1975, and, in a modified version, at the meeting of American Academy of Religion (panel of the Society for the Study of Chinese Religion) in St. Louis, October 1976. This third version has been considerably reedited.

The following abbreviations are used in the notes:

CJS	*Chūgoku Jōdo sansoden*
FST	*Fa-shih tsan*
HKSC	*Hsü Kao-seng chuan*
HWSC	*Hsin-hsiu wang-sheng chuan*
JYSC	*Jui-ying shan-chuan*
KFSH	*Kuan-Fo san-mei hai ching*
KNFM	*Kuan-nien fa-men*
KWLSC	*Kuan-wu-liang-shou-Fo-ching*
LSVS	*Larger SVS*

NFC	Nien-Fo Ching
PCST	Pan-chou san-mei tsan
SSVS	Smaller SVS
SVS	Sukhāvatī-vyūha-sūtras
WSC	Wang-sheng chuan
WSLT	Wang-sheng li-tsan
ZDIK	"Zendō den no ichi Kōsatsu"
ZTK	Zendō Dashi no Kenkyū

1. Many western writers on Chinese and Japanese Buddhism mention his name, but no extensive biography or analysis of his teaching was available until the publication of R. Fujiwara's *The Way to Nirvana* (Tokyo: Kyoiku Shincho Sha, 1974). This work was expected to fill a major gap in our understanding of the Chinese Pure Land movement, but unhappily it only deals with Shan-tao's concept of *nien-fo (nembutsu)*, and, moreover, its viewpoint is rather sectarian. See my book review in *Journal of Asian Studies* 36 (November 1976): 145–146. More recently, Ingram S. Seah has extensively examined Shan-tao's life in his "Shan-tao, His Life and Teachings" (Ph.D. dissertation, Princeton Theological Seminary, 1975), pp. 102–216. See also my "Shan-tao's Commentary on the *Amitāyur-Buddhānusmṛti-sūtra*" (Ph.D. dissertation, McMaster University, 1973), pp. 145–215.

2. The primary source material for Shan-tao's biography is contained in four or five compilations of the *Taishō Shinshu Daizōkyō* (hereafter cited as *T*):

    a. *Hsü Kao-seng chuan (HKSC)*, *T* 50.684a.11–19

    b. *Wang-sheng hsi-fang ching-t'u jui-ying shan-chuan (JYSC)*, *T* 51.105b.23–c.8

    c. *Ch'iu-sheng hsi-fang ching-t'u nien-Fo ching (NFC)*, *T* 47.120–133, attributed to Tao-ching and Shan-tao

    d. *Ching-t'u wang-sheng chuan (WSC)*, *T* 51.119a.25–b.13, composed by Chieh-chu (985–1077)

    e. *Hsin-hsiu wang-sheng chuan (HWSC)*, *T* 83.158a–c, an enlarged edition of (d) by Wang Ku in 1084. This text contains two separate Shan-tao biographies: *HWSC-A* and *HWSC-B* (*T* 83.158b.23–c.29).

Besides these primary sources, there are a great number of secondary sources, in Chinese and Japanese, and a vast amount of studies (books and articles) on Shan-tao, mostly in Japanese. Since this biography does not claim to be complete, I merely rely on these significant modern Japanese works, critically chosen from among the vast number:

    a. B. Matsumoto, T. Sekimoto, and S. Mochizuki, *Zendō Dashi no kenkyū (ZTK)* (Kyoto: Ryukoku Daigaku, 1927)

    b. H. Iwai, "Zendō den no ichi kōsatsu" (ZDIK), *Shigaku zasshi* 41 (1930): 57–94, 244–257, 446–482, 528–568, 916–973

    c. S. Nogami, *Chūgoku Jōdo sansoden (CJS)* (Kyoto: Bun'eidō, 1970), pp. 137–189.

3. *T* 37.246b.1–3.

4. *JYSC*, *T* 51.105b.24–27.

5. *HWSC*, *T* 83.158b.26–27.

6. Between A.D. 633, when he was twenty years of age, and A.D. 649, when he is said to have taken up his residence in Ch'ang-an.

7. *T* 59.684a.12.

8. *T* 83.158b.28–c.2.
9. *T* 51.105b.26.
10. *T* 83.158c.2–5.
11. *T* 83.158a.19–20.
12. ZDIK, p. 546.
13. ZDIK, p. 545.
14. While the *JYSC* omits the reference to this temple, both the *WSC* and the *HWSC-A* connect the incident of Shan-tao's suicide with the Kuang-ming temple. According to these latter sources, however, the temple was only renamed Kuang-ming temple after Shan-tao's death: Emperor Kao-tsung (r. 650–684) changed the original name to Kuang-ming to commemorate the tradition that each time Shan-tao recited the name of Amitābha Buddha, light *(kuang-ming)* came out of his mouth. That this is a later legend appears not only from the intrinsic character of the story but also from the foregoing reference in the *HKSC,* which proves that the temple in question already was named Kuang-ming during Shan-tao's lifetime.
15. ZDIK, p. 549.
16. *T* 50.684a.14–15.
17. Monks and nuns, laymen and laywomen.
18. *T* 51.119a.28–b.1.
19. *T* 83.158b.3–8.
20. *T* 84.158c.23–24.
21. *T* 47.267a.6.
22. See Jan Yün-hua, "Buddhist Self-Immolation in Medieval China," *History of Religions* 4 (1965): 243–268. See also J. Gernet, *Les Aspects Économiques du Bouddhisme* (Saigon: PEFEO, 1956), p. 234f.
23. *T* 83.158b.9.
24. See my article "Shan-tao's Interpretation of the Meditative Vision of Buddha Amitāyus," *History of Religions* 14 (2) (1974): 96–116.
25. See my article "The *Kuan-wu-liang-shou Fo Ching:* Its Origin and Literary Criticism," in L. Kawamura and K. Scott, eds., *Buddhist Thought and Asian Civilization* (Berkeley: Dharma Publishing, 1977), pp. 194–218.
26. Kenneth Ch'en, *Buddhism in China* (Princeton: Princeton University Press, 1964), p. 149.
27. Ibid., p. 191.
28. Ibid., p. 179. See Kenneth Ch'en, *The Chinese Transformation of Buddhism* (Princeton: Princeton University Press, 1973), for a study of this development.
29. See R. Michibata, *Bukkyō to Jukyō rini* (Kyoto: Heirakuji, 1968), pp. 60–121; *Tō-dai Bukkyōshi no kenkyū* (Kyoto: Hōzōkan, 1957; 2nd ed., 1967), pp. 271–334.
30. Michibata, *Bukkyō to Jukyō rini,* pp. 248–295.
31. These three aspects are from the second fascicle of Shan-tao's commentary, *T* 37.259a.24–c.13.
32. *T* 85.1403–1404.
33. *T* 17.787–799.
34. See the English translation of the *Hsiao-ching* by Sister M. L. Makra, Asian Institute Translations, no. 2 (New York: St. John's University Press, 1961).
35. Ibid., p. 20f.
36. For Tsung-mi's views on filial piety, see Michibata, *Bukkyō to Jukyō rini,*

pp. 267–273; Kenneth Ch'en, "Filial Piety in Chinese Buddhism," *Harvard Journal of Asiatic Studies* 28 (1968): 92; Chen, *Chinese Transformation,* pp. 30–40; Jan Yün-hua, "Tsung-mi: His Analysis of Ch'an Buddhism," *T'oung Pao* 58 (1972): 22–23.

37. *Kuan-wu-liang-shou-Fo-ching shu, T* 37.272b.10–11.

38. See my article "Shan-tao's Interpretation."

39. This refers to the practice of six daily periods of worship.

40. *Wu-hsin* or *wu-hsün,* which are garlic, three kinds of onions, and leeks. The reason why is explained further when Shan-tao talks about preventing persons who eat (or drink) these forbidden articles from approaching the sickbed of a devotee: "He would lose the right *nien,* evil spirits would disturb him; he would die suddenly and sink down into one of the evil rebirths" (*T* 47.24c.1–2).

41. *T* 47.24a.26–b.20.

42. Respectively *T* No. 1979, 1981, and 1980.

43. *T* 50.684a.14; *T* 51.105c.6–7.

44. See A. Waley, *A Catalogue of Paintings Recovered from Tun-huang by Sir Aurel Stein* (London: British Museum and Government of India, 1931), p. xxi.

45. See P. C. Swann, *Chinese Monumental Art* (London: Thames and Hudson, 1963), who on p. 107 refers to this hypothesis formulated by W. Willets, *Illustrated London News* (February 1954), pp. 187–188.

46. Z. Tsukamoto, *Shina Bukkyōshi kenkyū: Hokugi hen* (Tokyo: Kōbuntō, 1942; reprinted 1969), pp. 371–380.

47. *T* 47.428c–429a.

48. Fujiwara calls Hōnen "the exclusive successor of Shan-tao's teachings" and quotes Hōnen as saying "I exclusively depend upon Shan-tao alone." See Fujiwara, *The Way to Nirvana,* pp. 152 and 154.

49. These are respectively the *KWLSC,* and *SSVS,* and the *LSVS.*

50. *T* 37.272a.29–b.13.

51. Among these interpreters are S. Mochizuki, *Chūgoku Jōdo kyōri shi* [The development of Chinese Pure Land Buddhism] (Kyoto: Hōzōkan, 1942–1964), p. 189; Ch'en, *Buddhism in China,* p. 346; R. Robinson, *The Buddhist Religion* (Belmont, Calif.: Dickenson, 1970), p. 86; and Fujiwara, *The Way to Nirvana,* p. 104.

52. *T* 37.277b.14–17.

5

Awakening in
Northern Ch'an

ROBERT B. ZEUSCHNER

Although the Northern line of Ch'an ("Zen" in Japanese) Buddhism is discussed in western literature on Chinese Ch'an, the description is usually based upon the writings of its bitter rival, the Southern tradition of Ho-tse Shen-hui (670–762). Ho-tse Shen-hui was the most vocal and the most popular of the disciples of Hui-neng (638–713), whom the later Ch'an tradition came to recognize as the Sixth Patriarch in their teaching lineage.

Accordingly, the Northern line is depicted by its rival, Southern Ch'an, as teaching a doctrine filled with errors and with making untrue claims about its origins. This strongly partisan account has dominated most of the histories of Ch'an, and it is these same, mostly legendary, accounts which have been repeated in contemporary scholarship. Now, however, the teachings of the Northern line are available in recently discovered manuscripts, and these are revealing substantial errors in the traditional accounts. About eighty years ago, numerous Buddhist texts, including Northern Ch'an writings, were discovered in the caves of Tun-huang along the ancient silk route in northern China. The following study is based primarily upon these Tun-huang manuscripts, identified and published by Ui Hakujū and D. T. Suzuki, and more recently the superb historical and textual studies of Yanagida Seizan.[1] In the following pages I shall outline the major doctrines and practices of the Northern line of Ch'an concerning the process of awakening, or enlightenment, as expressed in the seven texts available to me:

1. *Kuan-hsin lun* (Treatise on Clear Contemplation of Mind; hereafter

abbreviated *KHL*). The text was originally attributed to Bodhidharma (the first Ch'an patriarch), but Sekiguchi Shindai has shown that the text is by Shen-hsiu (605?–706), the influential founder of the northern tradition, who settled in the capital in the north of China during his teaching years.[2] The text can be found in the Taishō collection of Chinese Buddhist texts, *T* 85.1270–1273, where it appears as text no. 2833.

2. *P'o-hsiang lun* (Treatise on Breaking Through Form; hereafter *PHL*). This is a more polished and slightly revised version of *KHL* and is text no. 2009 in *T* 48.366c–369c. Another variant of this same text can be found in the Zokuzōkyō collection, *ZZ* I.15.5.411b–414b. D. T. Suzuki has compiled a comparative edition of five different variants in his *Suzuki Daisetsu zenshū: betsukan ichi,* supp. vol. 1 (Tokyo: Iwanami shoten, 1971), pp. 592–645.

3. *Miao-li yüan-ch'eng kuan* (Discernment of Marvelous Reality and Highest Truth; hereafter *YCK*), attributed to Shen-hsiu. The only copy of this text available to me was the excerpt quoted in text no. 2016 of *T* 48.943a.–b.6.

4. *Ts'an Ch'an-men shih* (Verses in Praise of Ch'an; hereafter *TCMS*). The initial pages, with the correct title, are missing from this manuscript, and so the editors of the Taishō collection have given it the title of a short series of verses appended at the end of this text. The structure of this text makes it clear that this is one of the versions of the *fang-pien (upāya)* series of writings. It is found in *T* 85.1291–1293, but two better versions of the original manuscript can be found in Ui Hakujū, *Zenshūshi kenkyū,* vol. 1 (Tokyo: Iwanami shoten, 1939), pp. 511–515, and in Suzuki, *Suzuki Daisetsu zenshū,* vol. III (Tokyo: Iwanami shoten, 1968), pp. 161–167.

5. *Ta-ch'eng wu-sheng fang-pien men* (The Unborn *Upāya* of the Mahāyāna; hereafter *WSM*). This is another of the Five *Upāya* texts. It is text no. 2834 in *T* 85.1273b–1278a and is in Ui, *Zenshūshi kenkyū,* vol. I, pp. 449–467.

6. *Ta-ch'eng wu fang-pien pei-tsung* (Five *Upāya* of the Mahāyāna: Northern Tradition; hereafter *WFP*). This is the longest of the Northern Ch'an texts and the most fully developed doctrinally of the *upāya* group. This text, which has been formed by compiling two versions of what appear to be identical texts, does not appear in the Taishō collection, but it can be found in Ui, *Zenshūshi kenkyū* (hereafter *ZSK*), vol. I, pp. 468–510. It also is found in Suzuki, *Suzuki Daisetsu zenshū* (hereafter *SDZ*), vol. III, pp. 190–212 and 221–235.

7. *Ta-ch'eng pei-tsung lun* (Treatise by the Northern Line of the Mahāyāna; hereafter *PTL*). This text is composed of three short poetic descriptions subtitled "The Mahāyāna Mind." It is text no. 2836 of *T*

85.1281c–1282a. Slightly improved versions can be found in Ui, *ZSK* I.447–448, and in Suzuki, *SDZ* III.190–212 and 221–235.[3]

Although there are numerous interesting and important topics which could be analyzed on the basis of these texts, this study focuses upon methods for the attainment of awakening. A few initial studies have already been made on the historical genesis of the Northern line, the meditation techniques which the Northern Ch'an drew upon, and the interchange between the Northern and Southern traditions during the early eighth century.[4]

A careful reading of the seven texts reveals that the Northern line used two methods to achieve awakening *(chüeh)*. The first method is the technique of discernment utilizing five Buddhist scriptures. We shall call this the method of "Five *Upāya*" or "Five Expedient Means" *(fang-pien)*. This method may have existed within the Northern line from the very beginning, for it appears in rudimentary form in one of the texts which I believe to be among the earliest existing Northern Ch'an documents.[5] The second method is that of the "contemplation of mind" *(kuan-hsin)*, which is related to the Northern Ch'an technique of "maintaining awareness of mind" *(shou-hsin,* literally "guarding the mind"). This approach is associated with seated meditation and with mental concentration exercises. By mastering these techniques, the practitioner achieved a state in which both mind and body are undisturbed by all those things in the world which ordinarily cause us to lose our balance, or our mental equilibrium, so that we are no longer able to see the interconnected unity of reality. To achieve a mind which can remain balanced and undisturbed is to achieve awakening.

THE "FIVE *Upāya*" IN NORTHERN CH'AN

The early teachers in the Northern tradition of Ch'an were very well read and encouraged the study of Buddhist texts. Although they drew from a broad range of Mahāyāna Buddhist texts, the documents from the caves of Tun-huang reveal six texts to be of special importance. Five of these six are sutras (texts which are supposed to record the actual words of the Buddha), and the sixth is a *śāstra* (a treatise or commentary).

The first of these six is the *Laṅkāvatāra Sutra,* which has been closely associated with the founder of the Northern line, Shen-hsiu.[6] The second is the *Saddharmapuṇḍarīka (Lotus) Sutra* and the third is the *Vimalakīrti Sutra,* both of which were very popular among all the Buddhist schools in China. The fourth sutra is the *Viśeṣacinta-brahma-paripṛcchā,* in which a layperson named Viśeṣacinti asks numerous questions of the

Buddha.⁷ The fifth sutra is the *Avataṁsaka,* a text which supplied the
basis for the Hua-yen school and its profound understanding of the universe as unimpeded mutual interpenetration.⁸ The sixth text upon which
the Northern tradition placed special reliance is the popular treatise
entitled *Ta-ch'eng Ch'i-hsin lun* (Awakening of Faith in the Mahāyāna),
and several of the technical terms appearing in this text were central to
the Northern Ch'an documents.

The importance of these six texts is seen clearly in a group of Northern
Ch'an texts which are divided into five sections, each with an explication
of a quotation or technical phrase taken from the last five of the six texts
mentioned above. The five divisions were called "Five *Upāya,*" and the
two-character Chinese phrase *fang-pien (upāya)* often appears in the
titles of these texts. In Northern Ch'an, *upāya* seems to indicate a technique to lead a pupil to a profound realization of the nature of things as
they truly are.⁹ Each division of the text is an *upāya,* and each division is
an explication of (or perhaps a meditation upon) a passage or theme
from one of the five texts. Now we shall discuss these divisions and outline the major themes of each section.

The First *Upāya*

In the *WSM,* the *WFP,* and the *TCMS,* this first section begins with a
quotation from the *Ch'i-hsin lun* ("Awakening of Faith") which explains
that to awaken is to become a Buddha, and being a Buddha consists in
having a mind which is undisturbed *(wu-tung),* so that the "mind itself
which is free from thinking" *(hsin-t'i li-nien)* is revealed.¹⁰ The text then
goes on to explicate various passages. Awakening is said to have three
meanings: self-awakening, which involves being free from misinterpret-
ing the information provided by the senses; awakening others, which is
being unattached to external forms or characteristics; and perfect awakening, which occurs when the mind is free internally and not attached
externally—this state the texts call the Buddha's universal *dharmakāya.*

Following standard Buddhist understanding, the texts explain that if
one's mind is actively conditioned by externals and misinterprets the
causally interdependent nature of things, the mind understands this
"realm of dharmas" as being defiled, and consequently one abides in the
realm of the ordinary sentient being. On the other hand, if there is no
arising of the dichotomizing mind and one is no longer trapped by one's
prior conditioning, the text says that one thereby abides in the pure *dharmadhātu,* the realm of all Buddhas. To abide here is to be unattached to
dharmas—to have a mind which is not distorted by one's desires, not distorted by one's conditioning, not fragmented by the world. This is
achieving the state which Northern Ch'an masters call being "free from
thinking" *(li-nien),* a key phrase borrowed from the *Ch'i-hsin-lun.* To be

free from thinking is to attain the state of clear awareness where sensory input is not dichotomized into subject and object, or self and other, in the midst of mental activity.

The first *upāya* also utilizes a common Chinese philosophical distinction between the thing in itself, or its essence *(t'i)*, and the way a thing acts or functions *(yung)*. Using a dual mode similar to the one mentioned above, the Northern Ch'an text explains that to be free from thinking is called essence *(t'i)* and the activity of the senses is called function *(yung)*. In comparing being free from thinking to empty space, the text seems to be asserting that just as empty space cannot be described properly using the predicates of language which applies to mental phenomena, so too these mental predicates cannot be applied to the state called "being free from thinking." For example:

> Empty space is without characteristics and is unconditioned *(wu-wei)*; being free from thinking is also without characteristics and is unconditioned. Empty space is neither increased nor destroyed; being free from thinking too is neither increased nor destroyed. . . . Because it [empty space] is free from the mental *(hsin)*, it is everywhere and there is nowhere it does not encompass. If one has thoughts, then it is not everywhere; but if one is free from thoughts, then it is everywhere.[11]

And, a little further on, the *TCMS* asserts:

> The eye sees, the mind is aware, knows, thoughts arise, and numerous concepts are born; there are divisions and barricades, and one does not understand. Just this is the defiled realm of dharmas, the realm of the sentient being. If the eye sees, the mind is aware, and one is free from thinking, then there are no barriers and divisions, and this is the pure realm of dharmas; it is the realm of Buddhas.[12]

This passage seems to describe a state where the practitioner does not dichotomize the world into subject and object. Such dualism creates "barriers and divisions." One does not eliminate one's own mental awareness to attain a true nondualistic state—this the text makes clear. One is simply free from thinking while remaining active in the midst of worldly affairs.

In other discussions in the first of the five *upāya*, other correlative pairs are discussed—such as events *(shih)* and principle *(li)*, inner tranquillity and outer illumination, form and emptiness, purity and impurity, expansion and contraction, and body and mind. The first section ends with a discussion of three types of *dharmakāya*.

The Second *Upāya*

The second section of the *upāya* texts, "Opening the Gateway of *Prajñā*," is inspired by a brief quotation from the *Lotus Sutra*. In the *WFP*, for example, the section begins by discussing the two-character compound *chih-hui,* which the Chinese used to translate the single Sanskrit technical term *prajñā* (nondual wisdom). The Northern Ch'an text separates these two characters, first discussing "opening the gateway of *chih*" and then "opening the gateway of *hui.*" The first is associated with internal wisdom (the mind becomes tranquil and undisturbed); the second is associated with wisdom in terms of the way one deals with the external world (the input of the sensory organs is not disturbing). When both internal and external are undisturbed, the gateway of full wisdom, or *prajñā (chih-hui),* is opened. To attain full *prajñā* is identical with attaining *bodhi* (enlightenment). The tendency of the Northern texts to discuss Buddhist ideas in pairs is seen clearly here, especially when one remembers that *prajñā* has no such dual aspect in the original Sanskrit.

The Northern line provided its own interesting interpretations of standard Buddhist terms, as did the other Buddhist schools. For example, in this second section a student inquires about the phrase "having the power to save sentient beings" and asks what is meant by "sentient beings" and what is meant by "power." The master responds that being undisturbed is power and erroneous thinking is sentient beings. Thus "body and mind undisturbed is called 'saving sentient beings'."[13]

Next the state of being undisturbed is related to *prajñā* and then related to *samādhi* (concentration). Being undisturbed is discussed first in terms understood by followers of the Hīnayāna path and then as understood by followers of the bodhisattva path. Hīnayāna followers are able to open the gateway of *hui* and achieve inner tranquillity, but they are frightened by activity and emotional involvement with the external realm and therefore attach themselves to a passive lifestyle and strive to attain a nirvana of emptiness and extinction.[14] The *WFP* explains:

> If you see that there is a disturbance, then this is being disturbed. Even if you see no disturbance, this too is being disturbed. Not seeing that there is any disturbance, not seeing that there is any nondisturbance—this is genuinely being undisturbed.[15]

In other words, the follower of the Mahāyāna path of the bodhisattva

> realizes that the six senses are fundamentally undisturbed from the very beginning, and therefore within there is illumination clearly shining while without he functions in absolute freedom. This is truly and genuinely being undisturbed according to the Mahāyāna.[16]

In addition to the distinction between *chih* and *hui,* many other pairs appear in this second division. For example, the text discusses the important distinction between fundamental enlightenment and subsequently achieved enlightenment (which results from cultivation). This tendency to group key ideas into pairs is seen in the rather forced explanations given to the titles of various Buddhist sutras. The authors of the five *upāya* texts want to fit all titles into a rigid framework of pairs, so each title is divided into two halves and each half is then explicated as meaning either "mind unmoving" or "forms unmoving" or both simultaneously. In the *WFP,* for example, we find:

> What is the meaning of *Marvelous Dharma Lotus-Flower Sutra?*
> Reply: Mind undisturbed is the "Marvelous Dharma." Body undisturbed is the "Lotus-Flower." Body and mind undisturbed is entering into the *anantanirdesa-pratiṣṭhāna-samādhi* [which the Buddha entered into before he preached the doctrine of infinity as recorded in the *Lotus Sutra*].[17]

> What is the *Buddha's Broad-and-Great Flower-Ornament Sutra?*
> Reply: Mind undisturbed is "Broad-and-Great." Body undisturbed is "Flower-Ornament." Body and mind at peace, tranquil and undisturbed, is the "Buddha's Broad-and-Great Flower-Ornament Sutra."[18]

The entire second section of these various texts takes its inspiration from a passage quoted from the *Lotus Sutra.* The passage does not seem important to the rest of the sutra itself, but the Northern Ch'an masters were inspired by it. The passage simply states that the Buddha entered into "the *anatanirdesa-pratiṣṭhāna-samādhi* in which his body and mind were undisturbed."[19] When the Buddha arose from his *samādhi,* he addressed Śariputra about the *prajñā (chih-hui)* of the Buddhas, which is profound and deep, difficult to understand, difficult to enter, which the Hīnayāna Buddhists cannot understand.[20]

The point of the second of the five *upāya* is summarized in the following passage. When a student asks why the Hīnayāna followers are unable to fathom the wisdom of the Mahāyāna, the reply is that these people "have discrimination and grasping. If they were free from conceptualizing and grasping, this is called 'being able to fathom the wisdom of the Buddha.' "[21]

The Third *Upāya*

This section is closely related to the *Vimalakīrti Sutra* and is entitled "Revealing the Inconceivable Liberation." Much of the material in this division is almost a line-by-line commentary upon interesting dialogues which occur in the third, fourth, and fifth chapters of the sutra. This structure is seen most clearly in the five-*upāya* text entitled *Ta-ch'eng wu-fang-pien pei-tsung (WFP).* At the beginning of this third *upāya,* reference is made to a discussion on inconceivability, triggered by Śariputra entering the tiny room of the layman Vimalakīrti and wondering to himself where all the glorious bodhisattvas are going to sit. Another paragraph comments upon a dialogue between Vimalakīrti and Mañjuśrī (from the fifth chapter). The discussion ranges far and wide and remarks upon huge lion-thrones and the powerful bodhisattvas who can take the largest mountain from the center of the universe and put it into a tiny mustard seed without the mountain getting smaller or the seed gaining in size. The commentary is very free. In the following passage the words from the *Vimalakīrti Sutra* are italicized and the Northern Ch'an commentary appears below:

> *He caused thirty-two thousand lion-thrones, high, broad, and utterly pure, to come and enter the room of Vimalakīrti.*
> "Three" symbolizes the Three Bodies.
> "Ten thousand" symbolizes the profound meaning.
> "Two" symbolizes wisdom *(chih-hui)*.
> "One thousand" symbolizes the gate of cultivation. [22]

Another example of this commentary style is:

> *At the time he preached the dharma, five hundred of the sons of heaven* . . .
> These are the five senses.
> *from within the midst of the dharmas* . . .
> This is the organ of thought *(i-ken)*.
> *achieved the dharma-eye of purity.*
> The six senses simultaneously become pure and clear. [23]

This third division continues in a similar manner with the same key technical terms repeated again and again, especially "being undisturbed" *(wu-tung)*, mind and body both suchness, and the pair essence (or substance) plus function. The commentary also utilizes other technical terms in this explication of the sutra, such as the Ten Varieties of Inconceivability, the Three Poisons, and the Ten Evil Things. The stress is generally upon being free from conceptualizing, dichotomizing, and analyzing, reality. The inconceivability of reality when approached by dichotomizing and analysis is the major topic of this third section. This point is nicely summarized in the following passage from the *Ta-ch'eng wu-sheng fang-pien men (WSM)*:

> To give rise to the mind of conceptualization and description is to be fettered and not achieve liberation. Not to give rise to the mind of conceptualization and description is to be free from *(li)* attachments and fetters and is the achievement of liberation. [24]

The Fourth *Upāya*

This division, entitled "Revealing the True Nature of All Dharmas," is based upon a long quotation from a sutra entitled *Viśeṣacinti-brahma-*

pariprcchā. In the *WFP,* the main theme of the fourth *upāya* is summarized in the opening paragraph:

> The mind not discriminating, the mind is suchness.
> The mouth not discussing, the body is suchness.
> Body and mind [both] suchness is the inconceivable suchness liberation.
> Liberation is the true nature of all dharmas.[25]

The general structure seen in this quotation is typical of all the Northern Ch'an *upāya* texts and reflects a stylized format utilized extensively by the authors of these manuscripts.

In a discussion of the true nature of all dharmas, the texts also consider such fundamental notions as that of self-nature *(svabhāva),* desire-limit, consciousness, and the very nature of thinking. The following paragraph quotes again from the *Vimalakīrti,* tying it in nicely with the previous discussion. When the layman sage Vimalakīrti first meets Manjuśri, he welcomes him with these words: "Well-come, Manjuśri. You have the characteristic of not-coming and yet you come; you have the characteristic of not-seeing and yet you see." The Northern Ch'an text glosses it as follows:

> *Vimalakīrti said, "Well-come Manjuśri . . . "*
> "Vimalakīrti said" is the pure essence, "Manjuśri" is the wondrous insight, and when there is the union of pure essence and wondrous insight, the mind does not arise, and this is "well" and it is concentration. Consciousness unborn is "come" and is "insight." Thus it is said, "Well-come."
> *"You have the characteristic of not-coming . . . "*
> This is the mind not arising, and is concentration.
> *" . . . and yet you come."*
> Consciousness unborn; this is insight.
> *"You have the characteristic of not-seeing . . . "*
> The mind not arising; this is concentration.
> *" . . . and yet you see."*
> Consciousness unborn; this is insight. This is Manjuśri's wondrous insight, following upon concentration, awakening insight *(hui).* Following from insight, being oriented externally, it is the dharma-gateway of tranquil illumination.[26]

The text continues in the same way, treating each portion of a phrase as either "consciousness unborn is insight" or "mind not arising is concentration." The author picks pairs of correlative concepts, or creates such pairs (sometimes rather arbitrarily), reverses each member of the pair, and then discusses the union of the pair. Although the move is interesting initially, it often becomes a ritualized formula repeated mechanically and sacrificing meaning to form. Perhaps it is being used more as a device to induce meditative states than an explication of the text.

Another example of this process appears in the following response from the *WFP* concerning concentration and insight:

> Mind not arising is concentration; consciousness unborn is insight. Being free from self-nature is concentration; being free from desire-limit is insight.
> The highest truth is concentration; the worldly truth is insight.
> Great *prajñā* is concentration; great compassion is insight.
> Principle *(li)* is concentration; events *(shih)* are insight.
> Essence *(t'i)* is concentration; function *(yung)* is insight.
> The unconditioned *(wu-wei)* is concentration; the conditioned is insight.
> Benefiting oneself is concentration; benefiting others is insight.
> Nirvana is concentration; birth-and-death is insight.
> Being free from the transcendental *(li-kou)* is concentration; abiding in dharmas is insight.[27]

It is in the third and fourth divisions of the five *upāya* texts that the influence of the *prajñā-pāramitā* literature is most clearly seen. This is the group of texts which stress wisdom and emptiness, usually discussed within a framework of paradox and contradiction. Although this literature is closely associated with the rival Southern tradition of Ho-tse Shen-hui, it was important to the Northern masters as well. Drawing from the longest of the five *upāya* texts (the *WFP*), for example, we see the following interchange:

Question: When there is no-coming, does one still come?
Reply: Even not-to-come is coming.
Question: Is it the body which comes or the mind which comes?
Reply: There is constant coming.
Question: What is "constant coming"?
Reply: It is the essence of coming; thus we say "constant coming."
Question: What is the "essence of coming"?
Reply: Nonattachment is the essence of coming.
Question: Is it departing or not-departing?
Reply: Departing.
Question: Is there departing when there is no departing?
Reply: No-departing is departing.
Question: Is it body departing, or mind departing?
Reply: Constant departing.
. . . .
Question: In what place does one abide?
Reply: One abides in nonabiding abiding.
Question: What is this nonabiding abiding?
Reply: Nonattachment is the nonabiding abiding.[28]

The Fifth *Upāya*

The last of the five *upāya* sections, "Comprehending That There Are No Differences," asserts that when one has grasped the serene and undisturbed nature intrinsic to all things, the pathway of liberation which is without obstruction opens and one penetrates into the truth of nondifferentiation. Anyone familiar with Chinese Buddhism will immediately recognize this theme as deriving, at least partially, from the *Avataṁsaka Sutra* and its theme of the mutual interpenetration of all dharmas. Affiliated with this doctrine are central concepts such as *li* (principle), *shih* (events), and the Buddha-nature (*Tathāgatagarbha* in Sanskrit). In the longest version of the five *upāya* texts (the *WFP*), the last portion involves quotations from the *Lotus Sutra,* the "Awakening of Faith," and the third chapter of the *Vimalakīrti Sutra.* It may be that some pages from the previous sections became mixed into this last portion unintentionally.[29] In the *Ts'an Ch'an-men shih (TCMS),* this last portion is very brief, perhaps amounting to only a single page in English translation. In the *Ta-ch'eng wu-sheng fang-pien men* the last section is either misplaced or lost. It is of rather substantial length in the *WFP,* however.

The central insight which informs the entire fifth *upāya* is simply that when the mind is not dichotomizing, all dharmas are perceived as they truely are—without any fundamental differences. And when one perfectly comprehends that there are no differences, this is the way of unobstructed liberation.[30]

As in all the previous sections, we find the same basic structure employed to explicate the themes—that is, pairs are established and then broken into sets of three in a rather artificial manner. For example:

Subjectivity not obstructing objectivity,
This is the unobstructed way.
Objectivity not obstructing subjectivity,
This is the liberated way.
Neither subjectivity nor objectivity,
This is the nonabiding Way.[31]

Using much the same format, the text discusses the Dharmakāya Buddha, the Sambhogakāya Buddha, and the Nirmaṇakāya Buddha using the triad of activity, tranquillity, and the unobstructed exercise of one's senses.[32] In the same section we encounter another discussion of the nature of *prajñā,* again divided into *chih* and *hui.* When the two of these are attained, body and mind become undisturbed, the world of birth and death is no longer a cause of unhappiness *(duḥkha),* and one does not grasp after or reject any dharma. In this state, the mind does not dichotomize and one does not engage in irrelevant discrimination or conceptualization. Now all dharmas are perceived in their real state of suchness and original nondifference. The practitioner can genuinely understand that Mount Sumeru and the mustard seed can be called the same, that the great ocean and the tip of a hair are the same, a long life and a short life are the same, and the self and others are the same. The true nature of all things is manifested and there is no longer any obstruction caused by mind, mentation, or consciousness *(wu-hsin, wu-i, wu-shih)*.[33]

Many more examples of the Northern Ch'an tendency to personalize Buddhist technical terms can be found in this division. For example, the questioner asks what sentient beings are, and the master responds: "All the various thoughts which arise and cease, which are false thinking, inverted-and-backward, calculating—it is these that are 'sentient beings'."[34]

Although the technical term *wu-hsin* (no-mind) is very important in the rival Southern tradition of Hui-neng and Ho-tse Shen-hui, the term appears but rarely in the writings of Northern Ch'an. However, we do find *wu-hsin* in a few places in this fifth *upāya*. For example:

> Empty space is without edges or boundaries; mind too is without edges or boundaries. Empty space is incalculable; mind too is immeasurable. To have mind *(yu-hsin)* is to have edges and boundaries; to be free from mind *(wu-hsin)* is to be without edges or boundaries.[35]

Use of the Five Upāya in the Northern Texts

The Northern tradition of Shen-hsiu has taken the idea of five different expedient methods, or *upāya*,[36] and used them to structure its doctrines and philosophy. These five *upāya* were understood as leading to the experience of awakening, as we see in the *WFP:*

Question: Why does one study these *upāya?*
Reply: It is due to one's desire to accomplish the achievement of Buddhahood.[37]

There remain many unanswered questions about these five *upāya*. Are they to be understood as five sequential stages, with the first for beginners and the fifth leading to the highest enlightenment? Possibly they are five different but equivalent means for the attainment of Buddhahood. Although the interconnected sequential development of the five sections suggests the traditional *p'an-chiao* scheme of progressive insight, each level a more profound revelation of the truth, the texts themselves are silent on this matter. Thus a good case might be made for either alternative at this point.

Although these five *upāya* were essential to later developments within the Northern Ch'an tradition, we can assume that they were not suffi-

cient by themselves for the achievement of awakening. The extended discussions concerning meditation and meditative states in Northern Ch'an
writings indicate that meditation was considered equally essential to the
quest.

MEDITATION IN NORTHERN CH'AN

The central focus of the Northern Ch'an meditative techniques seems to
be control *(she)* over the mind. One important element in this effort is
what Shen-hsiu called the "clear contemplation of mind" *(kuan-hsin)*. In
the *PHL,* when asked "What method should be cultivated to seek the
Buddha-way?", Shen-hsiu replied: "Simply cultivate the single method
(fa) of clear contemplation of mind. It includes all methods."[38] The questioner is skeptical, however, and asks how one can achieve an end to the
major obstacles to the goal, such as being ensnared within the Six Paths
of Rebirth and the Three Realms, by merely contemplating mind. Shen-
hsiu's reply to the question is quite interesting:

> One knows that all good karma arises due to one's own mind. Simply be able
> to control *(she)* the mind and you will be free from falsehood and evil. The
> karma working for rebirth in the Three Realms and the Six Paths of Rebirth
> will naturally of itself cease and be extinguished. To be able to extinguish all
> *duḥkha* is liberation.[39]

The questioner remains unconvinced and argues that the Buddha spoke
of struggling for awakening for three great aeons in order to become a
Buddha. How could it be achieved by the mere clear contemplation of
mind? Shen-hsiu explains that "three great aeons" is a metaphor used by
the Buddha to symbolize the three poisons of anger, craving, and ignorance, which exist within the minds of human beings. "If you can discard
craving, ignorance, and anger, which are the three varieties of the poisons of mind, this is called 'salvation achieved after three great aeons'."[40]

Controlling the mind in order to be free from falsehood and evil is at
least one of the goals of Northern Ch'an meditation. In order to control
the mind, however, one must also control that which is understood to be
the cause of mental disturbance—that is, falsehood and evil. Since the
input of the senses is one important cause of the Three Poisons, the mind
must be controlled in order to minimize the disturbances generated by
one's reaction to sensory stimuli. Doing this, the mind is called "purified." This point is clarified when the questioner asks for more elaboration:

> You say that if we desire to grasp the pure Buddha, we must purify our own
> minds. And to be in accord with that mind which is pure is the Buddha's Pure

Land. . . . Now you speak of the six senses being pure and clear. . . . What then is the meaning of the Six Virtues *(pāramitā)* of the bodhisattva?[41]

Shen-hsiu replies:

> If you desire to cultivate the Six Virtues, you must purify the six senses. If you desire to purify the six senses, you must first get rid of the Six Thieves [the six senses when one is attached to what one perceives]. If you can cast out the eye thief, you will be free from all realms of forms and the mind will be free from stinginess. This is what we call charity [the first of the six *pāramitā*].[42]

Shen-hsiu treats the other five virtues in the same manner, advising the questioner to cast out the "hearing thief," the "taste thief," and so forth. Then he says:

> If you cast off forever the Three Poisons and consequently purify the six senses, body and mind become deep and clear, and within and without are pure and clear.[43]

And again:

> The Way [of the Buddha] is awakening; and this is cultivating all practices of awakening, moderating, and subduing the six senses. Pure practice for a long time without ceasing is called "practicing the Way during the six periods of the day."[44]

These passages clearly refer to meditative practices, but the texts do not supply details. Shen-hsiu does speak of some practices explicitly, such as fasting, but he redefines them to fit his own categories. For example, he writes:

> What we call fasting is controlling the body and mind, not allowing them to disperse or become agitated. . . . One certainly must restrain the six passions, and one certainly must govern the Three Poisons, diligently investigating the pure body and mind.[45]

Again we find reference to the control of body and mind, which here seems to mean that we are not to allow our concentration to become unfocused or agitated. For one who can follow this method of practice, Shen-hsiu promises great rewards:

> Simply be able to control the mind for inner illumination, and realize that insight is constantly shining. You will be free from the Three Poisons which will be forever destroyed, the Six Thieves will not be allowed to cause disturbances, and, of themselves, merits will accumulate.[46]

The text has revealed that at least one of the goals of Northern Ch'an meditative practices is to "control the mind for inner illumination and to realize insight for external clarity." Achieving this goal was called attaining the state of "mind and body undisturbed" *(wu-tung),* and to do this one must control the Six Thieves. But still there remains a puzzle. What precisely are we to *do* to accomplish this? What is the meditator to do, physically and mentally, in order to achieve this state of being undisturbed?

To discover the specific practices of Northern Ch'an meditation, we must begin with a brief examination of the technical terminology. The Northern Ch'an texts utilize the terms *ch'an* (often treated as a transliteration of the Sanskrit term *dhyāna*) and *san-mei* (usually treated as a transliteration of *samādhi*), but by far the most popular technical term referring to meditation is *ting. Ting* seems to have been a character which was not used to translate any single technical Sanskrit meditation term but, rather, corresponded in a general way to a number of technical terms.[47] The Chinese appear to have relied upon the ordinary meanings of *ting* in Chinese ("to be settled, stable, fixed") to carry the multiple meanings found in a number of interrelated and overlapping terms of the Indian meditation traditions and texts. Thus, in the broad range of possible meanings for *ting,* we find everything from the simplest introductory exercises, where the meditator concentrates upon breathing as an aid to develop sustained concentration *(ānāpānasati),* to the highest states where one who has mastered the levels of *dhyāna* achieves a state of heightened mental clarity describable only as equanimity *(upekkha)* and concentration *(samādhi).*

In general, then, we can guess that *ting* suggested a state of single-minded or one-pointed concentration. To be proficient in this skill was often considered a prerequisite for the achievement of *prajñā* and thus a prerequisite for the attainment of awakening. Although some might want to reserve the use of the term *ting* to render only *dhyāna,* or only *samādhi,* or only the highest mental states achieved by meditation techniques, the Chinese did not do this.[48] When translators encounter the term *ting,* they must be aware of the ambiguity of usage even though the term is rendered as either "meditation" or "concentration." *Ting* can describe strictly physical or bodily experiences as well as mental states generally achieved by the means of these physical practices. The question I have raised is: How did the Northern line of Ch'an understand *ting*? Was it applied strictly to only one aspect of meditation practice, or was it used in a broad sense to include physical practices and resultant mental states?

Because we have nothing which corresponds to a manual of meditation techniques for the Northern line of Ch'an, a definitive answer does not seem possible at this time. In all likelihood, the basic techniques of meditation were taught to the beginner by a teacher among the senior monks of the monastery; this knowledge would not be expected to be learned from written materials. Inasmuch as this part of the instruction could be imparted by a monk who had not yet attained the final goal, there would always be a surfeit of teachers. Those who wanted to learn meditation would simply go to the organized group of Ch'an monks and be assigned an instructor upon acceptance as a disciple. There would be little reason for the Northern line to write down the details of its techniques. In fact, it seems likely that its practices were not particularly unique and would have been similar to the methods taught in the other schools of Chinese Buddhism, particularly the T'ien-t'ai school, which spent much energy producing written meditation manuals and analyses.

In the absence of detailed manuals spelling out the techniques, we are forced to infer the particulars of its practices from the descriptions found in Northern Ch'an writings. Numerous passages clearly refer to meditation practices, but the exact details are not supplied. At the beginning of the *Ta-ch'eng wu-sheng fang-pien men,* for example, we find:

> Each of you must resolve to sit in cross-legged meditation *(chia-fu tso).* To identify oneself with the mind of a son of the Buddha which is perfectly undisturbed is called "purity."[49]

The text amplifies upon this remark in a subsequent paragraph:

> If you behold *(k'an)* the mind, and if it is pure, it is called the realm of the pure mind. You should not focus inwardly upon body-mind, and you should not focus outwardly your body-mind. There should be a relaxed, vast, and far-reaching inspecting *(k'an),* an inspecting which everywhere encompasses the empty sky.[50]

From the preceding passage it is clear that the monks at some stage (just beginners?) are required to sit cross-legged and, once seated, they should practice the "inspection" or "beholding" *(k'an)* of the mind. This does sound like the practice previously described as the "clear contemplation (or observation) of mind" *(kuan-hsin).* Many questions still remain, however. It is not clear whether the practice of inspecting brings about a pure mind, or whether one is simply inspecting the mind to become aware of its innate purity. A third possibility is that the inspecting itself is the functioning of the pure mind—its actualization, so to speak. Although the phrases "inspecting mind" and "clear contemplation of mind" suggest an inward-looking practice, the text says that the activity of inspecting should be "far-reaching" and this is compared to the empty sky. Perhaps the student is not to focus just inwardly upon mind; perhaps mind itself is not conceived of as existing inside the head. As we discovered in the "Five *Upāya*" discussion:

> Empty space is without edges or boundaries;
> mind too is without edges or boundaries.
> Empty space is incalculable; mind too is immeasurable.
> To have mind is to have edges and boundaries;
> to be free from mind is to be without edges or boundaries.[51]

It seems reasonable to read this passage as implying that the inspecting itself may cause the student to recognize the innate purity of the mind. Consequently the inspecting itself is not focusing one's attention inwardly, not concentrating upon the contents of consciousness, as is suggested by the English term "meditation." This conclusion is strengthened by the following:

> Inspecting is oriented toward what is before you and far-reaching; inspecting is oriented toward what is behind and far-reaching; inspecting simultaneously encompasses everywhere in the four directions, up and down; inspecting encompasses empty space; inspecting continuously uses the pure mind's eye. In this inspecting one is not cut off or worried about how much time is spent. In one who has achieved this, body and mind are harmonized and function unobstructedly.[52]

One might reasonably assume that this meditation technique is not aimed at the absolute beginner, for one must wonder whether the beginner could maintain this mental state for very long. Although this kind of sitting is situated within the context of cross-legged sitting, it could just as easily be interpreted as a mental state which is independent of one's physical posture. The Northern Ch'an texts do not go into sufficient detail about these practices to provide a definitive answer to the question about the necessity of physical posture for the attainment of a pure mind. If one were a follower of the Northern line during the eighth or ninth centuries, the preceding description would undoubtedly be sufficient to recall the details of the technique.

In subsequent passages from the Northern Ch'an text, we find a discussion of the six consciousnesses becoming pure, clear, and free from obstruction. When everything is free from obstruction, one has achieved awakening, which is liberation. The text asserts:

> Body and mind not arising is constantly keeping awareness *(shou)* of the true mind. . . . Mind not arising is the mind of true suchness; form not arising is form as true suchness. Because mind is true suchness, mind is emancipated; because form is true suchness, forms are emancipated. With mind and forms both free *(li)*, there is not a single thing, and this is the great tree of *bodhi*.[53]

Like the preceding passage, this statement raises as many questions as it answers. How, for example, is the state of "body and mind not arising" to be brought about? Is it the result of specific physical exercises, specific mental exercises, or both? Or is it perhaps the result of the inspecting which the text discusses in a previous paragraph? Is this a natural state of mind and body, or is it a temporary state attained as a result of concentrated mental manipulation? This latter view is suggested by the use of the term *shou,* which can be translated "maintaining awareness of" but can also be translated "keeping guard over." In this case, the passage would be rendered: "Body and mind not arising is constantly keeping guard over the true mind." Clearly this state would require some effort to achieve, and probably it would require effort to maintain.

"Guarding the mind" might suggest that the meditator achieve some sort of insensate trance or a shutting off of all sensory awareness. The texts are quite clear on this point, for they explicitly condemn all practices which shut one off from the world. Isolation of this sort is condemned as an inferior tool utilized by the followers of the "lesser vehicle" (Hīnayāna). One Northern Ch'an text deploys an interesting image from the *Nirvāṇa Sutra* to distinguish three kinds of people: the ordinary person; the follower of the Hīnayāna; the bodhisattva. The text states:

> For an ordinary person, when a sound exists it is heard, and when there is no sound, or when the sound has diminished and disappeared, there is no hearing.
> For the [followers of the] Two Vehicles, whether there is a sound or no sound, or the sound has diminished and is no longer heard, they do not hear.
> For the bodhisattva, whether there exists a sound or no sound, or whether the sound has diminished into inaudibility, there is constant hearing.[54]

Since the Northern line identifies its own methods with those of the bodhisattva path, it condemns any closing off of sensory perception. However, it also distinguishes its practice from the sensory awareness of the ordinary person. The Northern line advocates a sort of pure awareness, a "constant hearing" whether there is sound to attract our attention or simply silence. The importance of this pure sensory awareness is obvious in the following:

> Whether there exists a sound or no sound, or the sound diminishes [into inaudibility], there is constant hearing, and this is to be constantly in accord with the practice of being undisturbed *(wu-tung).* With the achievement of this technique *(fang-pien, upāya),* one achieves correct concentration *(ting)* and achieves perfect tranquillity, and this is the great nirvana [of the bodhisattva].[55]

In related passages, the Northern texts distinguish between two types of concentration *(ting):* correct and incorrect. The incorrect variety is the result of attempting to extinguish all sensory awareness until no sensations are allowed to penetrate into consciousness. Correct concentration is just the opposite: a pure sensory awareness which does not interfere with the undisturbed (*wu-tung,* "unmoving") nature of the mind and senses. As the text says, when the senses are undisturbed the Three Poisons are not awakened and the Six Thieves no longer function. This is what the Northern tradition calls the purification of the senses. It is not a state in which the meditator is in a trance and entirely oblivious of the external world. Rather, the goal is complete spiritual freedom; the meditator maintains a state of complete and constant mental alertness and unobstructed awareness, and the mind is not trapped by trying to create mental conceptualizations of suchness. The problem is not with the senses and not with the objects of the senses; the problem is with the mind which dichotomizes and misperceives as a result of conditioning and conceptualizing. This point is clear in the following dialogue:

Question: Can the entrances [senses] be purified?

Reply: When mind functions correctly, there is no awareness of any "entrances" and no awareness of any "exits." To be aware of an entrance is disturbance. To have an entrance or exit is a disturbance. Even to be aware of no-entrance is disturbance. To be free from both entrance and no-entrance is to be truly undisturbed.[56]

At this point we conclude our brief analysis of meditation according to the Northern Ch'an tradition, even though we have not resolved a number of interesting questions. As more texts from the Northern Ch'an teaching lineage are discovered among the Tun-huang manuscripts, we might expect a more detailed picture to emerge. Nevertheless, we seem safe in concluding that the ideas of the Northern teachers are quite in accord with the major themes of Mahāyāna Buddhism. In fact, it is likely that the majority of techniques were not unique to this tradition alone, but were shared by most schools of Chinese Buddhism which relied upon meditation as a means to the goal of Buddhahood.

CONCLUSIONS

As we have discovered, the Northern line of Shen-hsiu utilized at least two methods in its quest for awakening. The first was discussed in the context of intellectual discernment, although this expression was not intended to imply that the texts were not used in the context of meditation as well. This method was called the method of Five *Upāya* because several Northern Ch'an manuscripts are divisible into five sections, each based upon a different Mahāyāna Buddhist text. Moreover, the term *upāya* appears in the title of one of these manuscripts, and the complete expression "Five *Upāya*" appears in the complete title of another.

Finally, the text states that one studies these *upāya* because one desires to achieve Buddhahood.

The second method used by the Northern tradition of Ch'an is "contemplation of mind," which seems equivalent to other expressions encountered in Northern Ch'an writings: "maintaining awareness of mind," "guarding the mind," and "beholding (inspecting) purity" *(k'an-ching)*. These practices are associated with the cross-legged meditation posture, but the texts clearly state that this is not to be understood as an introspective practice which shuts off the external world. If anything, the exercises are directed outward in an attempt to generate a state of nondichotomizing awareness of the world. Through the cultivation of these techniques the student can achieve what the Northern masters called "both mind and senses undisturbed." This state is equated with awakening.

The relationship between these two methods is not clearly spelled out in the manuscripts. Was the student expected to practice the method of the textual study of the Five *Upāya* as a preliminary to the meditative exercises, or were the meditative techniques understood as a preliminary to the discernment aspect? Did the Northern Ch'an masters envision the path as conceptualization followed by meditation or as meditation followed by intellectual understanding?

When studying Buddhism one must be particularly wary of either/or situations, for almost invariably the situation is better understood as both/and. Using this model, one might reasonably expect that the disciples practiced both techniques simultaneously, each reinforcing the other, allowing the student to plumb deeper into the fundamental insights of Ch'an. The passages in the Five *Upāya* texts might be meditated upon and tested by the student's own experiences, and consequently the meditation may become more profound, especially as the student comes to understand the real nature of all dharmas, their inconceivability, their ultimate nondifferentiation, their nonsubstantiality, and their mutual interpenetration. Then the universe dissolves into an ever-changing process and all one's presuppositions ("But things *must* be like this!") dissolve as well. Although the meditation exercise might provide this insight by itself, it is likely that the meditative exercises are informed by this textual study as well, so that the final experiences are provided with a framework which is compatible with the history of Buddhist thought.

Ultimately one might conclude that there are not two different methods here but rather one method seen from two different vantage points. Through the study of the Five *Upāya*, students are provided with the categories by which they can describe the experiences that result from the pure unattached awareness of the world. The likely conclusion of the combination of meditation and discernment is neatly summarized by Shen-hsiu's *Kuan-hsin lun:*

> Simply be able to control the mind for inner illumination, and realize contemplation for outer clarity. You will then be cut off from the Three Poisons, which will be destroyed forever. Close up the Six Thieves, which will not be allowed to cause disturbances, and of themselves merits as numerous as the sands of the river Ganges will accumulate. . . . You will transcend the ordinary and achieve the level of sagehood. It will be right before your eyes and not far off in the distance. Enlightenment takes place in a moment.[57]

NOTES

1. Apparently there are other texts identified as belonging to the Northern line which are circulating in hand-copied or xeroxed versions, but I have not had access to them for this 1977 study.

2. Shen-hsiu, founder of the Northern line of Ch'an, is credited with a lengthy commentary upon the *Avataṁsaka Sutra* and was also known as a student of the *Laṅkāvatāra Sutra.* He had a reputation as a brilliant scholar, and this reputation for scholarship carried over into his lineage. This point is often contrasted with the attitude of the Southern line of Ch'an toward intellectual study, but the later Southern line was not so opposed to textual study as many of the popular writings about Ch'an have implied. It is clear from the writings of the Ch'an masters that they knew well a large number of passages from many different sutras. This is especially clear in the text attributed to the Sixth Patriarch of the Southern line, Hui-neng, who is usually taken as the paradigm of the illiterate anti-intellectual Ch'an master. In his *Platform Sutra,* and in the writings of his chief disciple, Ho-tse Shen-hui, more than a dozen different sutras are quoted. See Philip Yampolsky, *The Platform Sutra of the Sixth Patriarch* (New York: Columbia University Press, 1967). See also Kanehara Haruhide, "Kataku Jinne to in'yō kyōten" [A study of sutras quoted by Ho-tse Shen-hui], *Indogaku Bukkyōgaku kenkyū* 20 (March 1972): 641–642.

3. Determining authors and dates for the various Northern Ch'an texts is quite difficult. If we assume that the Northern line begins when Shen-hsiu left Hung-jen (the Fifth Patriarch), approximately A.D. 662, we can assume that the writings of Shen-hsiu date from this period and 706, the year of his death. I have listed the texts in the order in which I believe they were composed, but this sequence is by no means certain. Yanagida Seizan comes to a different conclusion in his "Hokushū Zen no shisō," *Zen bunkyō kenkyūjo kyō shiō* 6 (1975): 88–90. My choice of sequence is based upon the fact that each text seems to be an elaboration of the material in the text listed previously. Even if my conjecture about the sequence of composition is mistaken, none of my conclusions are based upon the order I have listed.

4. The most complete historical analysis of the Northern tradition of Ch'an remains unpublished at this time. It is the doctoral dissertation of John McRae, "The Northern School of Chinese Ch'an Buddhism," Yale University, 1983. For a study of the philosophical differences between the Northern and Southern lines of Ch'an see Robert B. Zeuschner, "The Philosophical Criticisms of Northern Ch'an Buddhism" (Ph.D. dissertation, University of Hawaii, 1977). See also

R. Zeuschner, "The Understanding of Mind in the Northern Line of Ch'an (Zen)," *Philosophy East and West* 28 (1) (January 1978): 69–79, and R. Zeuschner, "The Concept of *li-nien* in Northern Ch'an Buddhism," in Lewis Lancaster and Whalen Lai, eds., *Early Ch'an in China and Tibet* (Berkeley: Asian Humanities Press, 1983).

5. As mentioned in note 3 above, the dating of these texts is difficult. The text alluded to is the *Ts'an Ch'an-men shih, T* 85.1291–1293.

6. In a memorial inscription written for Shen-hsiu shortly after his death in 706, we find: "He received the *Laṅkāvatāra Sutra* and transmitted it as the mind-essential." (The Chinese text is in Yanagida Seizan, *Shoki Zenshūshisho no kenkyū*, Kyoto, 1966, p. 499.) The influence of the *Laṅkāvatāra* is especially clear in the *Ts'an Ch'an-men shih* (*T* 85.1291–1293), which discusses numerous topics taken directly from the sutra. The sutra is equally important in the *Leng-chia shih-tz'u chi*, a Northern Ch'an biographical text compiled between 708 and 741 which lists Shen-hsiu as the Seventh (not the Sixth) Patriarch (*T* 85.1283–1290).

7. *T* 15.33a–62a. A brief passage from this text is translated in Lucian Stryk, *World of the Buddha* (New York: Anchor Books, 1969), pp. 270–271.

8. The Hua-yen school of Chinese Buddhism has been regarded as epitomizing the highest development of Chinese Buddhist metaphysics. Good introductory studies of this school are available; see Francis H. Cook, *Hua-yen Buddhism: The Jewel Net of Indra* (University Park: Pennsylvania State University Press, 1977), and Garma C. C. Chang, *The Buddhist Teaching of Totality: The Philosophy of Hwa Yen Buddhism* (University Park: Pennsylvania State University Press, 1971).

9. *Upāya* is defined in Edgerton, *Buddhist Hybrid Sanskrit Dictionary* (Delhi: Motilal Banarsidass, 1972), p. 146b; for its meaning in Northern Ch'an, see Paul Demiéville, *Le Councile de Lhasa* (Paris: Presses Universitaires de France, 1952), p. 17.

10. A study of this phrase and its possible interpretations can be found in Zeuschner, "The Concept of *li-nien*."

11. *WFP* in Ui, *ZSK* I.469, no. 4. See also Suzuki, *SDZ* III.192, no. 3.

12. *WFP* in Ui, *ZSK* I.470; Suzuki, *SDZ* III.192.

13. *WFP* in Ui, *ZSK* I.471, no. 9; Suzuki, *SDZ* III.193–194, no. 2.

14. *WFP* in Ui, *ZSK* I.472; Suzuki, *SDZ* III.195.

15. *WFP* in Ui, *ZSK* I.473; Suzuki, *SDZ* III.196, no. 9.

16. *WFP* in Ui, *ZSK* I.473; Suzuki *SDZ* III.196.

17. *WFP* in Ui, *ZSK* I.476, no. 18; Suzuki *SDZ* III.199, no. 17.

18. Ibid.

19. The passage from the *Saddharmapuṇḍarīka* can be found in English translation; see for example, the translation by Senchu Murano, *The Sutra of the Lotus Flower of the Wonderful Law* (Tokyo: Nichiren Shu Headquarters, 1974), p. 21. See also Bunnō Katō, Yoshirō Tamura, and Kōjirō Miyasaka, *The Three Fold Lotus Sutra* (New York: Weatherhill, 1975), p. 51.

20. Ibid.

21. *WFP* in Ui, *ZSK* I.477, no. 25; Suzuki, *SDZ* III.201, no. 22.

22. *WFP* in Ui, *ZSK* I.481; Suzuki, *SDZ* III.206.

23. *WFP* in Ui, *ZSK* I.480, no. 30; Suzuki, *SDZ* III.205, no. 2.

24. *WSM* in Ui, *ZSK* I.465.

25. *WFP* in Ui, *ZSK* I.485; Suzuki, *SDZ* III.209 and 222.

26. *WFP* in Ui, *ZSK* I.486; Suzuki, *SDZ* III.222–223.

27. *WFP* in Ui, *ZSK* I.485; Suzuki, *SDZ* III.225.

28. *WFP* in Ui, *ZSK* I.488; Suzuki, *SDZ* III.226.

29. Since we find only four of the five divisions in the *Ts'an Ch'an-men shih* (*T* 85.1291–1293), we are unable to compare other lengthy versions of this *upāya*. It is not clear in the manuscript whether the text is so early that the standardized division into five was not yet firmly developed or whether the authors of the text, or later editors, intentionally or accidentally omitted the missing section. In his Japanese study of Chinese Ch'an, D. T. Suzuki suggests the former view (Suzuki, *SDZ* III.7–8). The discussion of the fifth *upāya* is very short in this text, and it is not present in the *Ta-ch'eng wu-sheng fang-pien men* (*T* 85.1273b–1273a). Thus we are unable to determine whether the inclusion of these other sources in this *upāya* was accidental or intentional.

30. *WFP* in Ui, *ZSK* I.489, no. 39; Suzuki, *SDZ* III.223, no. 1.

31. *WFP* in Ui, *ZSK* I.490; Suzuki, *SDZ* III.229.

32. *WFP* in Ui, *ZSK* I.490–491; Suzuki, *SDZ* III.229–230.

33. *WFP* in Ui, *ZSK* I.496; Suzuki, *SDZ* III.234.

34. *WFP* in Ui, *ZSK* I.493. The passage is not present in the Suzuki text.

35. *WFP* in Ui, *ZSK* I.498–499. One might note that the compound "no-mind" *(wu-hsin)* appears here. This is one of the central technical terms of the rival Southern line of Ch'an and appears rarely in the Northern Ch'an texts examined by the author. *Wu-hsin* was not an uncommon expression in Chinese Buddhism, however, and it does not seem to be given any special emphasis in this passage; rather it is treated as part of a general sequence of negations related to discriminative and dichotomizing mental activity which creates conceptual contraries—these are part of the either/or mentality which Buddhism in general finds inadequate when dealing with things as they really are. To be preferred is the nondichotomous awareness described previously, associated with *prajñā* *(chih-hui)*. The important technical term for the Northern line which seems to correspond to the Southern line's emphasis upon no-mind is *li-nien* ("to be free from thinking").

36. The idea of Five *Upāya* is not present in the few texts which have been identified as being by the founder of the Northern line, Shen-hsiu, but the concept does appear to have been familiar to Ho-tse Shen-hui of the Southern line. Ho-tse Shen-hui died approximately fifty years later than Shen-hsiu, so we might conjecture that the Five *Upāya* structure developed from the period of Shen-hsiu's two outstanding disciples, P'u-chi (651–739) and I-fu (658–736). Nevertheless, the idea of Five *Upāya* was not an innovation of the Northern tradition. The concept appears in numerous texts prior to the time of Shen-hsiu (d. 706). For example, in the fifth century there was a text known as the *"Five Upāya Sutra,"* but it appears to have been lost already by the beginning of the sixth century; it is known to us only through its title, which is mentioned in *T* 55.36b. Chih-i, of the T'ien-t'ai lineage of Buddhism, writes of Five *Upāya* in one of his *chih-kuan* texts (*T* 46.166c), but these are not even similar in content to the Five *Upāya* discussed in the Northern Ch'an manuscripts. The *Tso-ch'an san-mei ching* (*T* 15.285c) also relates Five *Upāya* to the practice of concentration and meditation. Thus even though the idea of Five *Upāya* was popular prior to the development of Northern Ch'an, none of the texts in which this idea appears were ever quoted by the Northern masters. For more details on the Five *Upāya* in early Ch'an, see Yanagida Seizan, *Shoki Zenshūshisho no kenkyū* (Kyoto: Zen bunka kenkyūjo 1966), pp. 115–116, n. 9.

37. *WFP* in Ui, *ZSK* I.493; Suzuki, *SDZ* III.232.

38. *PHL, T* 48.366c.
39. *KHL, T* 85.1271a.11–13.
40. *KHL, T* 85.1271a.20–21.
41. *KHL, T* 85.1271b.15–17.
42. *KHL, T* 85.1271b.17–18.
43. *KHL, T* 85.1271c.22–23.
44. *KHL, T* 85.1272b.5.
45. *KHL, T* 85.1272b.12–13.
46. *KHL, T* 85.1273a.29–b.2.
47. That *ting* was used to refer to a broad number of meditative techniques, some of which may well have been Taoist, is apparent in the Chinese version of the *Mahāprajñāramitā-śāstra (Ta-chih-tu lun)*, where we find in the twenty-eighth chapter:

All of the *dhyāna (ch'an-ting)* are also called *ting;* the four *dhyanas* ("absorptions") are also called *ting.* The *dhyāna (ting)* of the four *dhyāna* which excludes any remainder is also called *ting,* and so too *samādhi* and *dhyāna (ch'an).* [Quoted in Mochizuki Shinko, *Bukkyō daijiten* (Tokyo, 1955–1963), p. 3673a.]

The passage is somewhat garbled in English translation because the text is attempting to indicate that several different Sanskrit technical terms are being rendered by the same Chinese character, *ting.* And these technical terms were not the only ones rendered by *ting.* Mochizuki's *Bukkyō daijiten* lists the following Sanskrit terms as translated into Chinese by *ting: ānapānasati, samāhita, cittaikagratā, śamatha, anusmṛti.*
48. As A. E. Zurcher points out on p. 33 of his excellent study of early Chinese Buddhism, *The Buddhist Conquest of China* (Leiden: Brill, 1959):

The system of mental exercises commonly called *dhyāna (Ch'an)* in Chinese sources, but which is more adequately covered by the term "Buddhist yoga," comprising such practices as the preparatory technique of counting the respirations leading to mental concentration *(ānāpānasmṛti);* the contemplation of the body as being perishable, composed of elements, impure and full of suffering; the visualization of the internal and external images of various colors, etc. . . . Some of the *"dhyāna"* practices mentioned above, notably the *ānāpānasmṛti,* outwardly resembled certain Taoist respiratory techniques.

49. *WSM, T* 85.1273b.29–c.1; compare *WSM* in Ui, *ZSK* I.450, no. 1; Suzuki, *SDZ* III.168.
50. *WSM T* 85.1273c.4–6.
51. *WFP* in Ui, *ZSK* I.493.
52. *WSM, T* 85.1273c.9–12.
53. *WSM, T* 85.1273c.19–22. The practice of the "guarding" of the mind is briefly discussed in W. Pachow, "A Buddhist Discourse on Meditation from Tun-huang," *University of Ceylon Review* 21 (1) (April 1963): 47–62. There is an excellent translation and study of this text done by John McRae, which, unfortunately, remains unpublished at this time.
54. *WSM* in Ui, *ZSK* I.454; *T* 85.1274c.11–13.
55. *WSM* in Ui, *ZSK* I.454; *T* 85.1274c.19–22.
56. *WSM* in Ui, *ZSK* I.454–457; *T* 85.1275b.9–11.
57. *KHL, T* 85.1273a.29–b.4, amended in light of *PHL, T* 48.369c.9–11.

6
Faith and Practice in Hua-yen Buddhism: A Critique of Fa-tsang (643–712) by Li T'ung-hsüan (646–740)

JAE-RYONG SHIM

The Hua-yen school of Chinese Buddhism is one of the highest achievements in Chinese intellectual history. According to the traditional scheme, the Hua-yen sect was initiated by Tu-shun (557–640), developed by Chih-yen (602–668), elaborated by Fa-tsang (643–712), and further expounded by Ch'eng-kuan (738–839) and Tsung-mi (780–841). These are the so-called five patriarchs of the Hua-yen school and therefore its most authoritative spokesmen. During the Sung (960–1279) and Ming (1368–1662) periods, however, the preferred interpretation of the *Hua-yen (Avataṁsaka) Sutra* was not by Fa-tsang and Ch'eng-kuan but by Li T'ung-hsüan (646–740).[1]

In the landscape of medieval Korea, Pojo Chinul (1158–1210) stands out as the great synthesizer of the traditions of meditative practice (Sŏn; Ch., Ch'an) and doctrinal teachings (Kyo; Ch., Chiao), especially Hua-yen doctrine.[2] Although he drew upon the ideas of Tsung-mi and Ch'eng-kuan, he relied especially on Li T'ung-hsüan for the task of synthesizing Sŏn and Kyo.[3] Although Li T'ung-hsüan's ideas do not represent the views of Hua-yen, they express an important trend within Chinese Buddhism in his day and proved to be significant for later history, especially in Korean Buddhism. To understand his ideas clearly, it is helpful to contrast them with the position of his famous contemporary, Fa-tsang. More specifically, the point of departure for Li's interpretation of the *Hua-yen Sutra* lies in his emphasis on the importance of faith as the primary requisite for the attainment of Buddhahood. Accordingly, this shall be the starting point for our investigation.

FAITH

It should be noted that for Hua-yen, "faith" does not imply a blind belief in a superhuman deity responsible for the spiritual salvation of people from the world of suffering. Rather, in the context of Hua-yen Buddhism, faith is divided into ten degrees of intensity and the ten degrees together constitute the initial step toward ultimate enlightenment. There being no scriptural evidence for positing the ten degrees of faith in the *Hua-yen Sutra* itself, it was Fa-tsang who adopted the scheme of fifty-two steps of the bodhisattva's career by adding the ten degrees of faith from the *She-lun (She-ta-ch'eng-lun, Mahāyānasaṃgraha).*[4] Fa-tsang technically accepts the ten faiths as the initial stage toward enlightenment according to his Five Teachings, but his primary purpose for discussing faith lies in his distinct One Vehicle doctrine that "at the perfection of faith, one attains Buddhahood" *(hsin man ch'eng fo).* Let us examine Fa-tsang's explanation carefully:

> In the Perfect Teaching there are two categories. The first includes all the stages of practice displayed in the previous teachings; they are skillful means. The second refers to the distinct doctrine and there are three meanings.
>
> The first is explained through the intermediary of the stages [of the Three Vehicles and others]; that is, the six stages from the first stage of the ten degrees of faith up to the stage of Buddhahood are not the same [*as those of Three Vehicles*]. *If one stage is acquired, all stages are acquired. Why is this? Because each stage possesses the "six characteristics," because [of the infinite interrelationship] of "primary and secondary," because of "mutual inclusion," because of "mutual identity," and because of "perfect interfusion."* . . . Also since all [preliminary] stages and the stage of Buddhahood are identical with each other, then the cause [of practicing] and the result [of Buddhahood] are not different, and the beginning and end are mutually inclusive or nonobstructive. At each stage one is both a bodhisattva and a Buddha. . . .
>
> Secondly, when the stages are shown in their relationship to the results of action, then there are three lives. The first life forms the stage of "seeing and hearing" [the Buddha and the dharma]; that is, by seeing and hearing this inexhaustible dharma one forms the indestructible impressions *(bīja)* as taught in the chapter on the "Arising of the *Tathāgata* from Essential Nature" [in the *Hua-yen Sutra*]. The second life forms the stage of "comprehension and practice." . . . The third life is the stage of "realization of the ocean of result." . . .
>
> Thirdly, consider the stages with reference to practice. There are only two parts: practice itself and superior progress. This topic is explained above in discussing the life of "comprehension and practice." . . . [The bodhisattva in a causal state] can teach an indescribable number of beings in an instant and simultaneously causes them to arrive at the point just prior to "undefiled con-

centration." . . . From the perfection of faith and the acquisition of stages onward, the activities of this bodhisattva fill the *dharmadhātu.* According to the *Hua-yen Sutra:* "He does not abandon a single universe, nor does he arise from a single seat of meditation, yet he reveals the practices of countless bodies. . . . In a single instant, in all the worlds in ten directions, he becomes a Buddha and turns the wheel of the dharma at the same time . . ."

Therefore, know that this is completely different from the Three Vehicles. Why is that? Because the stages of the practice of the Three Vehicles are taught that way in order to produce faith and comprehension within the framework of teaching.[5]

This quotation is from the Treatise on the Five Teachings *(Wu-chiao-chang),* the magnum opus of Fa-tsang, which is said to represent the culmination of Chinese Buddhist philosophy. The reason why Fa-tsang is considered to be the most systematic philosopher in China is because of his logic of "nonobstruction among events" *(shih-shih wu-ai).* In fact, as we can see from the preceding excerpt, Fa-tsang's treatment of the practice and stages toward the ultimate attainment of Buddhahood is carried out under three categories: in terms of the stages themselves; in terms of the time span through three lives (of rebirths); and in terms of the practice itself. In the first case Fa-tsang utilizes a capsule summary of the main tenets of Hua-yen philosophy. (Note the italicized parts.) However, he uses the terminology and the system of the Three Vehicles' theory of stages toward final Buddhahood or ultimate enlightenment because, from the standpoint of Hua-yen, any stage can be identified with all other stages. Even the second category using the three-lives scheme from the logical standpoint of mutual nonobstruction can be considered a mere expedient convention, for, he argues, there is no distinction between causal state and the final result of enlightenment. Even though there is some disagreement whether this temporal schematization of three lives can be elicited from the actual epic of the pilgrimage of Prince Sudhana, Fa-tsang himself made it clear that the theory of three lives must be subsumed under the perfection of faith. In his *Record in Search of Mystery (T'an-hsüan-chi),* we have the following:

In what stage is Sudhana? Answer: He can be in any stage. When he is in the stage of faith, he is there; in the stage of abode, he is there, too, for with his one body he travels through the five stages, and he permeates all stages wherever he finds himself.[6]

That he can be in any stage does not mean that he attains a certain stage according to the result of his practice but that his attainment in any stage can be self-sufficient in the realm of the One Vehicle wherein all stages are equal and where cause and result are identical. Furthermore, Fa-tsang made a definite statement in the *Questions and Answers About the Hua-yen (Sutra) (Hua-yen wen-ta):*

Question: Are the three stages such as "seeing and hearing," "comprehension and practice," and "final realization" the correct stage of universal dharma?

Answer: No. I present such a theory simply to accommodate the Three Vehicles. In speaking of the correct stage of universal dharma, there is no stage that cannot be called a stage. All the six ways [of transmigration], triple worlds, and all the *dharmadhātus* are correct stages of the universal dharma.[7]

Bearing in mind Fa-tsang's philosophical appeal to the identity of all stages, the third category, that of practice, reveals Fa-tsang's real emphasis: "From the perfection of faith, the activities of this bodhisattva fill the whole *dharmadhātu*." During one's spiritual progress through the various stages, the pivotal point of nonregression is reached only when a bodhisattva fulfills the practice of resolute faith. That the logic of interfusion aims primarily at the formulation of reality as Fa-tsang perceives it is undeniable. Yet in the *Record of Mind's Journey in the Dharmadhātu of the Hua-yen (Hua-yen yu-hsin fa-chiai chi)* Fa-tsang makes resolute faith the fundamental requisite for attainment of Buddhahood:

Now those who wish to enter the *dharmadhātu* of nonobstruction must awaken the penetrating, resolute faith. The reason is that faith constitutes the basic foundation and ground for the multitude of practices. All practices are born from resolute faith. Thus resolute faith is listed first and it is made the point of departure.[8]

Faith is not only prerequisite; it is also a sustaining power that drives the devotee through to the ultimate result: the attainment of Buddhahood. Upon the acquisition of resolute faith, one can go on to comprehend the basic Hua-yen world view—that is, the dependent co-origination of mutual conditioning *(yüan-ch'i-hsiang-yu)* and the perfect interfusion of dharma-nature *(fa-hsing yung-t'ung)*. But understanding *(chieh)* is dependent upon practice *(hsing),* for unless practice is completed, true understanding is not gained. And both understanding and practice must necessarily come from resolute faith:

If resolute faith does not exist, though there be a great amount of understanding, it is nothing but inverted opinion. The reason is that understanding without resolute faith does not lead to practice, and inverted opinion is not real understanding.[9]

Faith, therefore, plays a vital role from the beginning to the end of a bodhisattva's career. In fact the intricate complexity of the Hua-yen world view can be summarized and concentrated in the statement that one becomes a Buddha at the perfection of faith. All the theories are directed toward the practical attainment of Buddhahood. Despite this clear emphasis on the importance of resolute faith, Fa-tsang has often been criticized for his predilection to theory. The reason for this can be found in the common belief among Mahāyāna Buddhists that the result *(kuo-fen),* that is, the ultimate enlightenment, is incapable of being fully expressed, whereas the cause *(yin-fen),* that is, the preparatory (progressive or abrupt) spiritual cultivation, can be elaborated in full.[10] Yet the primary concern of Fa-tsang's grand system of Hua-yen metaphysics is to intellectualize the accomplished state of enlightenment. This metaphysical speculation on the mutual nonobstruction of events yields little room for the practical aspect of cultivation and the role of the individual person in his system of Five Teachings.

At this juncture we can introduce the novelty of Li T'ung-hsüan's viewpoint on the *Hua-yen Sutra* vis-à-vis Fa-tsang's approach. These two Hua-yen commentators were contemporaries, although we have no evidence of any personal interaction. In fact, Fa-tsang never even refers to Li, although Li refers to Fa-tsang whenever he differs from him. In general Li follows Fa-tsang's interpretation so far as the traditional framework such as Ten Mysteries or Six Characteristics is concerned. In the practical application of the Hua-yen philosophy, however, Li is more radical than Fa-tsang in that Li deepens Fa-tsang's insight and articulates this standpoint in a short, clear-cut manner.

Let us consider Li's viewpoint on faith. He, like Fa-tsang, assumes that faith must be a point of departure for the bodhisattva's career. Yet whereas Fa-tsang merely refers to the text where faith is understood as a belief in the possibility of attaining Buddhahood through a long period of practical cultivation, Li asserts:

> If anyone in the state of the ten degrees of faith does not believe that his own body is none other than the Buddha-body and that there is no difference between the causal state [practical cultivation] and the result state [final enlightenment], he cannot be said to accomplish the perfection of faith supported by insight.[11]

This is Li's explanation why faith must be the pivotal point in becoming a Buddha. The very identity of one's body with Buddhahood is the focus for resolute conviction or faith. The usual interpretation of faith as a belief in the possibility of becoming a Buddha through the step-by-step procedure of faith, understanding, practice, and realization *(hsin chieh hsing cheng)* was changed into the new idea that faith is the resolute conviction that one is already identified with Buddhahood. This conviction regarding each person's primordial attainment of Buddhahood is the basis of the Ch'an doctrine of sudden awakening.

UNMOVABLE WISDOM

Li T'ung-hsüan has proposed that "unmovable wisdom" accompanies this faith. Fa-tsang and his predecessor Chih-yen never discussed unmovable wisdom as an essential characteristic of sentient beings, while Ch'eng-kuan mentioned it only in terms of the *śūnyatā* doctrine.[12] The orthodox patriarchs of the Hua-yen lineage emphasized Vairocana Buddha, the eternal *dharmakāya,* to be the principal figure of the *Hua-yen Sutra,* but Li T'ung-hsüan stressed unmovable wisdom or "wisdom of universal illumination" as the single underlying common ground of both ignorant sentient beings and enlightened Buddhas:

> According to the sermon in the Hall of Universal Illumination [in the *Hua-yen Sutra*] there are ten Buddhas, starting from the Buddha of Wisdom of Nonobstruction. . . . These ten Buddhas of the various wisdoms have the Buddha of Unmovable Wisdom for their fundamental basis. . . . The Buddha of Unmovable Wisdom represents the first degree of faith. The Buddhas of Nonobstruction, of Liberated Wisdom, and so forth represent the progress and the result of that first degree of faith. Unmovable wisdom is based upon the universally illuminated wisdom, which is based on the wisdom of nonabiding, which then is based upon all sentient beings such as Prince Sudhana. When Sudhana had an interview with Bodhisattva Maitreya, he ordered Sudhana to see Mañjuśri [representing faith and wisdom]. The profound significance of this story lies in that the final completion of five stages [of a bodhisattva's career] is not separate from the initial faith. . . . If anyone says that there is no final attainment in the beginning of ten degrees of faith, his faith is not perfect. *From the beginning to the end, all is the result of unmovable wisdom. The subject of faith is the result. The object of faith is also the result. The agent, throughout his career of practice, is also the result.* Only if one believes in that is his faith perfect. The cause and result of cultivation are never different from unmovable wisdom. . . . The various Buddhas representing the result of practice in the course of Ten Abodes, Ten Transfers of Merits, Ten Stages, and the like are simply the diverse names of the Buddha of Unmovable Wisdom.[13]

Li's emphasis on unmovable wisdom as the content of faith logically fulfills the Hua-yen doctrine that "faith perfected is Buddhahood attained." In order to push the doctrine to its logical limit, Li had to transform Fa-tsang's theory of attainment of Buddhahood through three lives of rebirth *(san-sheng ch'eng-fo)* into attainment of Buddhahood in an instant *(ch'a-na ch'eng-fo).* Having utilized the frame of the Three Vehicles, Fa-tsang had to support his theory of three lives by his logic of nonobstruction among the divisions of conventional times. Although Fa-tsang foreshadowed the movement from the numerous kalpas needed for the final attainment of Buddhahood to an instant of correct faith, he was not completely free from the framework of conventional time. Li T'ung-hsüan, however, was more radical in breaking away from such conventions:

> Prince Sudhana attains Buddhahood in his one life. Entering the first abode, his delusion is completely extinguished in an instant. He never thinks of three lives or even one instant. This is the true meaning of "one life." Not being attached to conventional time contrived by the deluded mind, he is free from any lives. He simply attains the result of Buddhahood.[14]

In short, Li eradicated the element of diachronic time from the religious domain of Buddhahood. What is required of a devotee free from the temporal divisions is an instantaneous decision that he himself, just as he is, *is* Buddha:

> One life does not admit rebirth into three lives. Herein lies the meaning of "one life." Both ordinary people and saints are originally appearances from the one self-identical substance. There is no substantial difference between them. This is why entering the stage of final attainment is called "one life," since the division into three lives is unreal. Such is true dharma. All other opinions are wrong.[15]

Here we see a close tie between Li's idea of faith in the unmovable wisdom and the notion of the unreality of conventional temporal divisions. It is natural for Li to oppose Fa-tsang's remark on temporal determination with regard to the sermon expressed in the *Hua-yen Sutra:*

> According to Fa-tsang, after his first enlightenment the Buddha preached the *Hua-yen Sutra* in the second seven days. . . . T'ung-hsüan does not rely on the foregoing theory of time, one that is contrived by deluded calculation, because the fundamental tenet of this sutra is the original wisdom within the *dharma-dhātu*. It is by nature both substance and function, reality and phenomena. The great compassion is the original reality. Hence opinions about the time of preaching—whether it is "long ago" or "presently"—are completely extinguished. The wheel of the dharma is turned always without beginning and without ending. Dharma is originally like this. . . . We necessarily cannot establish the divisions of time that are driven by our delusion. This sutra is a sermon of all times which is a time of no-time.[16]

Li T'ung-hsüan criticized Fa-tsang indirectly for his inconsistency. If we adhere to the logic of nonobstruction among events and its corollary with regard to time (that is, ten divisions of time are mutually interfused and identified with one instant according to one of the Ten Mysteries in the Hua-yen world view elaborated by Fa-tsang and other orthodox Hua-yen patriarchs), the conventional temporal determinations regarding the preaching of the *Hua-yen Sutra* cannot be limited to the second seven days after the initial enlightenment of the Buddha Śākyamuni. Likewise, the assembly at the Hall of Universal Illumination cannot be said to be held only twice (according to Fa-tsang) or thrice (according to Ch'eng-kuan). This view of time inevitably leads Li to a view of the whole organization of the *Hua-yen Sutra* that is entirely different from that of the orthodox Hua-yen patriarchs. If we follow the sutra literally, we can find only eight or nine assemblies (varying among different translations) in seven places consisting of thirty-four (according to the Chin translation) or thirty-nine (according to the T'ang translation) chapters. Fa-tsang, relying on the "literal interpretation" *(shih-hsiang shih)* of the text, did not cast any doubt on there being two assemblies at the same Hall of Universal Illumination. (The Chin text that Fa-tsang relied on refers to the hall only two times, while the T'ang text has three assemblies at the hall.) Li T'ung-hsüan, following the "dharmic interpretation" *(piao-fa shih)* of the text, does not rely on the conventional division of time or conventional determination of location. In fact, he includes the whole sermon of the sutra in "one *dharmadhātu* of emptiness comprising all lands and particles of dust."[17] This statement of Li is in agreement with Fa-tsang's "original teaching in accordance with dharma" *(ch'eng-fa pen-chiao),* the undiluted original insight of the Buddha's enlightenment. Whereas Fa-tsang tries to accommodate the other doctrines as "branch teachings for the needs of particular capacities of audiences" *(chu-chi mo-chiao),* Li strictly adheres to the fundamental teaching itself. Not only regarding the time and locale of the *Hua-yen Sutra* but also in terms of the agent or practitioner of dharma expressed in the sutra, Li T'ung-hsüan went a step further than Fa-tsang.

ENLIGHTENMENT FOR THE ORDINARY PERSON

Fa-tsang was a major pioneer in tackling the problem of integrating Buddhism into Chinese life by bringing the highest enlightenment within human reach.[18] We have already discussed how the Hua-yen view of time makes enlightenment possible instantaneously instead of requiring an infinite number of kalpas. Fa-tsang also makes the attainment of ultimate enlightenment realizable in this given body:

> According to the Perfect Teaching, the "ephemeral body" is not taught; one attains the top of ten stages by the "physical body." Since universal insight is gained by the naked eye, one knows that it is the physical body. Sudhana, for example, reached the ultimate of the causal state in the physical body.[19]

Some background information must be given to explain what Fa-tsang meant by the realization of ultimate enlightenment within this physical body. In his classification of Buddhist doctrines, Fa-tsang asserts that both Hīnayāna and the elementary Mahāyāna held that final attainment was reached in the physical body *(fen-tuan shen)*. The elementary Mahāyāna of direct advancement *(chih-chin shih-chiao)* has two interpretations: First, the physical body is used for practice in the seventh stage and below, but the ephemeral body *(pien-yi shen)* is required from the eighth stage and above; second, the physical body persists throughout the ten stages because the bodhisattva retains his human identity for the sake of practicing compassion in the world. The advanced Mahāyāna teaching explains that the physical body exists prior to the ten stages but only the ephemeral body remains after entering the first stage where all seeds of illusion are destroyed. Now the Perfect Teaching brings the observation back to a full cycle and stresses that ultimate enlightenment is realized in this physical body of human flesh born from human parents. Unno states that this view of Fa-tsang "completed the pattern of this-worldly interpretation" of Chinese Buddhism.[20]

If Fa-tsang maintained that the way of enlightenment is open to the physical body, it seems to follow that the text which preaches this doctrine must be open to everybody. Fa-tsang did not show any conscious effort to interpret the *Hua-yen Sutra* as a canon accessible to everybody, however, especially to ordinary beginners *(fan-fu ch'u-hsüeh)*. He extolled the *Hua-yen Sutra* as an expression of the primary, perfect, and highest enlightenment *(shih-ch'eng-cheng-chio)*, probably in reaction to T'ien-t'ai Chih-i's (538–597) claim that the *Lotus* and *Nirvana Sutras* are the ultimate teachings of the Buddha.[21] Thus Fa-tsang emphasized as much as possible the profundity and excellence of the Hua-yen teaching rather than its practical implications for ordinary people. No wonder Fa-tsang made the main part *(cheng-tsung fen)* of the *Hua-yen Sutra* the chapter on the "Arising of the *Tathāgata* from Nature," which is the best exposition of the world of light as it appears to those who attain perfect enlightenment. He simply does not show any interest in relating his profound speculation on the Buddha's enlightenment with actual religious practice. Furthermore, he eliminated ordinary people and heretics from the grand panorama of the chapter "Entering the *Dharmadhātu*" *(Ju fa-chiai p'in)*. From the outset Fa-tsang's intention is to reveal systematically that the universal dharma and thus the position occupied by the Perfect Teaching cannot accommodate those ordinary people who still suffer in the sea of defilement and passion. Although his philosophical justification for the universal dharma lies in the peculiar logic of nonobstruction among every dharma or event, the rigid scheme of his Five

Teachings barred him from recognizing ordinary people as legitimate recipients of the universal dharma. Only at the very end of his discussion of human capacities does he qualify this position even slightly: "Every sentient being will in the long run enter this [universal] dharma, because the dharma is originally built in every sentient being."[22]

Li T'ung-hsüan took over Fa-tsang's system of elaborate speculation and applied it to the actual practice for the salvation of common, ordinary people. For Li the main part of the *Hua-yen Sutra* is the chapter on "Entering the *Dharmadhātu*," which depicts the pilgrimage of Sudhana, whereas Fa-tsang treats the same chapter as the "propagatory part" *(liu-t'ung fen)*. The chapter on the "Arising of the *Tathāgata* from Nature" *(Ju-lai hsing-chi p'in)*, which is the main part for Fa-tsang, is only the propagatory part for Li T'ung-hsüan although most Buddhist scholars consider the final chapter of a sutra to be the propagatory part. Li was aware of the heterodoxy of his shift of emphasis:

> Why do I consider the chapter on the "Arising of the *Tathāgata* from Nature" as the part for transmission and propagation in spite of the fact that it is not at the end of this sutra? Because it is at the end of this scripture, in the sense that this chapter is placed at the end of the five stages of a bodhisattva's career.[23]

Why did Li change the main part of the basic text from the chapter on the "Arising of the *Tathāgata*" to that on the pilgrimage of Sudhana?

In discussing the ten kinds of essence of the teaching *(chiao-t'i)* in the *Hua-yen Sutra,* Li T'ung-hsüan stated: "Every dharma in the *dharmadhātu* is originally true. Hence each is the essence of the teaching. All sentient beings, based upon this dharma, can be either pure or defiled."[24] If everything is to be considered as the essence of the teaching, we cannot single out a fundamental ignorance that is not the essence of the teaching. Extending this notion to the issue of the intended audience of the sutra, Li was more emphatic in saying, "If there is not an ordinary man who can be led to faith and ultimate realization through this sutra, it is of no use."[25] From this statement we can see why Li T'ung-hsüan singled out the chapter on "Entering the *Dharmadhātu*" as the main part of the sutra: For Li the aim of the Hua-yen philosophy was not so much a theoretical formulation of enlightenment as it was the practical application of one's fundamental, primal insight. Li's emphasis on practice was a revolt against the orthodox Fa-tsang line of theoretical interpretation of the *Hua-yen Sutra*. Li considered the story of Sudhana to be an expression of ultimate enlightenment achieved by an ordinary person. Unless enlightenment is achieved by an ordinary man of flesh and blood, the complicated theory is to no avail. Li explains the attainment of Buddhahood exemplified by Sudhana as follows:

At one moment in the first stage of the ten abodes, he is completely free from the conventional mode of thinking. No thought arises whether it took three lives or even a single moment [to achieve this stage of enlightenment]. That is why it is called "one life." Because he is free from illusion or from the conventional mode of temporal division, he is free from life [and death]. This is the accomplishment of Buddhahood in one life.[26]

Li goes on to describe this fundamental experience of self-transformation by an ordinary person: "At one thought illusion is not produced. One obtains an absolute freedom within his own mind; his nature is free from production, obtainment, and realization. This is the attainment of supreme enlightenment."[27] We find here a striking agreement with the "sudden awakening" by the Ch'an school (Sŏn in Korean; Zen in Japanese). By seeing into one's nature, one attains Buddhahood. And yet Li himself did not mention a word about Ch'an in his work. It was only after the decline of the Hua-yen school that scholars began to see the possibility of reading the *Hua-yen Sutra* according to an interpretation sympathetic to Ch'an.

Let us pause and examine the crucial moment of Sudhana's pilgrimage when he entered the tower of Maitreya:

Sudhana now asks the bodhisattva Maitreya to open the tower and allow him to enter. The bodhisattva approaches and snaps his finger, and lo! the doors open. How gladly Sudhana enters, and then they close by themselves as mysteriously as they had opened before![28]

This moment is explained as follows: "This illustrates a case of the sudden realization of the *dharmadhātu* by a young pilgrim, Sudhana, when he practiced in accordance with the principles of the Hua-yen *dharmadhātu* and attained the highest stage."[29] From the viewpoint of Fa-tsang's system of speculative metaphysics and its theory of the nonobstruction among all dharmas, the young pilgrim Sudhana was reduced to a mere example for Fa-tsang's grand philosophical system. Araki Kengo observes in this connection the difference between Fa-tsang and Li T'ung-hsüan:

Fa-tsang stops short of presenting a human model who represents his philosophy of the nonobstruction among all things as supported by his logic of the identity of opposites; he does this rather than recognize Sudhana's radical transformation from fundamental ignorance to original wisdom. We can go so far as to say that Fa-tsang could do without Sudhana if he could still establish his system of *dharmadhātu;* whereas Li T'ung-hsüan's interpretation of the *Hua-yen Sutra* depends entirely on Sudhana, without whom his philosophy ceases to function.[30]

Araki further quotes P'eng Chi-ch'eng (1740–1796) to show the identical character in the interpretations of Li T'ung-hsüan and Hui-neng's insight: "Fang-shan's [Li T'ung-hsüan's] discussion directly cuts through the fundamental root. He breathes through the self-same nose as those of Shao-lin [Bodhidharma] and Ts'ao-ch'i [Hui-neng]."[31]

Another feature of Li T'ung-hsüan's interpretation lies in his radical formula for the attainment of Buddhahood. In the course of the historical development of Buddhist ideas, the Buddha's stature was raised from that of an enlightened historical teacher who taught the eradication of all cravings into a transcendental father figure similar to the conception of god in many theistic religions. The Lord Buddha came to be endowed with all kinds of miraculous power. He was described with a grotesque conglomeration of human and inhuman features including, for example, a tuft of white hair between his eyebrows which constantly gives off a glow. These features were put in a capsule formula of thirty-two primary marks and eighty secondary marks of a Buddha.[32] The life of Buddha was similarly formulated into a rigid framework in the so-called eight aspects of the Buddha's attainment *(pa-hsiang ch'eng-tao)*.[33] But Li's formula is much simpler as the following definition shows:

> One's desire for enlightenment is stirred first by wisdom or *prajñā*—insight. One then diligently seeks for the Buddha wisdom by cultivating *samādhi*. When he finally attains wisdom, he is born into the family of the *tathāgata* and becomes his true son. This is called the attainment of Buddhahood.[34]

Now the Buddha is completely stripped of the glorious ornaments that had been accumulated in the course of his deification. What is required of one's becoming a Buddha is no more than the essential transformation of one's standpoint. In other words, an ordinary person is radically changed into a Buddha not by accumulating ornamental qualities or supernatural powers but by transforming his standpoint from ignorance to Buddha-wisdom. This is the crux of Li's interpretation of the *Hua-yen Sutra:* Everybody is originally a Buddha *ab aeterno (pen-lai ch'eng-fo)*. Time and again Li urges us to see the identity between Buddha and sentient beings—that is, between wisdom and ignorance:

> Buddha is the Buddha within sentient beings. In terms of their fundamental capacity they are no different. If you want to know the source of all Buddhas, awake that ignorance which is originally enlightenment.[35]

Is there anyone who became a Buddha without being ignorant prior to his enlightenment? Ignorance is not to be cut off; it is to be seen through. Li's observation in this respect is remarkably similar to the Ch'an experience which recognizes the everyday affairs of ordinary people to be the existential fulcrum for the fundamental transformation into enlightenment.

CONCLUSION

At this point we can see how the Korean monk Chinul found Li T'ung-hsüan to be an inspiration in resolving the Sŏn and Kyo controversy that had been raging for over a century in Korea. Li T'ung-hsüan's interpretation of the *Hua-yen Sutra* provided Chinul with a strong weapon against the scholastic theoreticians of the orthodox Hwaŏm (Ch. Hua-yen) sect of Korea. With knowledge of Li's practical application of the Hua-yen metaphysical theory established by Fa-tsang, Chinul was ready to clear the ground for the direct experience of Ch'an. Thus we find that in every important passage Chinul refers to the religious exultation he feels upon reading Li's *Commentary*. Chinul was particularly fascinated by Li's idea of faith. At the end of his summary of Li's *Commentary*, Chinul succinctly observes:

> I have carefully examined that which was clarified in this *Commentary*. It states that the ultimate enlightenment is reached, according to the Three Vehicles, only after one has passed through the ten stages; according to the One Vehicle, however, the enlightenment of a Buddha comes about in the initial degree of ten faiths. Speaking of stages, enlightenment exists in the first abode of excitation of mind *(ch'u fa-hsin chu)*. If one is initiated into the first degree of faith, then he directly reaches the first abode without any effort. If he reaches the first abode, he naturally reaches the ultimate stage [of enlightenment]. This being the case, what is most essentially required for an ordinary person in the sea of suffering is the first awakening into correct faith.[36]

Hence Chinul emphasizes religious practice based upon Li's idea of faith. In fact, Chinul's summary of Li's *Commentary* is aimed at the ordinary individual with a resolute commitment in actual practice rather than one who is interested in producing a fixed doctrine constructed by elaborate speculation on principles such as identity and the interdependence of things.

It is true that ideas move the world and thought precedes action. But those ideas and thoughts are not to be established by argument; they must be revealed by life in action, motivated and driven by conviction. The peculiarity of faith or conviction lies in its circularity; faith implies action. Until faith results in action, the cry "I believe!" rings hollow. Hence the primacy of faith must reverberate all the way through to the ultimate achievement of Buddhahood. However ironic it may sound, we cannot say that one has perfected faith until one has attained Buddhahood. This is the reason why Chinul emphasizes faith repeatedly when he tries to convert scholars in the textual study school to the way of the patriarch's school, that is, Sŏn.

In conclusion, this analysis has substantiated Chinul's conviction that the central axis of Li's interpretation of the *Hua-yen Sutra* is faith rather than the theoretical argument, although this faith must meet three criteria. First, it must be supported by the eternality of dharma. Second, it must have actual efficacy in the religious practice of compassion or universal love represented by Bodhisattva Samantabhadra. And third, it must be able to be enacted by an ordinary person such as Prince Sudhana.[37]

NOTES

This study is part of the author's Ph.D. dissertation, "The Unity of Sŏn and Kyo in Chinul (1158–1210)—the Philosophical Foundation of Korean Chogye Sŏn Buddhism," Department of Philosophy, University of Hawaii, Honolulu, 1978.

1. The principal source for Li T'ung-hsüan's biography is Chinul's *Changja haengjang* attached to the end of his summary of Li's *Commentary*. According to Chinul, Li is said to be an offspring of the T'ang imperial family, a native of Ch'ang-chou (presently Shan-hsi). Late in his eighties Li devoted his life to elaborating on the T'ang translation of the *Hua-yen Sutra*. For his thought and life, see Takamine Ryōshū, *Kegon shisōshi* [History of Hua-yen thought] (Kyoto: Hyakkaen 1942), pp.200–208.

2. Besides my dissertation on the philosophical aspect of Chinul, there are two excellent treatises on him. The first is Yi Chong-ik's *Kōrai Fushō Kokushi no kenkyū–sono shisō taikei to Fushōzen no tokushitsu* [A study of Pojo, national precepter of Koryŏ–his thought system and characteristics of Pojo Sŏn] (Seoul, 1974), which was accepted by Taishō University in Japan as his doctoral dissertation in 1975. The second is Keel Hee-Sung's "Chinul, the Founder of Korean Sŏn [Zen] Tradition" (Ph.D. dissertation, Harvard University, 1977).

3.Chinul discovered that instead of the theoretical formulation of the *dharmadhātu*, the realm of absolute reality, Li t'ung-hsüan emphasized the direct personal experience of *dharmadhātu*. Accordingly, late in his life Chinul devised a three-fascicle summary of Li's forty-fascicle *Commentary on the Hua-yen Sutra* (*T* 36.721–1008) in order to help ordinary people attain enlightenment. Although Chinul recognized that the original was unrefined, difficult to analyze, and not well known, he considered it to be "the finest mirror for the mind through which ordinary persons with resolute faith can enter the gate of awakening perfectly and suddenly." See *Han'guk Kosŭng chŏngjip* [Complete works of eminent Korean monks], Koryŏ Period 2 [hereafter abbreviated as *HKC-K2*], ed. Pulgyohak Yon'guhoe [Buddhist Study Society] (Seoul, 1974), p.5, lines 7–8).

In his preface to the summary, Chinul also described the role this text had played in his own life:

I retreated to the mountain and began perusing the great Tripiṭaka in order to discover the Buddha-words which conform to the tenet of the Mind sect. Three cycles of hot and cold passed until I finally discovered the following simile in the chapter "Arising of the *Tathāgata*" of the *Hua-yen Sutra:* A particle of dust contains a thousand volumes of sutras. Later it concludes, "The wisdom of a *tathāgata* is also like that. It is complete within the bodies of the sentient beings. Yet the ignorant do not know it." [*T* 10.272c]

I put the sutra upon my forehead and unself-consciously shed tears of joy. I was, however, not clear as to how an ordinary person can first enter the gate of faith. I was reading the *Commentary on the Hua-yen Sutra* authored by Elder Li [T'ung-hsüan] commenting on the first degree of ten faiths. It says: "There are three meanings of the *Bodhisattva chüeh-shou* [the head of enlightenment]: First, he is awakened to the fact that his body and mind are originally the *dharmadhātu,* for they are pure and free from defilements. Second, he is awakened to the fact that his body and mind and even his discriminating faculty itself are originally Buddhas of Unmovable Wisdom. Third, he is awakened to the fact that the wonderful wisdom by which he can well discern the right from the wrong is none other than Manjuśri. At the initial stage of faith, one is awakened to these three facts [dharmas]. Hence he is called Chüeh-shou [the head of enlightenment]. . . . The reason why an ordinary person has difficulty in being initiated into faith is because he admits that he is an ordinary person but does not admit that his own mind is no other than the unmovable wisdom of a Buddha." [*T* 36.815a and 819b]

This quotation shows how the idea of Li T'ung-hsüan played a crucial role in interpreting to Chinul the meaning of a pivotal experience in his life which was to form the basis of his religious synthesis. (The corresponding parts in Chinul's summary are found in *HKC-K2,* 280 and 272. The whole quotation is from Chinul's preface to his summary of Li's *Commentary;* see *HKC-K2,* 3–4.)

4. This information is from Nakamura Hajime and Kawada Kumatarō, eds., *Kegon shisō* (Kyoto: Hōzōkan, 1960), p. 28.

5. *T* 45.489b–c and 490a.

6. *T* 35.454a.

7. *T* 45.607b.

8. *T* 45.645b.

9. *T* 45.646a.

10. *T* 45.503a.

11. *T* 36.744b and *HKC-K2,* 124.

12. Cf. *T* 35.591b.

13. *T* 36.870a–b.

14. *T* 36.761b.

15. *T* 36.940c.

16. Fa-tsang's theory concerning the time of preaching or composing the *Hua-yen Sutra* is found in *T* 35.127c and also in *T* 45.482b. Li T'ung-hsüan's repudiation of Fa-tsang's theory is in *T* 36.759a and Chinul's summary (*HKC-K2,* 204).

17. *T* 36.762, 763b.

18. See Taitetsu Unno, "The Dimensions of Practice in Hua-yen Thought," *Yūki Kyōju shōju kinen Bukkyō shisō ronshū* (Yūki Festschrift) (Tokyo: Daizo Shuppan, 1964), pp. 51–78.

19. *T* 45.492b.

20. Unno, "Dimensions of Practice," p. 59.

21. For the T'ien-t'ai classification of Buddhist doctrines, see Leon Hurvitz, *Chih-i (538–597), Mélanges chinois et bouddhiques* 12 (1960- 1962): 229–244; and

see David Chappell, ed., *T'ien-t'ai Buddhism: An Outline of the Fourfold Teachings* (Tokyo: Daiichi-shobō, 1983).

22. *T* 35.117b.

23. *T* 36.770c–771a.

24. *T* 36.771c.

25. *T* 36.770c and 756c.

26. *T* 36.761b.

27. *T* 36.941b.

28. D. T. Suzuki, *Essays in Zen Buddhism,* 3rd series (New York: Samuel Weiser, 1971), p. 132. There is as yet no complete English translation of the *Hua-yen Sutra.*

29. *T* 45.640c.

30. Araki Kengo, *Bukkyō to jukyō: Chūgoku shisō o keisei suru mono* [Buddhism and Confucianism: the formation of Chinese thought] (Kyoto: Heirakuji Shōten, 1963), p. 184.

31. Ibid., p. 185.

32. For more detail, see Hurvitz, *Chih-i,* pp. 353–361.

33. There are two different versions. According to the *Ta-ch'eng ch'i-hsin-lun* a future Buddha must (1) descend into and abide in the Tuṣita heaven, (2) enter into his mother's womb, (3) abide there visibly preaching to the *devas,* (4) be born from his mother's side in Lumbini, (5) leave home at age nineteen (or twenty-five) as a hermit, (6) after six years of suffering attain enlightenment, (7) roll the dharma-wheel, (8) at age eighty enter nirvana (see *T* 32.581a). Another version in the *T'ien-t'ai ssu-chiao-i* omits stage 3 and adds "driving away *mara*" between stages 5 and 6 (*T* 46.777b–c).

34. *T* 36.935a.

35. *HKC-K2,* 569, 571, 575, 595.

36. *HKC-K2,* 457.

37. For a brief summary of Li T'ung-hsüan's thought, see Ko Hyŏng-kon, "Han'guk pulgyo ŭi chont'ong sasang" [Traditional thought of Korean Buddhism], in *Tongbang sasang nonch'ong: Yi Chong-ik paksa hagwi kinyŏm nonmunjip* (Seoul, 1975), pp. 240–248.

Buddhism and Taoism
in Chinese Society

7

Religious Aspects
of Emperor Hsüan-tsung's
Taoist Ideology

CHARLES BENN

During the fourth month of 741, shortly after concluding an audience in the fifth watch (3:00 to 5:00 A.M.), Hsüan-tsung (r. 712–755), sixth emperor of the T'ang dynasty (618–906), dozed and dreamed. In his vision the pure form of Lao Tzu appeared and said to him:

> I am your distant ancestor. A statue of me, just over three feet tall, is at a place one hundred *li* or more southwest of the capital [Ch'ang-an]. No one today knows how long it has been there. If you send someone to seek it out, however, I will respond [with an omen so that he can find it]. You will be blessed with an extended life span and shall enjoy a reign without end. I myself shall determine the extent of your time. Now let us meet at the Hsing-ch'ing palace precinct. There you will receive great fortune of which I shall not speak now.[1]

The emperor immediately dispatched a commissioner and a group of Taoist priests from the inner palace to conduct a search in the region southwest of Ch'ang-an. After several days of fruitless inquiry, the commission witnessed the appearance of a purple cloud over Lou-kuan at Chou-ch'ih. The priests took this sign to be the response promised in the emperor's dream. Excavation of the area beneath the cloud began and soon yielded a jade statue. Having fulfilled its mission, the group returned to the capital to present the image to Hsüan-tsung.

The emperor suspended all government activities in Ch'ang-an and ordered his officials to attend ceremonies celebrating the arrival of the statue. He personally accepted the statue in the Ta-t'ung palace of the Hsing-ch'ing palace precinct, noting that it looked exactly like the figure which appeared to him in his dream. After a brief period for veneration in the palace, Hsüan-tsung had the image removed to the newly established Temple for the Emperor of the Mysterious Origin (Hsüan-yüan Huang-ti Miao) in the Ta-ning ward, a part of Ch'ang-an's northeast section. There he had it dressed in court regalia and placed on a throne so that the public could worship it. In the fifth month of the same year he ordered court painters to make copies of the statue and disseminated those icons throughout the empire.

In itself Hsüan-tsung's dream was not particularly unusual. Dreams had long been an important channel of communication between deities, spirits, or the supernatural and mortals. Traditional beliefs and theories held that they were portents sanctifying human actions or omens forecasting future events for rulers and subjects alike. Hsüan-tsung's experience in 741 was unique, however, in that it conveyed spiritual approbation for the emperor's innovative program to make Taoism, both as a philosophy and as a religion, a state doctrine, to propagate it as a dynastic, monarchical, and bureaucratic ideology. In the first month of 741 Hsüan-tsung issued a decree founding three new institutions promoting that end. He ordered both capitals (Ch'ang-an and Lo-yang) and all districts (the empire was divided into 331 administrative units at the time) to establish Hsüan-yüan Huang-ti Miao for the veneration of Lao Tzu and Ch'ung-hsüan Hsüeh (Schools Exalting Taoist Learning) for the education of potential officeholders in the Taoist classics. Simultaneously, he inaugurated the Tao-chü (Taoist Examination) for recruiting students and scholars well versed in Taoist texts into the civil service.[2] Taoism had played a role in the politics and government of previous dynasties—notably the Han (206 B.C.–A.D. 220), Liu-Sung (420–476), and Northern Wei (424–535) dynasties—but it had never before received official patronage on the scale that Hsüan-tsung accorded it nor had it been as thoroughly integrated with state institutions and ideology as it was in the T'ien-pao era (742–755).

The justification for Hsüan-tsung's development of Taoism as a dynastic ideology, the idea which caused and conditioned his vision, was a claim, enunciated early in the T'ang (620), that Lao Tzu was an ancestor of the reigning Li house. That claim was, in turn, derived from a tradition recorded in the *Shih chi*'s biography of Lao Tzu that his surname was Li. At the end of the biography Ssu-ma Ch'ien (145–88 B.C.), author of the history, appended the genealogy of a Li clan which capitalized on that tradition and included Lao Tzu among its forebears. In the same manner the royal house of the T'ang dynasty maintained that it descended from Lao Tzu, whom it called the Sacred Ancestor (Sheng-tsu). He appears as an archivist in its genealogy (the earliest fragment of which can be found in the *Pei shih,* a dynastic history written between the years

627 and 650). Hsüan-tsung's family undoubtedly had no real blood ties to the sage widely recognized as the author of the *Tao-te ching*. Nevertheless, the pretense of being related to him enhanced the prestige of the royal clan which was not ranked in the highest stratum of aristocratic society before it seized the throne from the Sui dynasty (589–618). Lao Tzu's eminence as a master of classical thought was, perhaps, second only to that of Confucius at that time. In a society acutely sensitive to the status of a clan's forebears, a family which claimed such a master as an ancestor could demand considerable respect from its noble peers and the highest social status, especially when it held supreme political power.[3]

Conversely, the T'ang's genealogical claim committed the court to the support of Taoism as a dynastic and state ideology. That commitment ultimately induced Hsüan-tsung to create official Taoist school and examination systems, an unusual step in view of Confucianism's near monopoly of conventional institutions of education and recruitment. Since the royal house also thought of Lao Tzu as one of the most venerable and powerful deities in the Taoist pantheon, the claim shaped the emperor's policy toward Taoist priests. Acting on a suggestion from the imperial chancellor, Hsüan-tsung placed the clerics under the jurisdiction of the Bureau of Imperial Family Affairs (Tsung-cheng Ssu) in recognition of their status as his clansmen—that is, as intellectual heirs of his ancestor.[4]

Naturally the T'ang devoted most of its attention to the cult of Lao Tzu Deified in its efforts to marshal ideological support from religious Taoism. The first references to imperial descent from Lao Tzu in historical records occur in the context of certain portents and prophecies which the deity delivered to Kao-tsu (r. 618–627), the dynasty's founder. Two of the portents, a white cloud and a pair of deer, appeared at Lou-kuan during an offering which the temple had made, at the emperor's request, to secure divine blessing and assistance for his struggle against anti-Sui rebels who refused to accept his authority. According to tradition, Lou-kuan, which was a center of Taoist religious learning in the Period of Disunion (317–589), rested on the site where Yin Hsi had built his home. In Taoist legend Yin was the guard of a pass through which Lao Tzu left China at the end of his political career. He requested and received a copy of the *Tao-te ching* from Lao Tzu. Hence the discovery of Lao Tzu's statue at Lou-kuan in 741, whether viewed as the consequence of divine intervention or the result of connivance between Hsüan-tsung and his officials, was hardly an accident.[5]

The deification of Lao Tzu occurred during the second century A.D. Emperor Huan (r. 147–168) of the Han dynasty officially recognized it in 165 when he sent one of his eunuchs to perform sacrifices to the god at what was supposed to be his birthplace, Hu-hsien (Po-chou during the T'ang, in modern Honan province). In 166 the emperor personally sacrificed to Lao Tzu in a garden of a palace in Lo-yang. An inscription written to commemorate the rites at Hu-hsien characterized Lao Tzu as a deity who existed during the primordial chaos preceding creation and as coeternal with the sun, moon, and stars. It also asserted that he had appeared in various epochs of high antiquity to serve as preceptor to the legendary sage-kings.[6]

Subsequent literature depicted him as the creator of the cosmos. Like P'an Ku, the mythological first man, he changed parts of his body to form the entities of the universe. His left eye became the sun, his right eye the moon, his flesh the four-footed animals, his stomach the sea, his body hair the trees and grass, and so forth. According to one text Lao Tzu issued the three primordial *ch'i* (breaths) which congealed and formed heaven, earth, and water. It was this cosmogonic role which inspired the honorifics that Emperor Kao-tsung (r. 650–684) of the T'ang bestowed on Lao Tzu. The emperor gave him the title Most Exalted Emperor of the Mysterious Origin (T'ai-shang Hsüan-yüan Huang-ti).[7] Hsüan-tsung, in turn, shortened it to Hsüan-yüan Huang-ti and adopted it as the name for the temples he founded for Lao Tzu.

In a decree issued after he personally sacrificed at Lao Tzu's temple in 741, Emperor Hsüan-tsung presented the image of Lao Tzu which he wished to propagate:

> Those who wish to safeguard mankind revere the Great Way. Those who have successfully maintained the mandate have steadfastly relied on their illustrious predecessors. They have venerated especially the Great Sage, Emperor of the Mysterious Origin. His Way illumines the Great Ultimate. He sprang forth before the origin during chaos, widely propagating the true doctrines and everywhere inducing transformations. Although he rides the seasons and mounts the wind, he transcends all and ascends to the pure region of Shang-ch'ing. There he amasses all blessedness and issues all good fortune. Always trusting and helpful to his descendants he has blessed Our dynasty in like measure with Heaven. Therefore from the establishment of Our dynasty to the present time he has repeatedly conferred good fortune on Us and many times graced Us with the appearance of his true image. The purity of Heaven, the peace on earth, the abundance in the life of Our subjects, the operation of natural forces in their proper seasons, and the submission of the barbarians on all borders have all been responses of the Sacred Ancestor and the Great Way.[8]

Clearly the emperor's conception of Lao Tzu included a great deal more than simply the deity's role as creator of the universe.

The decree's description of Lao Tzu Deified is an integration of concepts about divinity drawn from three sources. First, Hsüan-tsung accepted the tenet of ancestor worship that the spirit of a forebear (Lao Tzu in this case) watches over, protects, and aids its descendants. Second, he adopted the notion of religious Taoism that Lao Tzu resides in a celestial region from which he disseminates sacred teachings, effects all transformations, and promotes human welfare and prosperity. Finally, the emperor compared Lao Tzu to Heaven, the chief deity of the state cult and special guardian of the monarchy. Like Heaven, the Sacred Ancestor guarantees the perpetuity of the dynasty and the ruler's tenure (the prophecy in Hsüan-tsung's dream) as well as the peace, prosperity, and stability of the empire when the emperor venerates Lao Tzu and governs according to the principles of proper statecraft (the Great Way).

Hsüan-tsung maximized the political value of Lao Tzu's image. He declared that he and his dynasty enjoyed divine favor because they were descendants of the sage, his devotees, and followed the precepts of Taoist statecraft. For these reasons the empire had not suffered from calamities (floods, droughts, famines, internal rebellions, foreign invasions, and the like) but, to the contrary, flourished because nature and men responded favorably to the T'ang's benign administration. The emperor's objective in projecting this image was to persuade the people that he and his dynasty served their best interests and would endure eternally under Lao Tzu's protection. Thereby he could foster a climate of public opinion which would contribute to the political stability of the empire and the perpetuation of T'ang power.

Prior to the year 741 emperors who favored the cult of Lao Tzu sponsored rites and bestowed patronage on capital temples, the Po-chou shrine, and other places sacred to the traditions which had grown up around the deity. The temple at Lao Tzu's reputed birthplace received the major share of the imperial largess. Hsüan-tsung had it renovated and enlarged in 741, and in 742 he appointed a director *(ling)* to manage its affairs. Through gradual accretions in the T'ang it grew to mammoth proportions, eventually embracing more than seven hundred *chien* (an architectural unit defined as the space between four pillars). Its grounds contained more than a thousand trees and housed a guard unit of five hundred troops.[9]

Hsüan-tsung initially intended to follow the example of previous emperors. He founded the first Hsüan-yüan Huang-ti Miao in Lo-yang only. In the fifth month of 740 he ordered that a mansion he had acquired as a prince be converted into a temple under that title. What caused him to change his mind and order Ch'ang-an and all districts to establish similar temples eight months later is not clear from existing historical records and official documents. Apparently he had decided that he should disseminate the cult throughout the empire to provide greater exposure for his ideology.[10]

Miao (temples) served the needs of at least three forms of worship: the veneration of nature gods, ancestral spirits, and prominent mythological or historical personalities (sage-kings, classical masters, emperors of past dynasties, loyal ministers, valiant warriors, and the like). Insofar as they were dedicated to the memory of a single renowned philosopher, Hsüan-yüan Huang-ti Miao belonged to the second category and closely reassembled the K'ung Tzu Miao (Confucian temples) which Emperor T'ai-tsung (r. 627–650) ordered all official schools of districts and subdistricts to establish in 630. Lao Tzu's temples housed the official Taoist schools, the Ch'ung-hsüan Hsüeh. In Ch'ang-an and Lo-yang they also contained statues of major Taoist personalities (Chuang Tzu, Wen Tzu, Lieh Tzu, and Keng-sang Tzu). An imperial edict of 742 required students in the various Ch'ung-hsüan Hsüeh of the capital to act as ritual attendants *(chai-lang)* during sacrifices offered to Lao Tzu. The Hsüan-yüan Huang-ti Miao performed an important function in inspiring student devotion and focusing student commitment on the schools' leading thinker.[11]

Lao Tzu's temples also had some of the characteristics of the third type of *miao*. Generally speaking, families erected ancestral temples in their native villages, towns, or cities. However, clans fortunate enough or strong enough to ascend the throne established a special temple, the T'ai-miao, in the capital to conduct rites for their forebears. During the T'ang the T'ai-miao made no offerings for Lao Tzu, but the Hsüan-yüan Huang-ti Miao in Ch'ang-an assumed a major responsibility for performing imperial ancestral observances during the T'ien-pao era. In 742 the emperor ordered ritual officials to make fresh offerings, *chien-hsin,* there before doing so at the T'ai-miao. *Chien-hsin* theoretically supplied the souls of ancestors with sustenance in the form of wine, grain, fruit, and fresh meat. Normally the director of the Bureau of Imperial Sacrifice presided on such occasions.[12]

In 749 the emperor ordered the bureau to arrange performances of *ti-hsia* sacrifices at Lao Tzu's temple in Ch'ang-an as well. During these ceremonies the *chao-mu* (spirit tablets recording the names and achievements of clan forebears) were placed in front of the Ta-tsu (Grand Ancestor) from whom the family traced its descent. *Ti* rites required that the tablets appear one by one to be worshiped individually. During *hsia* sacrifices all tablets were set in a group to be worshiped collectively. Only the most important ancestors enjoyed these honors. In Hsüan-tsung's reign that group included the first five T'ang emperors and four clan leaders who lived before the establishment of the dynasty. The *K'ai-yüan li,* an official manual on state rites commissioned by the emperor, scheduled the performance of *ti* every five years with *hsia* following three years after each *ti.* When these occurred in the Hsüan-yüan Huang-ti Miao, Lao Tzu served as the Grand Ancestor.[13]

Finally, the emperor inaugurated *chien-hsien* (offerings) in Lao Tzu's temple at Ch'ang-an during 754. Ritual canon demanded that these ceremonies be performed in the first month of each season (the first, fourth, seventh, and tenth months of the lunar calendar) and shortly after the winter solstice (in the twelfth month). The rite included three offerings and three genuflections. The participants burned incense during each of the offerings.[14]

Although officials of the Bureau of Imperial Sacrifice usually conducted these rituals, Hsüan-tsung, acting in his capacity as chief priest of the empire, undertook this duty on a substantial number of occasions during the T'ien-pao era, perhaps to express his deep commitment to the cult of Lao Tzu. According to historical records and official documents, he personally presided over offerings at Lao Tzu's temple in Ch'ang-an during 742, 743, 749, 751, and 754. In 750 he coined a new term, *ch'ao-hsien,* for imperial offerings there to distinguish them from rites conducted by officials, *chien-hsien.* He also composed ritual music for sacrifices to Lao Tzu.[15]

As Hsüan-tsung endowed Lao Tzu with the attributes of Heaven, it should come as no surprise that he combined offerings to Heaven with ancestral rites to the Sacred Ancestor. In 751 he ordered *chien-hsien* performed at Lao Tzu's temple and the T'ai-miao during the imperial sacrifice to Heaven in the suburbs of the capital. He declared that the additional sacrifices would bring greater blessings to the dynasty. The importance of Lao Tzu's cult in the complex of state rites and doctrines increased throughout the T'ien-pao era. By the end of the period sacrifices offered at Lao Tzu's temple in Ch'ang-an took precedence over those conducted at the Altar of Heaven and at the T'ai-miao.[16]

While Hsüan-yüan Huang-ti Miao possessed a number of the *miao*'s characteristics, they were regular Taoist temples which were normally called *kuan.* Hsüan-tsung never applied the term *kuan* to them, but shortly after establishing them he did give them a designation more consistent with Lao Tzu's status as a Taoist deity. In the ninth month of 742 he renamed them T'ai-shang Hsüan-yüan Huang-ti Kung. *Kung* (palace) normally referred to imperial residential quarters and only rarely to Taoist temples. In a subsequent decree issued in the third month of 743 the emperor justified this change by saying: "The Sacred Ancestor truly exercises jurisdiction in the heavens. Since he desired to descend as spirit to guarantee that We should receive his statue, should We not honor him with a title? Should We not call his temples palaces?"[17] Lao Tzu's earthly shrines deserved a title commensurate with his dignity as a celestial monarch.

The emperor further emphasized this elevated status of Taoist temples by substituting new phrases for T'ai-shang Hsüan-yüan Huang-ti in the decree of 743. He gave the temples in Ch'ang-an, Lo-yang, and the districts the titles T'ai-ch'ing, T'ai-wei, and Tzu-chi respectively. T'ai-ch'ing was one of the three pure regions *(san-ch'ing ching)* located directly beneath Ta-lo, the highest heaven in the Taoist hierarchy of celestial realms. According to Taoist canon Lao Tzu presides over this region.[18]

T'ai-wei, a constellation of ten stars located south of the Pole Star, and Tzu-chi, which may have been another name for the Pole Star or the Tzu-wei Constellation (a group of stars north of the Pole Star), had formerly been the names of palaces in the Han dynasty and Period of Disunion. Indeed, the custom of naming buildings after celestial regions or mansions originated with the imperial court. Only much later did it become a practice for Taoist temples; the most notable example was the Hsüan-tu Kuan, the official capital temple of the Sui dynasty.[19] Hsüan-tsung adopted this custom in order to give Lao Tzu's temples a cosmological and religious power and imagery.

Like their titles, the ritual functions assigned Lao Tzu's temples reflected their Taoist character. In the founding decree for the Hsüan-yüan Huang-ti Miao, Hsüan-tsung charged them with the task of performing rituals each year in accordance with Taoist liturgy. The *Ta-T'ang liu-tien,* a manual describing government institutions, procedures, and regulations compiled under imperial auspices and completed in 738, lists seven types of rites which may have been those officially sanctioned during Hsüan-tsung's reign and those to which this provision of the decree refers:

1. *Chin-lu chai,* which harmonizes the positive and negative forces of nature, averts natural calamities and disasters, prolongs the life of the emperor, and ensures prosperity for the empire

2. *Huang-lu chai,* which secures salvation for all ancestors

3. *Ming-chen chai,* which students perform to exhaust prior causation (and obtain release from phenomenal existence?)

4. *San-yüan chai,* in which supplicants confess their sins and gain remission

5. *Pa-chieh chai,* through which Taoist adepts seek immortality

6. *T'u-t'an chai,* which saves everyone from peril

7. *Tzu-jan chai,* which brings blessings to all people[20]

All of these rites were services which any unofficial temple might perform for their clerics, the nation, or people living in the vicinity.

Despite the enormous importance of Lao Tzu's cult to the emperor's ideology, several of the principal aspects of his program to marshal religious support for his authority and that of his dynasty involved K'ai-yüan temples and monasteries. In 738 Hsüan-tsung ordered all districts and both capitals to select one temple and one monastery within their jurisdictions for conversion into official institutions under the title of his reign era, K'ai-yüan. This act was hardly an innovation. Emperor Kao-tsung, Empress Wu (r. 684–705), and Emperor Chung-tsung (r. 705–710) had all set precedents for it. The most important precedent was the network of Ta-T'ang Chung-hsing (Restoration of the Great T'ang) temples and monasteries founded in 705 and renamed Lung-hsing (Dragon Rising) in 707. These religious communities enjoyed an official status because they conducted rites for the state and received payments from the state for their services.[21] The K'ai-yüan temples differed from the Hsüan-yüan Huang-ti Miao in several respects. They were not devoted to a single cult, they had well-defined responsibilities for inspiring devotion to emperor and dynasty, and they had a Buddhist counterpart. The latter may explain Hsüan-tsung's preference for them as instruments for promoting his ideological ends. He could reach a larger audience by using the K'ai-yüan temples and monasteries.

In 739, on advice from the Bureau of Imperial Sacrifice, the emperor commanded priests, priestesses, monks, and nuns of district and subdistrict temples and monasteries to perform rites and burn incense on Kuo-chi Jih (days of national mourning) at K'ai-yüan temples and monasteries. (Previously Lung-hsing temples and monasteries in eighty-one large districts carried out this task.) Kuo-chi Jih marked the anniversaries on which prominent imperial ancestors, especially the first five emperors and their consorts, passed away. During the K'ai-yüan era there were twenty days of national mourning in the official calendar. Statutes required that all government business be suspended and that high-ranking officials participate in memorials at the temples and monasteries on the ten days set aside for commemorating former emperors and their consorts. These were very solemn occasions. Anyone caught violating the mourning by performing music was subject to a punishment of one hundred strokes with a heavy bamboo rod.[22]

Hsüan-tsung's enactment transformed imperial ancestor worship from a restricted observance of the court and certain officials into a national cult—national in the sense that it involved officials at the local and capital level. The emperor demanded that these officials demonstrate the same filial devotion to his ancestors that they showed for their own and thereby strengthened bureaucratic allegiance to the dynasty. Ancestor worship created cohesion within the family. The adulation of former kinsmen, personal expression of grief for them, and belief that the family's good fortune depended on their goodwill intensified the individual's commitment to the group, past and present. By imposing an obligation to openly display the same sort of reverence and sorrow for his deceased clansmen, Hsüan-tsung used these familial sentiments to augment and reinforce loyalty, the traditional ethical force which bound ministers to the royal house. Hence he created greater solidarity between the court and the bureaucracy.

Besides enhancing public respect for the Li clan, the K'ai-yüan temples and monasteries also served as instruments for stimulating adulation of Hsüan-tsung himself. In 739 the emperor entrusted the celebration of Ch'ien-ch'iu Chieh, the Festival of a Thousand Autumns (a euphemism for long life), to them. At a banquet in 729 Chief Minister Chang Yüeh proposed that Hsüan-tsung make his birthday, the fifth day of the eighth month, a national festival under the title Ch'ien-ch'iu. To give force to his argument the minister mentioned that the birthdays of Buddha and Lao Tzu were celebrated in all parts of the emperor's domain.[23]

The following year, on advice from the Bureau of Imperial Sacrifice, Hsüan-tsung ordered all villages to assemble at their altars every Ch'ien-ch'iu Chieh, sacrifice to the White Emperor *(sai pai-ti),* and make offerings to the founder of agriculture (Pao T'ien-tsu, also known as Shen-nung). Afterward the villagers were to sit and drink to the emperor's health and long life.[24] In contrast to Kuo-chi Jih, the Ch'ien-ch'iu Chieh were occasions for revelry.

The association of sacrifices to the White Emperor with the celebration of the emperor's birthday was not accidental. The emperor was born in the year *i-yu* (685), the twentieth year in a cycle of sixty. According to the theory of five elements, which postulated that each element had a corresponding color, mountain, direction, season, and so on, *yu* represented metal, the west, autumn, white, and Mount Hua (the western member of the Five Sacred Peaks, in modern Shensi Province). Consequently Hsüan-tsung believed that Mount Hua and the White Emperor were the special guardians of his destiny. Sacrifices to the latter pleased the master of his destiny and, it was hoped, helped ensure the emperor's good fortune and prolonged life.[25]

The Festival of a Thousand Autumns was a major advance in the development of the imperial personality cult. Previously the celebration of imperial birthdays was a court function. By enlarging it to include all levels of society down to the village, Hsüan-tsung created an instrument for periodically stimulating veneration of himself and focusing popular allegiance on the throne. In an age when mass communication was practically nonexistent, the value of such a device was immense. All of his subjects could readily identify with the monarch and no doubt felt a sense of participation in national affairs, at least on those days. As the repository of all legitimate political authority, the physical embodiment of the state and the community, the emperor possessed a universal appeal unrivaled by any other institution or figure. Any effort to enhance his image, to intensify reverence for him, promoted social solidarity and strengthened the state.

Hsüan-tsung's development of political iconography contributed to this growth in the imperial personality cult. The emperor's preoccupation with disseminating religious images, in turn, influenced this development. As noted, he had copies made of the statue discovered at Lou-kuan in 741 and distributed them to K'ai-yüan temples in every district. In 748, during his annual visit to the Hua-ch'ing Kung, a palace at a spa on Mount Li east of Ch'ang-an, he and his ladies saw the face of Lao Tzu in the sky over a pavilion. The emperor ordered his artisans to make copies of it, and he dispatched the copies to temples (unspecified) in all districts.[26]

The relationship between this kind of activity and Hsüan-tsung's efforts to foster his own cult is evident from the manner in which he chose to have his icons erected in the districts. In the third month of 744 he commanded all districts and both capitals to cast bronze statues of Yüan-shih T'ien-tsun (the highest deity in the Taoist pantheon and the most popular figure for statuary donated to temples at that time), Buddha, and himself for K'ai-yüan temples and monasteries. Each community was to receive a statue of its deity and one of the emperor. Hsüan-tsung stipulated that the districts should use official resources (public copper stores normally reserved for coinage?) to carry out this task.[27]

The T'ai-ch'ing Kung, Lao Tzu's temple in Ch'ang-an, contained the most elaborate staging of statuary. As shown in the accompanying figure, in the center at the rear of the temple was the image of Lao Tzu dressed in imperial ceremonial regalia and flanked by a pair of statues representing *chen-jen* (the Perfected Ones) on each side. To the left of that group stood Hsüan-tsung's statue. In 746 or 747 the emperor added statues of his Chief Ministers Li Lin-fu and Ch'en Hsi-lieh. (A statue of Yang Kuo-chung replaced Li's after Li's death and Yang's assumption of his post in 752.) Finally, Hsüan-tsung had statues of Confucius (who, according to some traditions, visited Lao Tzu seeking knowledge about certain questions and thereby placed himself in the status of pupil) and the four leading figures of the Taoist school erected in front of Lao Tzu's image.[28] The final arrangement of statuary, then, was rich in religious, philosophical, and political symbolism.

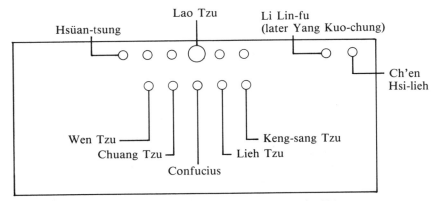

Reconstruction of the Main Hall of the T'ai-ch'ing Kung in Ch'ang-an.

Hsüan-tsung was the first emperor to realize the advantage in having icons of himself erected in shrines throughout the empire. Previous rulers had commissioned portraits to glorify themselves, and some had donated them to temples and monasteries. But none had ventured to evoke popular adulation for themselves by erecting statues in all districts or associating veneration of imperial images so closely with veneration of deities. Hsüan-tsung perceived that his statues could inspire mass allegiance for the throne as easily as religious icons could stimulate popular reverence for the gods. Imperial icons provided concrete objects to which his subjects could readily relate, objects which would, it was hoped, attract their fidelity for the distant and unseen monarch.

Several incidents illustrate how Hsüan-tsung's images were used for ideological purposes within the government. When Chang Hsün, an imperial general, was defending Yung-ch'iu (near K'ai-feng in modern Honan province) against the rebel An Lu-shan in 756, he had his officers pay homage to an imperial icon as they might to the emperor himself during an audience at the palace. When Hsüan-tsung moved the court to Szechuan after the loss of the capital to An Lu-shan in 756, he erected a gold statue of himself in a special chapel where officials made obeisance to it every day before taking up their duties. The elders of Yung-chou (in modern Honan province) during the Sung dynasty (960–1278) reported that the governor of their district in former times (Hsüan-tsung's reign?) paid homage to the emperor's image on the first and fifteenth days of every month before receiving his subordinates to conduct official affairs.[29] The last case is the most significant because it indicates that there was a fixed schedule for these observances. All instances demonstrate that the veneration of Hsüan-tsung's icon served not just to glorify him but also to create cohesion in civil and military bureaucracies and bolster morale, especially during national emergencies when confidence in emperor and state was shaky.

Certainly the innovations which the emperor introduced to promote his personality cult were unconventional, unprecedented, and self-serving. To justify them he needed concrete manifestation of spiritual approbation. On the thirteenth day of the third month of 745, Hsiao Ts'ung-i, a Taoist priest, observed a purple cloud over the San-ch'ing Gate, the west portal of the T'ai-ch'ing Kung in Ch'ang-an. As strange and wonderful music drifted down from the cloud, an extraordinary man appeared and said to Hsiao:

> I am Lao Tzu. You may report to my descendant [Hsüan-tsung] that he is one of the Perfected Ones *(chen-jen)* of the formless state *(shang-chieh)*. He is to stand next to me. I shall send heavenly artisans to assist in the completion of a statue for him. When it is finished, it will long protect him, and he will receive an unlimited mandate. Calamities will be eliminated, and the empire will be at peace.[30]

The prophecy not only sanctioned the placement of the emperor's statue in Lao Tzu's temple; it also conferred on Hsüan-tsung a new status as one of the Perfected Ones.

Originally the *chen-jen* was Chuang Tzu's ideal man of mystic detachment. By the late third century B.C. at least, however, the term had come to denote a state of physical immortality. Ch'in-shih Huang-ti (r. 221–209 B.C.), founder of the Ch'in dynasty (221–207 B.C.), became obsessed with finding an elixir which would enable him to avoid death and adopted *chen-jen* as the form of address by which he wished others to refer to him, anticipating that he would attain immortality. When Taoism developed into a religion (by the second century A.D.), it absorbed many of the techniques for prolonging life—yoga, alchemy, and the like—and *chen-jen* became an ideal state to be reached by an adept through self-cultivation.[31]

The emperor had tried for many years to find a key to immortality. In 744 word reached him that Sun T'ai-ch'ing, a Taoist adept in retirement on Mount Sung (in modern Honan province) had succeeded in concocting an elixir without using the usual ingredients (cinnabar and arsenic?). Intrigued, Hsüan-tsung sent Chief Minister Li Lin-fu to investigate. Li returned with a sample. The emperor took it with him when he went to pray at a Taoist altar in the inner palace on the eleventh day of the second month of 745. In response to his prayer a strange voice whose source he could not ascertain proclaimed that his life had been prolonged. When the emperor placed Sun's elixir on the altar, the voice warned him not to take it until the heat of the summer had passed.[32] The record of the emperor's actions after this incident does not reveal whether he actually consumed the concoction or not.

Chen-jen were not deities in the strictest sense. They did, however, share a number of attributes with the gods: immunity to death; invulnerability to all sorts of attack from weather, disease, animals, or weapons; and magic powers to accomplish extraordinary feats. The pretense of being one of the Perfected Ones greatly enhanced Hsüan-tsung's mystique and charisma. It permitted him to portray himself as a superhuman exempt from the natural laws which governed the destiny of lesser men and replete with mysterious powers far superior to those which his purely institutional status conferred. Furthermore, the pretense enabled him to assert that his authority was inalienable. The restraints which the theory of Heaven's Mandate (the threats of popular rebellion, natural calamities, and foreign invasion) imposed on the monarch did not apply to *chen-jen,* and the claim of having physical immortality implied that the emperor's power as well as his life would endure eternally.

Fan Tsu-yü (1041–1098), a Sung historian, upbraided Hsüan-tsung for cultivating a personality cult, charging that his actions reflected his unrestrained conceit. While undeniably there is truth in this criticism, it ignores the political problems the emperor had to face. He grew up during the reign of Empress Wu (690–705), who overthrew his clan and usurped the throne. Despite the achievements of early T'ang emperors, the royal house had not established itself firmly enough to prevent challenges to its authority. Furthermore, after the restoration of the T'ang in 705 factionalism and corruption seriously weakened both court and state. Long after he ascended the throne Hsüan-tsung remained sensitive to these weaknesses, and throughout his reign he strove to overcome them by institutional reform and ideological innovation.[33] The development of the imperial personality cult was one of his most important means for accomplishing his goal—an instrument for restoring confidence in the dynasty, focusing allegiance on the throne, and bolstering public and bureaucratic morale.

Religious doctrines and institutions, especially Taoist, proved remarkably well suited to the emperor's designs. The cult of Lao Tzu provided Hsüan-tsung with an opportunity, unparalleled in previous or subsequent dynasties, for unifying diverse rituals to secure spiritual protection for the dynasty and the monarchy from a single deity whose power was recognized by the family, the state, and the masses and whose image was both particular and universal, private and public. It supplied him and his dynasty with a claim to legitimacy by divine right as descendants of Lao Tzu, a claim repeatedly sanctioned by epiphanies, prophecies, and portents. Finally, it enabled the emperor to assure his subjects that his authority and that of his house would endure eternally, satisfying a deeply rooted popular aspiration for security and stability.

Taoist temples offered an excellent means for propagating the emperor's ideology. They were meeting places for the surrounding communities on festival days and, under the influence of Buddhism, had developed methods for communicating the tenets of their faith to the largely illiterate masses (scriptural recitations, story telling, murals, and so forth). Hsüan-tsung capitalized on the influence of these temples by converting a number of them into state institutions and assigning them responsibility for venerating himself and his ancestors. Taoism also contributed to the techniques and imagery for evoking reverence and adulation of the emperor. The worship of images facilitated the spread of Lao Tzu's cult and later the imperial personality cult. Its concept of the *chen-jen* furnished Hsüan-tsung with the means of asserting his semidivine status and the inalienability of his authority.

Institutionalized Taoist traditions with tightly organized communities of clerics spread throughout the empire to convert large segments of the population to their faiths developed in the Period of Disunion and reached an apex in the T'ang dynasty. Hsüan-tsung effectively exploited this development for his ideological ends. His success influenced rulers long after his death. Later T'ang emperors maintained or revived many aspects of his program to propagate Taoism as a state doctrine, and Sung monarchs found his ideology attractive enough to emulate it.[34]

NOTES

1. *Chin-shih ts'ui-pien,* compiled by Wang Ch'ang (Shanghai: Sao-yeh shan-fang, 1921), chüan 84, p. 3a; *Ta T'ang chiao-ssu lu,* compiled by Wang Ching, in *Shih-yüan ts'ung-shu,* compiled by Chang Chün-heng (n.p., 1913–1917), chüan 9, p. 1a; *Ts'e-fu yüan-kuei,* compiled by Wang Ch'in-jo and others (Taipei: Chung-hua shu-chü, 1972), chüan 53, pp. 19a–20b (*TFYK* hereafter); *T'ang hui-yao,* compiled by Wang P'u and others (Taipei: Shih-chieh shu-chü, 1968), chüan 50, p. 865 (*THY* hereafter); Tu Kuang-t'ing, *Tao-chiao ling-yen chi* (*Tao-tsang* 440–448), chüan 6, p. 2b; Robert des Rotours, "Cult des cinq dragons," in *Mélange de sinologie offerts à Monsieur Paul Demiéville* (Paris: Presses Universitaires de France, 1966), pp. 274–275; and J. J. L. Duyvendak, "The Dreams of Emperor Hsüan-tsung," in *India Antiqua* (Leiden, 1947), p. 105. This was not the emperor's first dream of Lao Tzu. In the eleventh month of 739 the Sacred Ancestor appeared to him in a vision to warn that a trip which he planned to take to the north would end in disaster. See *TFYK,* chüan 53, pp. 17a–18a; *Hun-yüan sheng-chi,* compiled by Hsieh Shou-hao, in *Tao-tsang chi-yao,* compiled by Ho Lung-hsiang (Taipei: K'ao-cheng ch'u-pan she, 1961), vol. 6, p. 2500b (*HYSC,* in *TTCY* hereafter); and Duyvendak, "The Dreams of Hsüan-tsung," p. 104. The present study is basically a reworking of materials presented in my dissertation,

which should be consulted for more information and analysis; see Charles David Benn, "Taoism as Ideology in the Reign of Emperor Hsüan-tsung (712–755)" (Ph.D. dissertation, University of Michigan, 1977).

2. The founding decree for these institutions can be found in *TFYK*, chüan 53, p. 18a; *HYSC*, in *TTCY*, vol. 6, p. 2502a; and *Ch'üan T'ang wen*, compiled by Tung Kao and others (Taipei: Hui-wen shu-chü, 1961), chüan 31, p. 13a–b (*CTW* hereafter). For discussion of discrepancies in dating the emperor's dream and the establishment of Taoist schools see Benn, "Taoism as Ideology," p. 377, n.1, and p. 397, n.2.

3. *Shih chi*, chüan 63, p. 180c–d (the K'ai-ming edition of the dynastic histories is used throughout this study, Shanghai, 1935); T'ang Lan, "Lao Tzu shih-tai hsin k'ao," in Lo Ken-ts'e, ed., *Ku-shih pien* (Hong Kong: T'ai-p'ing shu-chü, 1962), vol. 6, p. 605; and Homer Dubs, "The Date and Circumstances of Laodz," *Journal of the American Oriental Society* 61 (1941): 215–221. Three fragments of the T'ang genealogy have survived: *Pei shih*, chüan 100, p. 3050c–d; *TFYK*, chüan 1, pp. 25b–30a; and *Hsin T'ang shu*, chüan 70a, p. 3795a (*HTS* hereafter). When T'ai-tsung (r. 627–650), second emperor of the T'ang, commissioned a compilation of all clan genealogies in the empire, he discovered to his dismay that the editors had relegated his family to the second rank in their hierarchy of great houses. As late as the ninth century Emperor Wen-tsung (r. 827–841) complained that marriage alliances with the Ts'ui and Lu clans were preferred to those with the imperial family. See *Chen-kuan cheng-yao*, compiled by Wu Ching (Shanghai: Chung-hua shu-chü, *Ssu-pu pei-yao*, 1927–37), chüan 7, pp. 11a–12b; *THY*, chüan 36, p. 664; Ssu-ma Kuang, *Tzu-chih t'ung-chien*, with *yin-chu* by Hu San-hsing (Taipei: Ta-tung shu-chü, 1970), chüan 195, p. 1308a; and Howard Wechsler, *Mirror to the Son of Heaven: Wei Cheng at the Court of T'ang T'ai-tsung* (New Haven: Yale University Press, 1974), pp. 90–92. Lao Tzu's prestige derived, in part, from a tradition that Confucius visited him to inquire about rites, government, and the Tao. Confucians did not reject it in the Han dynasty, and it appears in works of their school. See *Chiao-cheng Chuang Tzu chi-shih*, compiled by Kuo Sung-t'ao (Taipei: Shih-chieh shu-chü, 1968), chüan 13, p. 477; chüan 14, pp. 516–517, 522–525, and 531–532; chüan 21, pp. 711–716; and chüan 22, p. 741; *Li chi chin-chu chin-i*, annotated by Wang Meng-e (Taipei: Shang-wu, 1970), chüan 7, pp. 255, 267, 269–270; *Shih chi*, chüan 63, p. 180c, and chüan 47, p. 161a; *K'ung Tzu chia-yü*, annotated by Wang Su (Taipei: Shih-chieh shu-chü, 1963), chüan 3, pp. 25 and 29; and Max Kaltenmark, *Lao Tzu and Taoism*, translated by Roger Greaves (Stanford: Stanford University Press, 1969), p. 8.

4. Tu Kuang-t'ing, *Li-tai ch'ung-tao chi*, in *CTW*, chüan 933, p. 5a; *Ta T'ang liu-tien*, compiled under imperial auspices by Li Lin-fu and others (Taipei: Wen-hai ch'u-pan she, 1968), chüan 16, p. 24a–b (*TTLT* hereafter); *T'ung-tien*, compiled by Tu Yu (Taipei: Hsin-hsing shu-chü, n.d.), chüan 25, p. 150c; *THY*, chüan 49, pp. 859–860; *TFYK*, chüan 54, p. 5b; *Traité des fonctionnaires et Traité de l'armée*, translated by Robert des Rotours (Leiden: 1947–1948), vol. 1, p. 388; and Yamazaki Hiroshi, "Tōdai ni okeru sōni sorei no mondai," *Shina Bukkyō shiseki* 3 (1) (1939): 1–4.

5. *Chin-shih ts'ui-pien*, chüan 41, p. 3a; *Ku Lou-kuan tzu-yün yen-ch'ing chi*, collected by Chu Hsiang-hsien (*Tao-tsang* 605), chüan 1, pp. 1a–4b; Tu Kuang-t'ing, *Tao-chiao ling-yen chi*, chüan 14, pp. 2b–3a; *HYSC*, in *TTCY*, vol. 6, p. 2491b; and *Chiu T'ang shu*, chüan 1, p. 3065d (*CTS* hereafter). For a discussion of variations in the accounts of these portents see Benn, "Taoism as Ideology," pp. 329–330, n. 18. On Yin Hsi and Lao Tzu see *Shih chi*, chüan 63, p. 180d;

Lieh-hsien chuan chiao-cheng pen, in *Li-tai chen-hsien shih-chuan* (Taipei: Tzu-yu ch'u-pan she, 1970), chüan 1, p. 2b; *I-wen lui-chü,* compiled by Ou-yang Hsün (Taipei: Hsin-hsing shu-chü, 1969), chüan 6, p. 4a; *Ch'u-hsüeh chi,* compiled by Hsü Chien and others (Taipei: Hsin-hsing shu-chü, 1966), chuan 7, p. 24b; and Kaltenmark, *Lao Tzu and Taoism,* p. 9.

6. *Hou Han shu,* chüan 7, p. 666d; *Hou Han chi,* compiled by Yüan Hung (Shanghai: Shang-wu, *Ssu-pu ts'ung-k'an,* 1919–1937), chüan 22, pp. 8b–9a and 11b–12a; *Tung-kuan Han chi,* compiled by Liu Chen and others (Shanghai: Chung-hua shu-chü, *Ssu-pu pei-yao,* 1927–1937), chüan 3, p. 5a; and Anna Seidel, *La divinisation de Lao Tseu dans le Taoisme des Han* (Paris: École française d'Extrême-Orient, 1969), pp. 36–38 and 62–63.

7. Kristofer Schipper, "The Taoist Body," *History of Religions* 17 (3–4) (1978): 358–363; and Tu Kuang-t'ing, "Shih Lao-chün sheng T'ang ts'e-hao," in *CTW,* chüan 944, pp. 10a–13b.

8. *TFYK,* chüan 54, pp. 4b–5a.

9. Tu Kuang-t'ing, *Tao-chiao ling-yen chi,* in *Yün-chi ch'i-ch'ien,* compiled by Chang Chün-fang (Taipei: Tzu-yu ch'u-pan she, 1962), chüan 117, p. 1632; *TFYK,* chüan 53, p. 19a; *CTS,* chüan 24, p. 3163d; and *T'ung-tien,* chüan 53, p. 305b.

10. *TFYK,* chüan 53, p. 18a; and *T'ang liang-ching ch'eng-fang k'ao,* compiled by Hsü Sung (Taipei: Shih-chieh shu-chü, 1963), chüan 5, p. 31a.

11. On *miao* dedicated to nature gods and historical or mythological personalities in the Period of Disunion see Miyakawa Hisayuki, "*Suikei chū* ni mietaru shibyō," *Tōyōshi kenkyū* 5 (1) (1939): 21–38. On K'ung Tzu *miao* see J. K. Shrylock, *The Origin and Development of the State Cult of Confucius* (New York: Paragon Book Reprint Corp., 1966), pp. 134–136. The regulations regarding statuary at Ch'ang-an's temple can be found in *CTS,* chüan 24, p. 3164d; *TFYK,* chüan 54, p. 13a; *THY,* chüan 50, pp. 865 and 881; and *Ta T'ang chiao-ssu lu,* ch'ian 9, p. 16. The statute concerning students serving as *chai-lang* is described in *CTS,* chüan 42, p. 3243c; *HTS,* chüan 48, pp. 3744d, 3745c–d, and 3746b; *Traité des fonctionnaires,* vol. 1, pp. 326, 382, 387, and 411; and *Pai K'ung liu-t'ieh,* compiled by Pai Chü-i and K'ung Ch'uan (Taipei: Hsin-hsing shu-chü, 1960), chüan 67, pp. 6b–7a.

12. *THY,* chüan 50, p. 866; *T'ung-tien,* chüan 49, p. 282c, and chüan 116, p. 608a–b; *Tōrei shūi,* compiled by Niida Noboru (Tokyo: Tokyo daigaku, 1964), pp. 203–204.

13. *CTS,* chüan 9, p. 3086a; *TFYK,* chüan 54, p. 14a; and *THY,* chüan 13, p. 305.

14. *THY,* chüan 50, p. 866; *Ta T'ang chiao-ssu lu,* chüan 9, p. 1a–b; and *HYSC,* in *TTCY,* vol. 6, p. 2505b.

15. *CTS,* chüan 24, pp. 3163d–3164a, and chüan 9, p. 3085b–c; *TFYK,* chüan 54, pp. 2a and 17b; Ssu-ma Kuang, *Tzu-chih t'ung-chien,* chüan 216, p. 1459b; *HTS,* chüan 5, p. 3646b; *T'ang ta chao-ling chi,* compiled by Sung Min-ch'iu (Shanghai: Ting-wen shu-chü, 1959), chüan 78, p. 443; Tu Fu, *Tu Shao-ling chi hsiang-chu,* annotated by Ch'ou Chao-ao (Hong Kong: Chung-hua shu-chü, 1974), pt. 9, chüan 24, pp. 97–106; and Shen Kua, *Meng-chi pi-t'an chiao-cheng* (Taipei: Shih-chieh shu-chü, 1965), chüan 1, pp. 9–13.

16. *TFYK,* chüan 54, p. 15a; and *Ta T'ang chiao-ssu lu,* chüan 9, p. 2a.

17. *CTS,* chüan 9, p. 3085b; *T'ung-tien,* chüan 53, p. 305b; and *THY,* chüan 50, p. 866.

18. *CTS,* chüan 24, p. 3163d; *THY,* chüan 50, p. 866; *T'ang ta chao-ling chi,*

chüan 78, pp. 442–443; *San-tung chu-nang,* compiled by Wang Hsüan-ho (*Tao-tsang* 780–782), chüan 7, p. 33a; *Wu-shang pi-yao* (*Tao-tsang* 768–779), chüan 84, p. 16a–b.

19. Hsin ?, *San Ch'in chi,* in *Shuo-fu,* compiled by T'ao Tsung-i, unabridged edition (n.p.: Wan-wei shan-fang, 1647), pt. 61, p. 2b; Paul Wheatley, *The Pivot of the Four Quarters* (Chicago: Aldine, 1971), pp. 442–443; P'an An-jen, "Hsi-cheng fu," in *Chao-ming Wen-hsüan,* collected by Hsiao T'ung (Taipei: Tung-hua shu-chü, 1969), chüan 10, p. 134; Li Pai, "Shang-huang hsi-hsün nan-ching ko," in *Li T'ai-pai chi,* annotated by Wang Ch'i (Taipei: Ho-lo t'u-shu ch'u-pan she, 1965), vol. 3, chüan 8, p. 37. According to one tradition, the divine ruler of T'ai-wei taught Lao Tzu Taoist doctrines. According to another, Lao Tzu ascended to T'ai-wei after transmitting scriptures to Yin Hsi. See Tu Kuang-t'ing, *Tao-te chen-ching kuang sheng-i* (*Tao-tsang* 440–448), chüan 3, pp. 16a–17a; and *Shang-ch'ing kao-shang chin-yüan yü-chang yü-ch'ing yin-shu ching* (*Tao-tsang* 1038), pp. 16a–b and 25a–b. One source declares that Lao Tzu resides in Tzu-wei when acting as chief of the flying immortals; see *Wei shu,* chüan 114, p. 2197b.

20. *TTLT,* chüan 4, pp. 42b–43b.

21. *THY,* chüan 50, p. 879; Michibata Yoshihide, "Tōchō ni okeru Dōkyō taisaku—toku ni kan Dōkan setchi to Dōkyo ni tsuite," *Shina Bukkyō shiseki* 4 (2) (1940): 32–42; and Shigenori Shizuka, "Tōchō no shūkyō seisaku," *Rekishi kyōiku* 11 (4) (1963): 17–22.

22. *THY,* chüan 50, p. 879; *TTLT,* chüan 4, pp. 47a–50b; and Kenneth Chen, *The Chinese Transformation of Buddhism* (Princeton: Princeton University Press, 1973), pp. 258–259.

23. Chang Yüeh, *Chang Yen-kung chi* (n.p., 1899), chüan 9, pp. 1b–2a; and Wang Ming-ch'ing, *Hui-chen lu* (Shanghai: Chung-hua shu-chü, 1964), chüan 1, p. 1.

24. *TFYK,* chüan 2, p. 7a.

25. E. Chavannes, *Le T'ai chan* (Paris: E. Leroux, 1910), pp. 234–235; *Chin-shih ts'ui-pien,* chüan 72, pp. 6a–8a; and *Pao-k'o ts'ung-pien* (Shanghai: Shang-wu, *Ts'ung-shu chi-ch'eng* ed., 1929–41), chüan 10, p. 310.

26. *TFYK,* chüan 53, p. 20b, and chüan 54, p. 12b; *CTS,* chüan 9, p. 3086a.

27. *CTS,* chüan 9, p. 3085d, and chüan 24, p. 3163d; *THY,* chüan 50, p. 880; and *TFYK,* chüan 54, p. 6b.

28. *T'ang liang-ching ch'eng-fang k'ao,* chüan 3, p. 18b; *THY,* chüan 50, p. 865; *CTS,* chüan 24, p. 3164; and *TFYK,* chüan 54, p. 13a. Kao Yen-hsiu gives different locations for the statues of Hsüan-tsung and his chief ministers. His work dates from the late T'ang when the statues may have been moved; see Kao Yen-hsiu, *Ch'üeh shih (Ts'ung-shu chi-ch'eng),* chüan 2, p. 35. The *Lu-i chi* states that Lao Tzu's statue was flanked by two statues of *chen-jen* on either side; see Tu Kuang-t'ing, *Lu-i chi* (*Tao-tsang* 327), chüan 7, p. 5b.

29. Ssu-ma Kuang, *Tzu-chih t'ung-chien,* chüan 218, p. 1488b, and chüan 224, p. 1531a; *HTS,* chüan 133, p. 3976d; *Yü-ti chi-sheng,* compiled by Wang Hsiang-chih, (Taipei: Wen-hai ch'u-pan she, 1962), chüan 56, p. 5b; and Edward Schafer, "The T'ang Imperial Icon," *Sinologica* 7 (3) (1963): 156–160.

30. *TFYK,* chüan 54, pp. 8a–b.

31. Henri Maspéro, "Les procédés de 'nourir le principe vital' dans la religion Taoiste ancienne," *Journal Asiatique* 229 (1937): 177–252, 353–430; Chou Shao-hsien, *Tao-chia yü shen-hsien* (Taipei: Chung-hua shu-chü, 1970), pp. 40–43; and Yü Ying-shih, "Life and Immortality in the Mind of Han China," *Harvard Journal of Asiatic Studies* 25 (1964–1965): 81–124.

32. *Wen-yüan ying-hua,* compiled by Li Fang and others (Taipei: Chung-hua shu-chü, 1965), chüan 562, p. 9a–b; *Chin-shih ts'ui-pien,* chüan 86, pp. 5b–8a; Ssu-ma Kuang, *Tzu-chih t'ung-chien,* chüan 216, p. 1461b; *TFYK,* chüan 54, pp. 7a–8a; and Arthur Waley, *The Poetry and Career of Li Po* (London: Allen & Unwin, 1950), pp. 53–54.

33. Fan Tsu-yü, *T'ang chien* (Peking: Ts'ung-shu chi-ch'eng, 1958), chüan 9, p. 79; Benn, "Taoism as Ideology," pp. 190, 193–194.

34. *CTW,* chüan 87, p. 11a; *THY,* chüan 93, pp. 1677–1678, and chüan 64, p. 1122; *Wen-yüan ying-hua,* chüan 476, pp. 2a–b; and Sun K'o-k'uan, *Sung Yüan Tao-chiao chih fa-chan* (Taipei: Tung-hai ta-hsüeh, 1965), pp. 80–86.

8

The "Political Career" of the Buddhist Historian Tsan-ning

ALBERT A. DALIA

When we turn to the Buddhist historical writings of the Sung dynasty, we find a large and unprecedented number of works. Within the period A.D. 960–1278, at least fifty works on Buddhist history were written. This means that about every eighth year a history of Buddhism was written during the entire epoch of the Sung dynasty. In this great movement of Buddhist historiography, Tsan-ning (919–1001) occupied a special place, because he was the earliest and most influential writer amongst Buddhist historians. His works are the main sources for the later Buddhist historians.[1]

One of the most important themes of Chinese intellectual history has been the emphasis given to synthesis or harmony. This theme has also been a recurring concern in the development of Chinese Buddhism. In his dual role as Buddhist monk and Han-lin Academy historian, Tsan-ning stands out as the great synthesizer of early Sung Buddhism. Because his achievements were made possible not only by his personal abilities and vision but also by his unique position with the Sung court, this essay explores the history and significance of Tsan-ning's "political career."

INTRODUCTION

The monk Tsan-ning (919–1001) stands in a similar relationship to imperial patronage of Buddhism by the Sung dynasty (960–1279) as Chih-i (538–597) did to the Sui state (589–618) and its support of the Buddhism of his time. Chih-i, with the support of the Sui emperor, and with the urgent needs of both the state and Buddhism clearly in mind, created a synthesis of the various Buddhist doctrinal schools in northern and southern China.[2] For the Sui emperor Wen such a synthesis was urgently desired in order to unite China by providing a common set of moral values. Buddhism was seen as fulfilling one aspect of this need, although

Sui Wen-ti also turned to Confucianism and Taoism to make the synthesis as complete and powerful as possible.[3] Chih-i, unlike Tsan-ning, limited his synthesis to Buddhist doctrines and practices. The differences in the orientation of Tsan-ning from Chih-i can be understood in terms of the new circumstances Tsan-ning had to face.

The Sung emperor's power, as a result of the destruction of the great aristocratic T'ang clans during the latter part of the T'ang and the Five Dynasties period, had greatly increased. At the same time a new ruling elite came into being, chosen primarily on the basis of ability. Their rise marks a strong revival of the Confucian ideal of government. The practical expression of that ideal manifested itself in the Sung use of the examination system as the primary source of civil service recruitment. The emphasis of this new elite partook of Confucian ideals. Aristocratic privilege gave way to achievement through ability, which in turn mirrored the practical solution by the Sung of the problem of recruiting a new ruling elite after the dissolution of the old T'ang aristocratic elite.

Tsan-ning, appointed by Sung T'ai-tsung, had to prove himself capable of meeting criteria that measured ability before he was accepted by the Han-lin academicians. Yet one must not lose sight of the fact that for both Chih-i and Tsan-ning their ability to master the Confucian literary tradition had also played an important role in their acceptance into their state's respective ruling classes. This is especially true for Tsan-ning, who was a prolific writer. As far as I can determine, he has twenty three titles attributed to him. Besides his works on a Buddhist history, the other titles indicate he wrote on such diverse topics as topography, bamboo shoots, tides, and the Han Confucian philosopher Tung Chung-shu (179?–104? B.C.) and that he composed gazetteer-type records, recorded stone inscriptions, and dealt with other topics outside the traditional concerns of Buddhism.[4] Respect for the Confucian literary tradition was thus a common denominator among all. The point to remember here, however, is that the Sung elite differed from the Ch'en-Sui dynasties of Chih-i's time and the Wu-Yüeh elite of Tsan-ning's background in its more persuasive emphasis on ability. A strong Confucian revival had contributed to the Sung rise to power; they were more skeptical of the Buddhist establishment.

The Buddhism that Tsan-ning came to know personally was more inclined toward historical-genealogical argumentation than doctrinal dispute. The major Buddhist controversy of the Sung dynasty seems to have been between the Ch'an and T'ien-t'ai schools over the question of orthodox lineages. This specific controversy did not stimulate the writing of philisophical tracts but rather of the composition of sectarian histories.[5] Sung Buddhism thus was characterized by an explosion of historical writing in contrast to T'ang Buddhism with its reputation as the high point for Chinese Buddhist philosophical thought.

Tsan-ning was the earliest of the Sung Buddhist historians. Yet we find in his extant Buddhist historical works a striking antisectarianism. One can sense an urgency in his constant attempts to reconcile various competing groups throughout the *Sung Kao seng chuan (Sung Edition of the Biographies of Eminent Monks)* and his other extant historical work, *Seng shih lüeh (An Outline History of the Saṇgha).*[6]

Tsan-ning recognized the weakened position of Buddhism and its urgent need to stop internal and external sectarian squabbling. He was in a unique position to appreciate the threat to Buddhism. Like Chih-i of the Sui dynasty, he was sponsored by the emperor in an attempt to unify some of the diverse religious elements for a young dynasty trying to consolidate its position. The second emperor of the Sung dynasty, T'ai-tsung (r. 976–997), commissioned three major religious works during his reign: the *SKSC,* the *SSL,* and *San-chiao sheng-hsien shih chi (A History of the Sages and Virtuous Ones of the Three Religions).* These three works are very characteristic of Sung Buddhist writings and have two interesting features in common. They are essentially histories, not philosophical works, as had been most of the works produced by Chih-i and his contemporaries. Furthermore, Tsan-ning had an essential role in writing all of them; he was the author of the first two and a major contributor to the third.

Tsan-ning's solution to the problems facing Buddhism in the early Sung was one of synthesis on separate levels. He, like many politically involved monks before him, sought to gain influence among the ranks of those who would be most hostile to Buddhism: the ruling class. Yet at the same time Tsan-ning came under attack from both the Buddhists and their potential "enemies." The reactions of Buddhists are hinted at in Tsan-ning's defense of the T'ang monk Tsung-mi who, like Tsan-ning, attempted to defend Buddhism through contact with the ruling class. Jan Yün-hua aptly points out that Tsan-ning's defense of Tsung-mi in the *SKSC* can also be regarded as a self-defense. Jan translates Tsan-ning's comments as follows:

> There are some people who blame Tsung-mi, saying that it was improper for him either to receive nobles and officials or to visit the emperor. I, Tsan-ning, would answer this charge with these words: "Buddha entrusted the dharma to kings and ministers. If one has no connection with kings and ministers, how can the religion be spread and flourish? Is Buddha's word about the helpful power of sovereigns [*Cakravartin*] and ministers incorrect? The sentiment of men in the present age is critical to anyone who is closely associated with the court. This is because the critics do not fully understand the purpose of those

who are associated with kings and ministers. Should their association be merely for personal fame or profit, I would be grateful for these critics. Should the association be only for the sake of religion, however, one should strive after the great acheivement rather than escape insignificant criticism. His critics objected to his actions and simply were jealous of him; but their criticism is meaningless if we understand the intention of the monk."[7]

This quote reveals some interesting convictions of Tsan-ning, above all his commitment to official position as a means for assuring the prosperiety of religion.

Tsan-ning believed that Buddhism must replace its internal and external squabbling with harmony. At many points in the *SKSC* we find him intervening, through his use of commentaries, in Buddhist sectarian issues as an advocate of unity. By working through the medium of history to synthesize the various schools of Buddhism, Tsan-ning used a technique widely applied by traditional Chinese historians—namely, to write history in order to speak to contemporary issues. Tsan-ning's commentary to Shen-hsiu's biography in the *SKSC* is an intriguing example of his use of historical incident to urge his contemporaries to stop their internal wrangling. He takes up the early T'ang "Northern-Southern" Ch'an controversy and compares both schools to two students who attempt to pay respect to their mutual teacher by washing his feet and in their haste end up breaking his legs. Tsan-ning asks if this is not like those who say they are upholding the dharma while they engage in forming factions and divisions within the dharma. Certainly by the early Sung the Northern-Southern Ch'an controversy had long since been settled and Shen-hui and Shen-hsiu's schools had both died out. Here Tsan-ning is using that famous controversy to warn his contemporaries of the harmful effects of such wrangling.[8]

Again in his essay, in the section of the *SKSC* on "Mediators," we find him defending the Ch'an school from Buddhist criticism. Most important for our understanding of Tsan-ning's position are the essay's closing remarks. He asks his fellow Buddhists to respect the different perspectives within Buddhism—the Ch'an school is just one of the many manifestations of the dharma—and thus allow the dharma to shine brightly. He does not end here, however, but links the health of Buddhism with the emperor by taking the position that a unified harmonious Buddhism is the means by which the emperor's benevolence in allowing them to become monks is rewarded.[9] The linking of the emperor to the harmonizing of sectarianism in Buddhism is expressed by Tsan-ning as the Buddhist concept of *hu-fa* or "protection of the dharma."

In his essay on "Protectors of the Dharma" in the *SKSC,* Tsan-ning sets forth his interpretation of *hu-fa,* again by relying on historical exam-

ple. He draws our attention to the Hui-ch'ang suppression of Buddhism
(824–845) and analyzes its causes. Both the Taoist master Chao Kuei-
chen and the Buddhist monks in the capital are blamed for the supres-
sion. Tsan-ning finds Chao gaining the confidence of the emperor and
using his position to spread rumors against Buddhism. But Tsan-ning
also believes that the rumors spread by the Buddhist monks against Chao
are the source of Chao's desire to get vengence against Buddhism. Hence
he warns his contemporaries against criticizing things that do not concern them as followers of the dharma. Taoism and Buddhism are like the
four limbs of the body, continues Tsan-ning, and by harming each other
they destroy the body. He then claims that the sages who established all
the various teachings never tried to take power from each other. This,
then, is the way to "truly protect the dharma." Tsan-ning urges that the
two teachings be harmonized, thereby protecting future generations
from persecution.[10] Ts'ao Shih-pang points out that Tsan-ning's position
allowed him to work in conjunction with the Taoist master Han Te-shun
in writing the imperially commissioned *History of the Sages and Virtuous Ones of the Three Teachings.*

In Tsan-ning's other extant work, the *SSL,* we find him extending his
synthesis to the Confucian school.[11] Using the analogy of the relationship between the four limbs and the body, Tsan-ning applied an organis-
mic viewpoint in formulating his idea of "truly protecting the dharma."
As a historian he was well aware of the various attempts at suppressing
Buddhism and came to the conclusion that in order to protect Buddhism
both internal and external harmony must be achieved. From his organis-
mic viewpoint he considered both internal and external factors to be inti-
mately related to the health of the whole body—the very fabric of Chinese society. An injury to one part affected the other parts. With such a
view it was quite understandable that not only did Buddhism need to get
its own house in order but also that order (harmony) must include the
other teachings and the state as well.

Since Chih-i ranked the various Buddhist doctrines and excluded Taoism and Confucianism, he can be placed within the late medieval tradition of Chinese Buddhism.[12] At the same time, both Chih-i and Tsan-
ning held positions that their respective patrons, Sui Wen-ti and Sung
T'ai-tsung, found complementary to their own needs. Yet it is important
to note that both monks sought their respective positions not from a
desire for personal fame or profit but from their firm conviction about
the needs of Buddhism vis-á-vis their contemporary historical situations.
We can see from Tsan-ning's defense of Tsung-mi that he had nothing
but contempt for monks who tried to win favor with the emperor to further their personal ambitions. Tsan-ning felt that the only justification

for government service on the part of the *sangha* was total dedication to the service of Buddhism—that is, to the protection of the dharma. While he advocates harmony with the other teachings he is clearly against any attempt to usurp Buddhist prerogatives, such as the Buddhist use of incense at state ceremonies or the use of Taoist ceremonies by Buddhist monks.[13] Tsan-ning believed in harmony between the three teachings yet he had quite forceful opinions on the supremacy of Buddhism. A knowledge and respect for Confucianism and Taoism were justified for two reasons. First, harmony is much more desirable than conflict. Throughout history, Tsan-ning contends, all three teachings suffer when conflict breaks out between them. Second, knowledge of Confucianism and Taoism is essential if one is to be able to defend Buddhism against their arguments.[14]

Yet Tsan-ning's attitude regarding the supremacy of Buddhism vis-á-vis the Taoists, I believe, is of a different nature than that suggested by Makita Tairyō in his article on Tsan-ning. Makita argues that the idea of "*Sangha* first, Taoists last" *(Seng hsien, Tao hou)* was an important point raised by Tsan-ning in the *SSL*. Makita contends that the real purpose for Fa-tao (or Yung-tao, 1086–1147) to republish the *SSL* was to realize this principle.[15] The status of Buddhism had fluctuated throughout Chinese history according to the feelings of the various emperors, and a principle to govern its status was lacking. Makita further argues that, given the lack of a guiding principle, "*Sangha* first, Taoists last" was an important point raised by the *SSL* and employed by Fa-tao to combat the inroads made by Taoism in gaining court support.[16] While this argument is certainly plausible, there is a problem of interpretation: Neither Tsan-ning nor Fa-tao specifically uses the phrase in Makita's context. In fact, Fa-tao never mentions the phrase in his introduction to the *SSL*. It only appears within the context of Tsan-ning's essay.

In attempting to determine the proper way of discriminating between Buddhism and other teachings, Tsan-ning asks that one employ one's "wisdom-eye" *(chih-yen)*. Without such penetrating discernment "jade and stone are destroyed together." But once the proper discernment has been restored, what can be done? Tsan-ning's answer is that in looking back at the past from the Later Chou through the Sui, T'ang, and into his own time one sees the fortunes of Buddhism have risen and fallen, prospered and declined, in cycles. Sometimes Buddhists ranked higher, sometimes the Taoists, and so on. But for Tsan-ning the fortunes of Buddhism as manifested in history cannot be but subject to prosperity and decline. Historical fortunes simply follow their phenomenal nature. Or to quote Tsan-ning: "Owing to the phenomenal aspect of things, how can they escape the continued influence of the four states of phenomena [that is, birth, being, change or decay, and death, which are considered to be the nature of all phenomena]?" He further explains that long periods of prosperity eventually lead to weakness; when the weakest point is reached, a return to prosperity begins; arising and declining are mutually interdependent. Tsan-ning then returns to the use of historical examples, noting that in different periods there were different court rankings assigned to the Buddhists and the Taoists. Finally, he notes that in his own time the *sangha* entered the court first and the Taoists entered last, with both groups standing parallel once on the court—the *sangha* on the east, the Taoists on the west, and at the sacrifice to heaven ceremony the *sangha* on the left with the Taoists on the right. He ends the essay by saying that he does not know the origin of this practice.[17] This is hardly a call for establishing the principle of having the *sangha* enter the court first followed by the Taoists. Rather, it is a statement of contemporary Sung court ceremony. If any principle can be discerned here it is surely that of applying the Buddhist concept of phenomena to an understanding of the *historical* fortunes of Buddhism. Tsan-ning's admission that he does not know of the origins of the early Sung court procedure involved here would hardly fit an argument for precedent on his part. In his preface of the *SSL* Tsan-ning says he was ordered to write a history of the *sangha*. Since there already existed a great deal of information on the *sangha,* he chose to outline only the most important points in his work.[18] Perhaps Fa-tao, writing 103 years after Tsan-ning's death, was using the "*sangha* first, Taoists last" phrase as a precedent for his own time. Yet given Tsan-ning's situation and the absence of this phrase in Fa-tao's introduction, such a use seems unjustified.

Makita quotes Fa-tao to support his contention about Fa-tao's use of the *SSL*. But when we examine the quote it seems that Fa-tao wanted to create an awareness of Buddhist historical foundations among the faithful through the reading of the *SSL*. Furthermore, just before the section quoted by Makita we find Fa-tao lamenting that the Taoists were "robbing" the Buddhist teachings to establish them as their own and that few people are aware of this. Tsan-ning, according to Fa-tao, had a complete understanding of both Buddhist and non-Buddhist teachings and thus the republishing of his works would aid in exposing Taoist plagiarism.[19] Makita is drawing his interpretation from the historical situation in Fa-tao's time, when the Taoist had been given favor over the Buddhists at court, and not from Tsan-ning or Fa-tao's own views as expressed in the works discussed here.

In explaining Tsan-ning's attitude toward the supremacy of Buddhism vis-á-vis the other teachings, I would suggest that it was based upon his insight into the nature of the Buddha's teachings—that is, it was fundamentally a spiritual understanding. History was the phenomenal manifestation of the dharma ("truth"), and one had to be careful in discriminating its manifestation as such. By doing so one realized that truth manifested itself in many forms. Thus Taoism and Confucianism also could be understood as dharma. At the same time, for Tsan-ning, it was the teaching of the Buddha that made such insight or discrimination possible. Hence monks who quarreled among themselves and with the representatives of non-Buddhist teachings were revealing a lack of insight and acting contrary to the Buddha's teachings. The protection of the dharma therefore required Tsan-ning to intervene in all such quarrels and restore this fundamental insight which, when properly understood, led naturally to harmony. When Tsan-ning urges the *sangha* not to attack the Taoists or sees the fortunes of institutional Buddhism fluctuating as all phenomena must, he is speaking from the same type of awareness that the Ch'an master Hui-hai (748–812) expressed in his conversation with a guest at his monastery:

> Then he [the guest] asked a further question: "Do Confucianism, Taoism, and Buddhism really amount to one doctrine or to three?"
> Master: "Employed by men of great capacity, they are the same. As understood by men of limited intellect, they differ. All of them spring forth from the functioning of the one self-nature. It is views involving differentation which make them three. Whether a man remains deluded or gains illumination depends upon himself, not upon differences or similarity of doctrine."[20]

Tsan-ning's talent as historian and administrator was conscientiously mobilized to protect such principles from dissolution. The fortunes of institutional Buddhism, as mere phenomena, were subject to cycles of rise and fall—such was the nature of history. Yet history, once its phenomenal nature is understood, allows insight into a deeper level of dharma. Tsan-ning worked from this insight to expose "illusory" distinctions through the use of historical examples. The final result was the ability to see harmony between all the teachings, Buddhist and non-Buddhist.

EARLY LIFE

Tsan-ning was surnamed Kao.[21] His family was originally from the P'o Hai district of present-day Hopei, but at the end of the Sui dynasty (618) they moved to the Te-ch'ing district of Wu-hsing prefecture, in present-day Chekiang.[22] His grandfather's given name was Ch'uan or Chiung, while his fathers,given name was Shen; they are described as being virtuous and modest in not seeking government service, which is probably an indication of the lack of information on their background. Moreover, the description of his relatives is very likely a polite way of saying they were commoners.[23] His mother was surnamed Chou.[24] There is one more interesting piece of information related to Tsan-ning's family background that appears in the Sung dynasty Buddhist work *Hsiang-shan yeh-lu* and also in the *Sung-jen i-shi hui-pien.*[25] The court astronomer-astrologer, Wang Chia-na, was reading Tsan-ning's fortune and asked him if his family had any contact with royalty.[26] Tsan-ning then said that his mother had told him that when he was born she had laid him on a straw bed. At that time the king of Wu-Yüeh, Ch'ien Wen-mu, took shelter from the rain under the grass roof.[27] Chronologically speaking, it was in fact possible that Ch'ien Wen-mu visited Tsan-ning's house in 919 and that the court astronomer could have had such a conversation with Tsan-ning.[28] The identification of his grandfather and father's given names and his mother's maiden name along with the family's geographic origins indicate that Tsan-ning's family background was known. The fact that nothing else is added plus the story of Tsan-ning's being placed on a straw bed at birth and the description of his house tend to indicate that his family was poor and lacked noble lineage.

Tsan-ning was born in 919 at a "villa" in the Te-ch'ing district of Wu-hsing prefecture, present-day Chekiang.[29] He left the "householder's life" to become a monk during the T'ien-ch'eng period (926–929) of the Later T'ang dynasty, which would make him between seven and ten years old at this time.[30] The sources vary concerning the identification of the temple in which Tsan-ning began his life as a novice monk.[31] Wang Yü-ch'eng says that during the beginning of the Ch'ing-t'ai preiod (934–935), Tsan-ning went to Mount T'ien-t'ai, where he received full ordination.[32] Chou Yu-liang, however, comments that Tsan-ning "was only about fifteen years old at that time. The full ordination probably took place some time later, but Wang did not give a precise date."[33] Usually full ordination took place when the novice monk had reached "adulthood" (approximately at the age of twenty).

Throughout the sources Tsan-ning is praised for his broad education, which seems to have taken place exclusively during his monastic life. Wang Yü-ch'eng notes, at the beginning of his introduction to Tsan-ning's collected works, that there were four types of learning in which Tsan-ning was broadly knowledgable: Buddhist studies, Confucian studies, poetry, and essay writing. In Buddhist studies Tsan-ning was a master of the *vinaya* (or monastic disciple) tradition. His Buddhist lineage was that of the "Four Division *Vinaya*" *(Dharmagupta)* of the Southern Mountain *vinaya* school.[34] With regard to Confucian studies, the *HSLA* say he studied the Six Classics and the histories. In addition, Tsan-ning is reputed to have also studied Lao-Chuang (that is, Taoist philosophy) and the "hundred schools of philosophy" of the Chou dynasty.[35] A reading of his two major works, the *Sung Kao seng chuan* and the *Seng shih lüeh*, amply supports these statements. Tsan-ning used this broad classical education to his advantage during his latter service in the Han-lin Academy. As for poetry and essay writing, the sources state that he was expert in either or both.[36]

THE WU-YÜEH KINGDOM AND BUDDHISM

Tsan-ning's educational background covers four categories of expertise: Buddhist and Confucian studies and poetry and prose writing. It is, in part, through his wide learning that he gained the attention of and, finally, entry into the royal court of the Wu-Yüeh kingdom—this in turn opened his way into the Sung court and to the highest monastic-administrative position. His entry into the Wu-Yüeh court, then, was a crucial point in Tsan-ning's career. My research has led me to the conclusion that his educational background was only one of three factors responsible for gaining the attention of courtly circles. The second was the nature of the Wu-Yüeh kingdom itself; the third was the influence of Tsan-ning's teachers, a factor that has gone unrelated or has even been completely disregarded.[37]

During the Five Dynasties and the Ten Kingdoms period (907–960), the kingdom of Wu-Yüeh (907–978) with its strong royal family, the Ch'ien, was a very interesting, if not unique, state both religiously and politically. The Wu-Yüeh political experience is aptly summed up by Edouard Chavannes:

> The saga of the Ch'ien family was not an isolated case in the history of China; several other officials profited from the weakening of the central power under the Five Dynasties for the sake of carving out their own independent principalities. But, by some infinitely rare destiny, the Ch'ien avoided the downfall which overtook the majority of the usurpers. They, of course, always kept the appearance of loyalism, while being in fact autonomous. They were sufficiently skilled diplomatically to preserve the appearance, with the various would-be successors to the imperial throne, of a relationship of subject to sovereign. When the Sung dynasty had finished reestablishing the absolute sovereignty of the son of heaven, they [the Wu-Yüeh] could submit themselves without waiting to be subjugated by force of arms and although dispossessed of their territories they lived surfeited with riches and honors. Such an exceptional success was a marval to the Chinese. . . . [38]

Each of the Five Dynasties arose over a short period of time and almost immediately changed. Lo-yang and K'ai-feng in northern China were their centers of power. As a result of the social turmoil brought about by these frequent changes, one finds few great developments within the Buddhism of that region. However, each region of the Ten Kingdoms had broken away from the power struggles of the central government. Compared to the central government they enjoyed longer periods of stability, which manifested itself in social, cultural, and economic benefits. Moreover, some of the monarchs of these kingdoms favored Buddhism. It was from these circumstances, then, that the most important Buddhist development arose. It is particularly the Buddhism of the Wu-Yüeh, Nan T'ang, and Min kingdoms that can be regarded as representative of this period.[39]

The growth and development of Chinese Buddhist culture has been, and still is, closely tied to the political culture.[40] The nature of the monastic-state relationship in the kingdom of Wu-Yüeh is an excellent example of this trend. The Five Dynasties period, as a whole, illustrates the full spectrum of monastic-state relations among the various dynasties and kingdoms—from the anti-Buddhist policies of the Later Chou to the almost Aśokan attitude of state sponsorship of Buddhism by the Wu-Yüeh king Chung-i.

Buddhist historiography both praises and defends the Wu-Yüeh kingdom; the kingdom did the same for Buddhism. The *Fo-tsu t'ung-chi* (1269), a Sung Buddhist historical work, cites several excellent examples of the reciprocal nature of the monastic-state relationship in Wu-Yüeh and gives us a picture of Buddhist attitudes toward that kingdom and more specifically toward its most devoted Buddhist ruler, King Chung-i. Although there are scattered references to the Wu-Yüeh kingdom through the *Fo-tsu t'ung-chi* (hereafter *FTTC*), it is in the biography of King Chung-i that the reciprocal attitudes can most readily be seen. The biography, which started with a brief historical background of the Ch'ien royal family, focuses on the personality of Chung-i and then turns to recording Buddhist events that are thereby associated with his character. He is said to have been sincere and generous by nature. Being naturally wise, he revered the Buddha. Admiring King Aśoka, the most famous Indian Buddhist monarch (third century B.C.), he built eighty-four thousand miniature pagodas, distributed sutras, built all the temples to the north and south of West Lake in Hangchou, revered several monks as his teachers, and supported the restoration of the T'ien-t'ai school scriptures by sending missions to Korea and Japan to secure those writings which had been lost. For this last undertaking he is, in turn, revered by the *FTTC* as a "protector of the teaching." It is not surprising, then, that he receives such warm praise in the *FTTC,* for it is a T'ien-t'ai work. The reciprocal relationship is most clearly evident, however, in the commentary which follows the main body of the biography. Quoted there are two contradictory views of the Ch'ien family reign. Ch'ing Yu-chao considered the family loyal to the central court and "benevolent enough to protect their subjects, wise enough to preserve their clan." Opposing this view is that of Ou-yang Hsiu, who said in essence that the Ch'ien family were tyrants having no merit or virtue. Chih-p'an, the compiler of the *FTTC,* concludes that Ou-yang Hsiu's comments are excessive and that Ch'ing Yu-chao's views are "indeed admirable."[41]

LITERARY ACTIVITIES IN THE WU-YÜEH KINGDOM

Besides the political and religious nature of the Wu-Yüeh kingdom, another aspect should be mentioned which is also of great importance in understanding the environment that facilitated Tsan-ning's rise to prominence—namely, the high regard placed upon literary talent and the active participation in such pursuits by the royal family. In the sources regarding the Wu-Yüeh kingdom there are repeated references to the royal family's great interest in literary pursuits. With regard to the founder of the Wu-Yüeh kingdom, Ch'ien Liu (852–932), the *Chiu wu-tai shih* says:

> Ch'ien Liu studied books and took pleasure in chanting rhymes. Now in Chiang-tung there was a certain Lo Yin who was a reputed poet and renowned throughout the empire. He had as his patron Ch'ien Liu, from whom he received the title Ts'an Tso. Ch'ien Liu often took pleasure in singing alternating rhymes with him.[42]

As we shall see, Lo Yin also plays an important role in the life of one of Tsan-ning's teachers. Ch'ien Yüan-kuan's (r. 932–941) literary interests are mentioned in the following passage from the *Wu-tai shih:*

> Ch'ien Yüan-kuan knew well how to command his officers and soldiers. He appreciated also the learning of lettered men and himself excelled in the writing of poetry; he ordered his counselor of state Chen Sung to organize an academy of chosen talents. Men of letters of the Wu region were selected and provided with a stipend.[43]

The last Wu-Yüeh monarch was King Chung-i, noted for his devotion to Buddhism and his study of the T'ien-t'ai scriptures. Wang Yü-ch'eng, in his introduction to the collected works of Tsan-ning (now for the most part lost), provides an interesting glimpse into the literary situation in Wu-Yüeh and the role played by King Chung-i. Wang says that Tsan-ning's "reputation prospered day by day," and that his literary ability flourished. At that time the Ch'ien royal family, including King Chung-i, discussed literary works together with Tsan-ning. Furthermore, at the same time the literati exchanged poems with Tsan-ning. As a Buddhist monk and a man of obvious literary talent, Tsan-ning would seem to have gravitated naturally into the literary circles at the Wu-Yüeh court. In considering his ascent, however, one is immediately faced with the problem of discerning the influences on the development of his talents.

The interest in literary pursuits consumed the attention of both the *sangha* and the ruling class in the Wu-Yüeh kingdom. As a result, the men who influenced Tsan-ning during the formative development of his talents were drawn from both monastic and secular ranks. Wang Yü-ch'eng notes that besides his literary discussions with the royal family and the literati, Tsan-ning also studied *wen-ke* with the monk Hui-cheng, who was titled *Kuang-wen Ta-shih* and *shih-chüeh,* and with Kung Lin, who had the title of *Ch'ien chin shih.*[44]

Furthermore, the Wu-Yüeh *sangha* was deeply affected by the strong literary tradition of both the Hangchou area and the Wu-Yüeh kingdom. Wang Yü-ch'eng, after mentioning Tsan-ning's literary contacts, says that in Ch'ien-t'ang (that is, the Hangchou area) at that time there were monks famous for their literary ability such as Ch'i-ning, who was called *Lun hu* ("Tiger of Critical Essay Writing"), Ts'ung-i, who was called *Wen hu* ("Tiger of Literature"), and Tsan-ning, known as *Lü hu* ("Tiger of the *Vinaya*"). In the Wu-Yüeh kingdom, it would seem that even the Buddhist rules of monastic discipline *(Vinaya),* when written about with literary skill, were considered good reading.[45] Makita Tairyō says that in Chiang-nan (the area south of the Yangtze River), Buddhist circles included many "scholar-monks" such as Kuan-ksiu, Ling-ch'e, and Ch'i-chi. No doubt this literary activity of the Wu-Yüeh kingdom stimulated interest in scholarship. Makita considers the "Four Tigers" to be the most prominent of the Wu-Yüeh scholar-monks.[46]

It is in this context that Wang Yü-ch'eng's remark that Tsan-ning's reputation grew day by day and his writings flourished is best understood.[47] Although Wu-Yüeh *sangha's* active interest in literary pursuits provided a climate conducive to Tsan-ning's pursuit of scholarly endeavors, the direct influences on Tsan-ning's career can be seen in his relations with his teachers.

We have seen how both the nature of the Wu-Yüeh kingdom and its *sangha* was conducive to the advancement of monks with literary talent. A third factor, the role of the master-disciple relationship, has been suggested as an equally important force in the advancement of Tsan-ning's career. We have discussed how Tsan-ning was probably of commoner family background; his family was neither rich nor of a discernible noble lineage. Yet by the time he was approximately twenty-nine years old in 948, when King Chung-i ascended the Wu-Yüeh throne, he was discussing literary works with the Ch'ien royal family, including King Chung-i. Stanley Weinstein, in his essay "Imperial Patronage in the Formation of T'ang Buddhism," has shown the importance of family ties in advancing the career of the brilliant T'ien-t'ai school synthesizer Chih-i. It is useful to quote Weinstein at length to illustrate how such relationships function:

> When Chih-i arrived in Chin-ling in 568, his father had been dead for some fourteen years, while his father's erstwhile colleague, the founder of the Ch'en dynasty, Ch'en Pa-hsien, had been dead some nine years. Yet many family friends, now in positions of authority, were still around to give sympathetic hearing to the new doctrines espoused by the thirty-year-old Chih-i. . . . Thus, the Ch'en imperial family, whose surname Chih-i shared, all had close links with the group surrounding Hsiao I in Chiang-ling in the early 550's, the same group in which Chih-i's father had held a prominent position. To the Ch'en imperial family, as well as to many powerful bureaucrats in Chin-ling, Chih-i was no obscure purveyor of a new gospel, but the son of an esteemed, now deceased, colleague.[48]

Tsan-ning, while enjoying no similar advantages in terms of blood lineage, did enjoy the benefits of his religious lineage. The Buddhist *saṇgha,* from its origins in India, was in many of its functional aspects similar to a secular family or clan. In this sense I would suggest that Tsan-ning reached the highest circles of Wu-Yüeh society not as some talented yet obscure *vinaya* monk but rather as the student of two respected and influential monks, Hsi-chüeh and Hui-cheng.[49] Just as Chih-i's father had become influential among the powerful in the Ch'en dynasty, so were Hsi-chüeh and Hui-cheng among the elite in the Wu-Yüeh kingdom. This influence would in turn manifest itself in the careers of both Chih-i and Tsan-ning as a means by which their entry into the power structures of their respective states would be facilitated.

Hsi-chüeh's contacts with those influential in the Wu-Yüeh kingdom developed early in his life. Hsi-chüeh came from a once fairly well-to-do family and as a young man worked as a clerk in the home of the supervising censor, Lo Yin. When Lo Yin discovered Hsi-chüeh's family name and home district, he asked him how a son of the Shangs of P'i-ling (in present-day Chiangsu) could end up in such a common occupation. Lo Yin, then, looked after Hsi-chüeh and urged him to continue his studies.[50] It is this same Lo Yin who is mentioned in connection with the literary interests of the founder of the Wu-Yüeh kingdom, Ch'ien Liu. The *Chiu wu-tai shih* refers to Lo Yin as a poet, specializing mainly in historical satirical poems, known throughout contemporary China. His relationship was close enough to Ch'ien Liu that one of his satires of the king (that is, King Wu-su or Ch'ien Liu) brought only an amused response.[51] Hsi-chüeh, after leaving Lo Yin's service, became a monk in 888. Lo Yin died in 924, which means he would have known Hsi-chüeh as a monk for thirty-six years. Hsi-chüeh was also on close terms with other influential figures in the Wu-Yüeh kingdom. Ch'ien Hua, the youngest brother of Wu-Yüeh King Wu-su, paid respects to Hsi-chüeh and possibly intervened on his behalf when he was falsely accused by certain other monks.[52] Moreover, King Wen-mu of Wu-Yüeh built a monastery, appointed Hsi-chüeh abbot, and personally conferred honors on him.[53] Hsi-chüeh died in the same year that King Chung-i, the last monarch of the Wu-Yüeh kingdom, ascended the throne: 948.

Hsi-chüeh and the students in his "dharma family" can be seen to form a close network of ties with the Wu-Yüeh royal family. The *SKSC* biography of Hao-tuan (890–961) states that he was Hsi-chüeh's student and had been ordered by King Wu-su, the first Wu-Yüeh ruler, to be a lecturer.[54] Wen-i (885–958), whom Hsi-chüeh considered to be his best student, went on to become an eminent Ch'an master.[55] In turn, one of the best students of Wen-i was the Ch'an master Te-shao (891–972). Te-shao's greatest student was Yen-shou (904–975) of Yung-ming temple. With regard to their relations with King Chung-i, the *FTTC* says: "[King Chung-i] revered monks such as Mount T'ien-t'ai's imperial teacher Te-shao and Yung-ming temple's Ch'an master Yen-shou. He treated them with the respect shown a teacher."[56] The *Shih-kuo Ch'un-ch'iu* states that King Chung-i honored Te-shao by making him imperial teacher. Chung-i honored Yen-shou by making him the abbot of the famous Yung-ming temple, where he is said to have had more than two thousand students.[57]

In the *HHC* it is mentioned that Tsan-ning had discussed literature with King Chung-i and five other members of the Wü-Yueh royal family. Four of the five were sons of King Wen-mu, who personally knew Hsi-chüeh; the other was the eldest son of King Chung-hsien (r. 941–947). Tsan-ning, then, was the disciple of a master highly regarded by the father of four of them, while the other, Ch'ieng Yü, King Chung-hsien's eldest son, would later study and write about bamboo with Tsan-ning.[58] Furthermore, we have seen King Chung-i's respect for both Te-shao and Yen-shou. When Te-shao died in 972, it was probably King Chung-i himself who ordered Tsan-ning, as monk administrator of the capital, to write the plaque for Te-shao's pagoda.[59] Again in the case of Yen-shou we find Tsan-ning crossing paths with another member of his "dharma family," for it is said that he and Yen-shou built a pagoda on a riverbank to stop the flooding of the Shih-t'ang narrows in Hangchou.[60] From this background we sense an interlacing network of relationships involving both the Buddhist and royal families, a network which aided Tsan-ning's entry into the upper classes. The intimacy of this relationship was intensified, moreover, by the small size of the Wu-Yüeh kingdom.

In the same sense, Hui-cheng, Tsan-ning's other teacher, was also part of this network. Hui-cheng was made monk administrator by King Chung-i.[61] While we have no specific information on Hui-cheng's use of his political influence for Tsan-ning, we can see how it was effective with regard to his former student Yung-an. The *Transmission of the Lamp* relates that after Hui-cheng informed King Chung-i of Yung-an's "merits," the king ordered Yung-an to take the position of abbot of Ch'ing-t'ai monastery.[62]

I am suggesting here that Tsan-ning's connection as a disciple of both Hsi-chüeh and Hui-cheng involved him in a far-reaching set of relationships which in turn made possible, as in the case of Chih-i, his sympathetic reception into the upper-class circles of the Wu-Yüeh kingdom. While the information that would provide us with specific details of Tsan-ning's entrance into those circles is lacking, we may generalize on the relationship between the forces that propelled Tsan-ning into one of the highest monastic-administrative positions at the Wu-Yüeh court and eventually led him to the highest monastic post at the Sung court. The fairly independent political status and general prosperity of the Wu-Yüeh kingdom allowed its educated elite to indulge in cultural pursuits which included both literary activity and a deep interest in Buddhism. This environment set the stage for the encouragement of a Buddhist monastic society highly talented in literary skills which, moreover, was very much a heritage of the traditionally high level of culture maintained in the Hang-chou area. It is within this context that human relationships, such as those examined above, came to play a crucial role. This, however, is by no means a unique phenomenon in Chinese history, since the same can be said for the example of Chih-i and other monks. Thus one must keep in mind that the network of connections linking the *sangha* and secular society could play a significant role in the career of a Chinese monk and, as Weinstein has shown, even in the success or failure of particular schools of Buddhist thought.[63]

DIPLOMATIC RELATIONS BETWEEN WU-YÜEH AND SUNG

Tsan-ning's political post in the Wu-Yüeh kingdom, given the diplomatic relations between that kingdom and the Sung dynasty, provided him with a stepping stone to the Sung court. According to the *HHC*, Tsan-ning held the position of superintendent of ordination platforms in the Wu-Yüeh kingdom and for several decades he was monk superintendent for the Liang-Che region (that is, the Wu-Yüeh kingdom). Wang Yü-ch'eng goes on to credit Tsan-ning's administration with restoring the "brightness" of Buddhism and bringing order to its monastic ranks. While this is probably an exaggeration by a close friend and admirer, it is reasonable to assume that Tsan-ning was a capable administrator because of his steady rise to the highest monastic-administrative position in both the Wu-Yüeh and Sung courts.[64] The *SMCT* adds that Tsan-ning was given the honorary name *Ming-i Tsung-wen* (roughly translated as "Illuminating the Meaning, Honoring Literature").[65]

In the four biographies of the *SKSC* where Tsan-ning's title is given, three of them call him *Tu seng-cheng* (monk administrator of the capital) and one simply refers to *Seng-cheng* (monk administrator). Furthermore, in one of the biographies his full title is given as *Liang-Che tu seng-cheng,* that is, Liang-Che (present-day Chekiang) monk administrator of the capital. The seeming discrepancy between the *HHC* and the *SKSC* can perhaps be explained by Tsan-ning himself. In his *Outline History of the Sangha (Seng shih lüeh),* he says that while the Ten Kingdoms of the Five Dynasties period were all followers of Buddhism, some of the kingdoms used their own titles for the various monastic-administrative positions. The Wu-Yüeh kingdom, he continues, did use the title of monk superintendent *(Seng-t'ung),* but afterward these titles changed.[66] It is difficult, if not impossible, to determine to which system Wang Yü-ch'eng and the *SKSC* compilers are referring when they speak of Tsan-ning's official title. The main point here, however, is that Tsan-ning apparently rose to the highest monastic-administrative post in the Wu-Yüeh kingdom. The eminence of his position is all the more apparent when we see that it is Tsan-ning who is sent to the Sung court to act as the Buddhist representative of the Wu-Yüeh kingdom. Our knowledge of Tsan-ning's activities with the royal family and various government officials at King Chung-i's court until he entered the Sung courts is based on this meager information.[67]

It was through diplomacy that the Wu-Yüeh kingdom was able to survive the Five Dynasties period and enter the Sung dynasty intact. Tsan-ning was part of this Wu-Yüeh diplomacy. During this period the relationship of the Wu-Yüeh kingdom to the Lo-yang and K'ai-feng political centers was very similar to that of the military governors *(chieh-tu shih)* to the central government during the latter half of the T'ang dynasty. The Wu-Yüeh founder, Ch'ien Liu, rose to power and consolidated his hold on the Chekiang area primarily through his military service to the T'ang, Later Liang, and Later T'ang dynasties, and at two points in his career he was given the post of military governor.[68] Ch'ien Liu's descendants inherited both his title of king of Wu-Yüeh and his ability to use the kingdom's capabilities in the service of the successive dynasties that controlled Central China down to the Sung dynasty.

This Wu-Yüeh tradition of diplomacy can clearly be seen in King

Chung-i's relations with the first emperor of the Sung, T'ai-tsu. In the first year of the Sung dynasty, King Chung-i was granted the title "supreme commander of the imperial cavalry" by Emperor T'ai-tsu. King Chung-i continued his military and financial support of the newly established dynasty, the latter support in the form of tribute, through the reign of T'ai-tsu and enjoyed a close relationship with the emperor. In so doing, Chung-i was following the tradition established by his ancestor Ch'ien Liu. Two years after T'ai-tsu's successor T'ai-tsung (r. 976–997) ascended the Sung throne, King Chung-i brought his kingdom under the direct control of the Sung.[69] His memorial to Emperor T'ai-tsung, petitioning for integration into the Sung empire, reveals the nature of the Wu-Yüeh kingdom's relationship not only to the Sung dynasty but also to the succession of major political powers in north-central China. Accordingly, in the memorial King Chung-i appeals to this relationship and builds upon it. He states that his family, from his ancestors down to his own time, have personally led "just" (that is, loyal) troops and have honored the "central capital." They have conquered the Liang-Che area, pacified it, and exterminated the rebels of that region who had cut the route to the imperial court and prevented those who wished to be of service to the court from reaching the capital. King Chung-i goes on to note that his ancestors received the orders of the imperial palace and protected the borders on the frontier areas for a hundred years.[70]

Since the main power struggles during the Five Dynasties period took place in Central China, the Wu-Yüeh kingdom's geographic distance from the center of struggle—as well as its political policy of supporting, as a loyal retainer, whichever faction held sway at the capital—afforded it a relatively independent existence. Following this policy down to the establishement of the Sung allowed the last king of Wu-Yüeh to enjoy amicable relations with the Sung emperors.[71] Much in the way that T'ang military governors were expected to guard the frontiers of the empire, the Wu-Yüeh kings protected the southeastern "frontier" of the fledgling Sung dynasty as it attempted to deal with its more powerful opponents in other regions.

The Wu-Yüeh kingdom's diplomacy, though based primarily on military cooperation and tribute, also included the use of Buddhism to further its interests. In effect, its diplomacy can be seen as reflecting the kingdom's main strengths: military, economic, and religious. The *Sung shih* mentions nothing about Tsan-ning's mission to the Sung court, but, as pointed out above, this silence is not unusual for Chinese secular histories.[72] The Wu-Yüeh court not only had close relationships with eminent Buddhists but also actively supported the spread of Buddhism within its territory. Furthermore, it would seem consistent with its pro-

Buddhist activities that these attitudes would naturally be extended into that kingdom's foreign policy.

It is useful when examining the Buddhist policy of the first Sung emperor to consider both the immediate circumstances of T'ai-tsu's rise to power and the Buddhist policies of previous dynasties in order to understand his policy within the broad context of traditional Chinese history. In 955, the Later Chou emperor Shih-tsung (r. 954–949) declared a "reformation" of the Buddhist establishment which resulted in the destruction of 3,336 out of 6,030 temples. Moreover, government control of the *sangha* increased and 61,200 monks and nuns were registered.[73] T'ai-tsu's Buddhist policy can be seen as a reaction to this overt suppression.[74] For example, the *FTTC* says:

> From the beginning of Buddhism down to the present, a country with moral principles has always exalted Buddhism and used it to exhort the country. When T'ai-tsu first saw the Chou dynasty's destruction of images [that is, Buddhism], he grieved over this saying, "Ordering the destruction of the Buddha is surely not to the good fortune of the country." After he ascended to the throne, he promptly handed down an imperial order of restoration. It can be said that a ruler of moral principles certainly exalts Buddhism.[75]

The *FTTC* then emphasizes T'ai-tsu's role in restoring Buddhism. Besides the restoration of Buddhism, T'ai-tsu is noted for having sent monks to India to search for Buddhist teachings, welcoming Indian monks who translated and transmitted Buddhist scriptures, establishing battlefield temples for the spirits of slain soldiers, ordering blocks to be cut for the printing of the Tripiṭaka, and for his efforts at spreading Buddhism during periods of hardship.[76] Furthermore, when he ascended the throne in 960 T'ai-tsu ordered the ordination of eight thousand monks on the anniversary of his birthday and "personally undertook the layman's vows, one of the few Chinese emperors to do so."[77]

Sung T'ai-tsu's restoration of Buddhism after the Chou repression and the unification of China parallels the promotion of Buddhism by Emperor Wen of the Sui dynasty (589–618) in his efforts to unify the empire after the division of China during the Northern-Southern Dynasties period and the persecution of Buddhism by the Northern Chou. One notes that Buddhism is used by both Sui Wen-ti and Sung T'ai-tsu in a very similar manner. As Arthur F. Wright, in "The Formation of Sui Ideology, 581–604," has remarked:

> The use of Buddhism was governed in part by the recent history of North China, notably the Northern Chou persecution of Buddhism and Taoism. While this persecution had created sufficient discontent to make a reversal of

policy appealing to one who sought power, Wen-ti must have been well aware of the abuses of clerical privilege that were in part responsible for the persecution. Even the most partisan Buddhist chronicles admit this. Wen-ti was a devout Buddhist, but he was also a shrewd and calculating man in pursuit of great power and universal dominion. . . . From beginning to end Buddhism was under firm state control and support of Buddhism, as well as the ideological use of Buddhism, were calculated in terms of the problems facing the dynasty.[78]

This "calculated" revival of Buddhism based first on the needs of the dynasty is also evident in T'ai-tsu's Buddhist policy. While he ended the Later Chou practice of destroying temples without government permission, he continued the practice of limiting both the number of new temples built and the number of monks and nuns ordained. With regard to the latter, T'ai-tsu carried on the Later Chou practice of requiring an examination in order for the monks and nuns to enter the *sangha*.[79]

T'ai-tsu's successor and brother T'ai-tsung, with whom Tsan-ning would meet as a representative of the Wu-Yüeh kingdom, carried on the same type of Buddhist policy. Specifically the *FTTC* credits T'ai-tsung with various works such as having 170,000 novices ordained upon his ascending the throne, establishing a hall for the translation of sutras, composing prefaces to the Buddhist scriptures, ordering name plaques for all "nameless" monasteries, and for having established the K'ai-p'ao Great Pagoda Reliquary.[80] T'ai-tsung's use of Buddhism was no less expedient than that of T'ai-tsu. While T'ai-tsu started the initial reunification of China under the Sung dynasty, it remained T'ai-tsung's task to complete it. Buddhism, the major religion of the population under Sui Wen-ti, T'ang T'ai-tsung, Sung T'ai-tsu, and Sung T'ai-tsung, was used in a calculated and selective manner by all four emperors. Arthur Wright, in his essay on T'ang T'ai-tsung's relationship to Buddhism, provides an excellent overview of how T'ang T'ai-tsung perceived this relationship and a good summary of the attitudes of all four emperors to the politics of Buddhism. In speaking of T'ang T'ai-tsung, Wright says:

Though markedly less devout than Sui Wen-ti, his policies towards Buddhism strike many of the same notes: The welfare of the state and dynasty is the first consideration; linked to this is concern for the morale of his people, and here Buddhist belief, if properly channeled and controlled, could be a positive influence. If the clergy and believers were not so controlled—he believed—corrupt and subversive practices would proliferate and have to be dealt with by drastic means. The imperial family, individually and collectively, stood to benefit from appropriate observances and acts of pious generosity, but never from excessive favor to the Buddhists or prodigal giving to their establishments; a measured patronage would reassure the mass of their subjects and enlist for the T'ang the benevolent assistance—present and future—of all the divinities and forces of the Buddhist universe.[81]

This statement applies equally well to both Sung T'ai-tsu and T'ai tsung. Moreover, although the Wu-Yüeh kingdom was more of a Buddhist kingdom than the Sung, its rulers too were governed by expediency in their dealings with the Buddhist establishment. Tsan-ning, one of the outstanding Buddhist leaders of the time, is credited with "restoring order" to the monastic ranks of the kingdom. Although one notes that this achievement coincides with an important concern of T'ang T'ai-tsung's Buddhist policy, this correspondence is not so unusual. The greatest of Indian Buddhist monarchs, King Aśoka, was also concerned foremost for the welfare of "state and dynasty."[82]

TSAN-NING AND THE SUNG COURT

Tsan-ning's first contacts with the Sung court were due to his role in the diplomatic relations between the Wu-Yüeh kingdom and the Sung court. Wang Yü-ch'eng says that in the year 978, when King Chung-i decided to merge his kingdom with the Sung dynasty, Tsan-ning made an offering to the Sung imperial palace of a miniature pagoda containing "the true body relic."[83] The *FTTC* combines Wang Yü-ch'eng's account with that of the *SMCT*. According to the *FTTC*, in the fourth lunar month of 978 King Chung-i offered his kingdom to the Sung dynasty. He ordered Tsan-ning, as monk superintendent, to offer the relic pagoda of Śākyamuni Buddha to the Sung imperial palace. The *FTTC* goes on to say that Emperor T'ai-tsung, having heard of Tsan-ning's fame, summoned him seven times in one day. The emperor conferred the name "Great Master T'ung-hui" upon Tsan-ning.[84] The *Sung shih* makes no mention of Tsan-ning's mission but focuses on the interaction between King Chung-i and Sung T'ai-tsung. For the fourth lunar month of 978, the *Sung shih* records a memorial sent by King Chung-i to the emperor in which the former attempts to negotiate his submission to the Sung dynasty.[85]

It is difficult to know exactly within what context the Sung emperor had initially heard of Tsan-ning's fame, if indeed this account represents actual fact rather than the biographer's own admiration. We do, however, have some information on the topics discussed by Tsan-ning and T'ai-tsung at their initial meeting. The *SKSC* says that Tsan-ning was questioned about the dimensions of a famous stone bridge at Fu-t'ien monastery on Mount T'ien-t'ai. Makita adds that Tsan-ning was also questioned about the five hundred arhats recorded in Hsüan-tsang's work, *Hsi-yü chi*.[86] The discussions foreshadow one of the major characteristics attributed to Tsan-ning throughout the literature dealing with him—that is, his encyclopedic knowledge which in these reports ranges from the physical dimensions of a bridge to the account of the five hundred arhats in Hsüan-tsang's writings. The impression this must have made on T'ai-tsung is immediately apparent, for Tsan-ning is given the honorary name T'ung-hui ("Thorough Knowledge"). Furthermore, T'ai-tsung appointed him to the Han-lin Academy.[87]

Tsan-ning's appointment to that exclusive institution was apparently a very rare privilege for a monk. Consulting volume 28 of the *Taishō shinshū daizōkyō sakuin* (the index for the major Buddhist canon) for references to monks nominated to the Han-lin Academy, I can find mention of only Tsan-ning and the Ming-dynasty monk Yüan-cheng. Both monks, judging from their respective biographical sources, seem to have been amply qualified to hold such a scholarly office.[88] This opinion about Tsan-ning does not, however, seem to have been shared by some of his Han-lin associates when he was first appointed. The *FTTC* says that some of his colleagues ridiculed him asking, "How could the academy accept this person?" In recounting this event both the *FTTC* and *SMCT* quote Tsan-ning's detractors as using the character *wu* in their reference to him—a derogatory term that connotes a "thing" rather than a "person."[89]

Because of this reaction, one might come to the hasty conclusion that this was an anti-Buddhist act to prevent a Buddhist monk from serving in an academy which was a bastion of Confucian orthodoxy. Yet we read that Tsan-ning, relying on the histories and the Confucian classics, "rolled endlessly" over his critics (Confucian scholars) and those who had ridiculed him "submitted from fear" to his arguments. Thus scholars like Wang Yü-ch'eng and Hsü Hsüan, having constantly doubted Tsan-ning, ended by respecting him once he had demonstrated his thorough grasp of the classical Confucian heritage.[90] I would suggest that the attacks on Tsan-ning were concerned more with his qualifications to join one of the empire's highest scholarly organizations than with the issue of whether or not a Buddhist monk should be accepted. If the issue was *solely* Tsan-ning's religious affiliation, it is difficult to see how any arguments, much less arguments based upon the Confucian classics, could have helped him against anti-Buddhist critics. More likely Wang Yü-ch'eng, Hsü Hsüan, and others correctly assumed that a Buddhist monk would not likely be qualified enough to hold a position in the Han-lin Academy. They quickly found that Tsan-ning was not an ordinary Buddhist monk, however. Wang became a great admirer and the biographer of Tsan-ning. Hsü Hsüan's acknowledgment of Tsan-ning's abilities can be seen in the poem he presented to Tsan-ning.[91]

Tsan-ning was approximately fifty-nine years old when he met with Sung T'ai-tsung and was appointed to the Han-lin Academy, yet his most productive years as a historian lay ahead of him. His appointment to the academy and his acceptance there represent the foundation of his political career with the Sung court. His initial conflict with his fellow scholars in the academy seems to have been resolved favorably, for there are no indications of further dispute during the rest of his career in any of our sources.[92]

From 978 to his death in 1001, Tsan-ning's rise at the Sung court was very rapid. In the sixth lunar month of 983, the emperor ordered Tsan-ning to compile *The Great Sung Edition of the Biographies of Eminent Monks (SKSC)* when Tsan-ning was sixty-four years old. He returned to the Ch'ien-t'ang district of his home region to begin the compilation of his greatest work.[93] The *SKSC* is unique in many aspects, not least of which is the fact that, unlike its two predecessors, it was commissioned by the emperor. This, in turn, had an influence on the approach used by Tsan-ning in compiling this impressive and fascinating work.[94] The emperor, at the same time, also ordered Tsan-ning to compile the *Seng shih lüeh (Outline History of the Saṇgha)*.[95] In 988, Tsan-ning presented the finished *SKSC* in thirty *chüan* to the throne. The emperor sent Tsan-ning a memorial praising the work and ordered it to be added to the Tripiṭaka. Tsan-ning was then ordered to move into T'ien-shou monastery in the capital. He was approximately sixty-nine years old by that time.[96] At the T'ien-shou monastery, Tsan-ning says he found the time to look over the available materials and do the research for writing the *SSL*.[97] In the first year of the Ch'un-hua period (990), Su I-chien was ordered to compile the *San-chiao sheng-hsien shih chi (History of the Sages and Worthies of the Three Teachings)*. Tsan-ning was asked to do the section relating to Buddhism, which he completed in fifty *chüan* and titled *Chiu-ling sheng-hsien lu* ("A Record on Sages and Virtuous Ones of Buddhists").[98] In the same year, at the age of seventy-one, Tsan-ning was commanded to fill the post of *Tso-chieh chiang-ching shou-tso* (senior sutra expounder of the Left Street).[99] The next year Tsan-ning was ordered to fill a post in the History Office as a compiler.[100] In 996, at the age of seventy-seven, he was appointed supervisor of religious affairs in the western capital.[101] In the next year Li Fang established the Association of Nine Elders in Lo-yang, attempting to carry on a cultural tradition begun in the T'ang dynasty by Po Chü-i. Both the T'ang association and its Sung imitator were dedicated to the appreciation of the arts and were composed of nine elderly gentlemen who were writers, poets, artists, or musicians. In both cases, there was one monk included among the nine elders: Ju-man in Po Chü-i's association and Tsan-ning in Li

Fang's.[102] Once again Tsan-ning's literary abilities were recognized by his cultural peers. In the Wu-Yüeh kingdom that recognition had been localized, whereas the recognition of his talent by the Association of Nine Elders represented a "national" recognition of his abilities.

Two years later, at the age of seventy-nine, he was appointed monk secretary of the Right Street. The Japanese monk Ennin noted in his diary for the eighteenth day of the first lunar month, 839, that the monk secretaries "control the monasteries of the whole land and regulate Buddhism." While this is obviously one of the highest monastic-administrative offices in the government, it must be pointed out, as Kenneth Ch'en has said, that "although monks held the positions of *seng-lu* and *seng-cheng,* it was clear that the real authority over the monastic community was held by the civil officials in the central government and the provinces."[103]

In 999, at the age of eighty, Tsan-ning was promoted to the Left Street as monk secretary.[104] Two years later, in the fifth lunar month at the age of eighty-two, Tsan-ning died.[105] He was buried in the Ch'ien-t'ang district of his home region in the former Wu-Yüeh kingdom. His pagoda was erected there during the T'ien-sheng period (1023–1031).[106] In 1105, Tsan-ning was posthumously honored by the emperor with the honorary title Yüan-ming ("Perfect Brightness").[107]

CONCLUSION

Tsan-ning's political career can be conveniently divided into two periods: his life in his home region (919–976) and the period of service with the Sung court (976–1001). The first period marks his rise from a common family background to the highest monastic-administrative position in the Wu-Yüeh kingdom. The second phase marks his acceptance into Sung court society and his establishment as a major Buddhist historian.

His rise during the first period was contingent on three major factors: education, the unique nature of the Wu-Yüeh kingdom, and the role of his teachers. Combined with Tsan-ning's own talent, these three factors interacted in a way that greatly facilitated his successful Wu-Yüeh career.

The Wu-Yüeh kingdom was distant from the power struggles of the Central China plain during the Five Dynasties period. Due to the astute political leadership of the ruling Ch'ien family the Wu-Yüeh successfully navigated the seventy-year period from the fall of the T'ang to the unification of China under the second Sung emperor T'ai-tsung.

As a result of Wu-Yüeh's independence and relative stability the attention of the literati was freed to follow cultural pursuits. In such an aristocratic atmosphere education was not only highly esteemed but required in order to master the highly specialized body of commonly revered Confucian literature.

Among the cultural pursuits of the Wu-Yüeh literati an active interest and respect for Buddhism was clearly evident. The pro-Buddhist attitude of the last Wu-Yüeh ruler, King Chung-i, manifested itself both in his patronage of the Buddhist establishment, especially the T'ien-t'ai school, and in his foreign policy. The Buddhist *sangha,* also literarily inclined, interacted easily with the Wu-Yüeh literati-ruling class. The result of this interaction was the formation of strong relationships between various monks and members of the upper class, thus benefiting the Buddhist-state relationship as a whole. Tsan-ning as a Buddhist monk highly skilled in both Buddist and non-Buddhist literature and educated by teachers with important secular connections rose easily into the Wu-Yüeh upper class. His religious lineage thus came to take the place of an aristocratic blood lineage in providing him with an introduction into upper-class circles. Furthermore, his ability as an administrator assured him of a high position within the kingdom's monastic administration. This government position provided him with a stepping stone into the Sung court.

To appreciate fully the transition from Tsan-ning's Wu-Yüeh career at the Sung court one must consider the diplomatic relations between Wu-Yüeh and Sung. The relationship can be characterized as that between a T'ang-style military governorship and the central government; its function was to support the central government militarily and financially. The Wu-Yüeh kingdom survived because this relationship safeguarded its own independence. Its policy toward the Sung, then, was very much based upon previous experience. The last Wu-Yüeh king, however, recognized that the Sung dynasty's power was much more stable than that of its immediate predecessors. King Chung-i therefore led his kingdom into peaceful union with the Sung.

Another aspect of Wu-Yüeh diplomacy that also reflected the kingdom's traditions was an appreciation for the political usefulness of Buddhism. The use of Tsan-ning as a diplomatic representative of the Wu-Yüeh kingdom would make little sense, however, if the Sung court did not place a reciprocal value on Buddhism. The early Sung, while not nearly so pro-Buddhist as the Wu-Yüeh kingdom, recognized the practical value of entering into a relationship with the Buddhist establishment much as Sui Wen-ti and T'ang T'ai-tsung had done. The mutual recognition of such a relationship by both the Wu-Yüeh and early Sung provided a viable role for Tsan-ning to play in the diplomatic relation between the two courts.

Nevertheless, once he became a member of the Sung court through his appointment to the Han-lin Academy by Sung T'ai-tsung, Tsan-ning was immediately faced with the problem of being accepted by a ruling elite who were much more ambivalent toward Buddhism than their Wu-Yüeh counterparts. Even so, the common denominator of a shared respect for the Confucian literary heritage provided Tsan-ning with the key to gaining social acceptance at the Sung court.

Tsan-ning's career at the Sung court parallels his most productive period of Buddhist historical writing. It is in this period that Tsan-ning established his position in the history of Chinese Buddhist historiography. His rise at the Sung court was a result of both his administrative and literary abilities and the needs of the Sung emperors. Tsan-ning was recognized in his own lifetime for his outstanding abilities in both areas by being invited to participate in Li Fang's literary association and by being perhaps the only Buddhist monk ever admitted to the Han-lin Academy as a historian.

Looking back on Tsan-ning's brilliant career, one cannot help but recall his words in defense of the T'ang monk Tsung-mi regarding monks who sought political association: "Should the association be only for the sake of religion, then one should strive after that great achievement rather than escape insignificant criticism." Later generations of Buddhist historians applauded Tsan-ning for his strenuous protection of the dharma, thus honoring him and his ideals of a "political career."

NOTES

The following abbreviations are used in the notes:

CKFHJMTT	Ming-fu. *Chung-kuo Fo-hsüeh jen-ming tz'u-tien*. Taipei: Fang chou ch'u pan she, 1974.
CTCTL	Tao-yüan. *Ching-te ch'uan teng lu* (published in 1004). *T* 51. 196–467.
CWTTT	Chang Ch'i-yün, ed. *Chung-wen ta tz'u-tien*. Taipei: China Academy, 1973. 10 vols.
DRZGGS	*Denritsuzu gengeshū* (published in 1684). In *Dai Nihon Bukkyō zensho*. Tokyo: Dai Nihon Bukkyō zensho hakkōsho, 1913–1922. Vol. 105.
FTTC	Chih-p'an. *Fo-tsu t'ung-chi* (published in 1269). *T* 49.129–475.
HCP	Chih-yüan (976–1022). *Hsien chü pien*. *ZZK* 101.27–109.
HHC	Wang Yü-ch'eng. *Hsiao hsü chi*. Shanghai: Szu pu ts'ung k'an chi pu, Shang wu yin shu kuan, n. d.
HHKFLHSC	T'ang-ngo (1285–1373). *Hsin-hsiu k'o fen liu-hsüeh seng chuan*. *ZZK* 133.210–490.
HJAS	*Harvard Journal of Asiatic Studies*.
HSLAC	*Hsien-shün Lin-an chih* (published in 1268). [Rare Books, Peiping National Library.] Microfilm roll 304.
HSYL	Shih Wen-ying. *Hsiang-shan yeh-lu*. In Tsao Ch'iu-yüeh, ed., *Hsüeh-hai lei-pien*. Taipei: Taiwan wen yüan shu chü, 1964. Vol. 6.
LHSC	*Lung-hsing (hsiang fu chieh t'an) szu chih*. In Ting Ping (1832–

1899), compiler, *Wu-lin chuang ku ts'ung pien* (dated 1883–1900). Vol. 16.

RK　　　　Gyōnen (1240–1321). *Risshū kōyō* (published in 1306). *T* 74.5–20.

ROSBD　　*Ritsuon sōbōden* (published in 1689). In *Dai Nihon Bukkyō zensho*. Tokyo: Dai Nihon Bukkyō zensho hakkōsho, 1913–1922. Vol. 105.

RSGKS　　Gyōnen (1240–1321). *Risshū gyōkanshō* in *Dai Nihon Bukkyō zensho*. Tokyo: Dai Nihon Bukkyō zensho hakkōsho, 1913–1922. Vol. 105.

SJISHP　　Ting Ch'uan-ching, ed. *Sung-jen i-shih hui-pien*. Peiping: Shan wu yin shu kuan, 1935.

SKCC　　Wu Jen-ch'en (1628–1689?). *Shih-kuo Ch'un-ch'iu*. Taipei: Kuo lao shu chu, 1962.

SKSC　　Tsan-ning. *Sung Kao seng chuan* (published in 988). *T* 50.709–900.

SMCT　　Tsung-chien. *Shih-men cheng-t'ung* (published in 1237). *ZZK* 130.357–463.

SSINL　　Ch'en Yüan. *Chung-kuo Fo-chiao shih chi kai-lun*. Peking: K'o hsüeh ch'u pan she, 1955.

SSL　　　Tsan-ning (919–1001). *Seng shih lüeh*. *ZZK* 150.234–257.
WLHHKSSL　Yüan-fu and Yüan-ching. *Wu-lin Hsi-hu kao seng shih lüeh* (published in 1256). *ZZ* 134.233–240.

　　1. Jan Yün-hua, "Buddhist Historiography in Sung China," *Zeitschrift der Deutschen Morgenländischen Gesellschaft* 114 (2) (1964): 362.

　　2. Stanley Weinstein, "Imperial Patronage in the Formation of T'ang Buddhism," in *Perspectives on the T'ang*, Arthur F. Wright and Denis Twitchett, eds. (New Haven: Yale University Press, 1973), pp. 274–291.

　　3. Arthur F. Wright, "The Formation of Sui Ideology, 581–604," in *Chinese Thought and Institutions*, John K. Fairbank, ed. (Chicago: University of Chicago Press, 1957), pp. 71–104.

　　4. *Wu-lin chuang ku ts'ung pien*, compiled by Ting Ping (1832–1899), is a treasure trove of information on Tsan-ning. In that collection the following works have information pertaining to Tsan-ning's various writings: vol. 26, *Shun-yu Lin-an chih*, chüan 4, pp. 14b and 15a; vol. 16, *Lung-hsing szu chih*, chüan 6, pp. 1b, 2a, 10a–b, 12a–b, 13b, 14a–b, 15a, 17a, 20a, 21b, 23b, and 24a. See also the *Wu-ch'ao hsiao-shuo ta kuan*, vol. 3, pp. 271–273, and Makita Tairyō, "Sannei toso no jidai" [Tsan-ning and his age], in his *Chūgoku kinsei bukkyōshi kenkyū* [Studies on Chinese Buddhist history in the recent period] (Kyoto, 1957), pp. 109–110.

　　5. *Chung-kuo Fo-chiao shih kai-shuo*, translated into Chinese from the Japanese by Shih Sheng-yen (Taipei: Taiwan Shang-wu yin shu kuan, 1971), p. 125.

　　6. *Sung kao seng chuan*, *T* 50, pp. 709–900 (hereafter *SKSC*); *Seng shih lüeh*, *HTC* 150, pp. 234–257 (hereafter *SSL*).

　　7. Jan Yün-hua, "Tsung-mi," *T'oung Pao* 58 (1972): 19.

　　8. *SKSC*, chüan 8, p. 756b.

　　9. Ibid., chüan 14, p. 790a.

　　10. Ibid., chüan 17, pp. 819c–820a.

　　11. Ts'ao Shih-pang, "Chung-kuo Fo-chiao shih-ch'uan yu mu-lu yüan ch'u

Lu-hsüeh sha-men chih t'an-t'ao" [A study on Chinese Buddhist biographies and bibliographies derived from the Vinaya sect, p. 3], *Hsin-ya hsüeh-pao* 7 (2) (August 1966): 145.

12. See Weinstein, "Imperial Patronage," p. 287, on the intention of Chih-i's classification.

13. For Tsan-ning's comments on the offering of incense at state ceremonies, see *SSL*, p. b, pp. 241b–242a. In the *Shih-men cheng-t'ung, HTC* 130, pp. 450b–451a, Tsan-ning is praised for "protecting the dharma" by his careful investigations into Buddhist history.

14. See Tsan-ning's essay on "Non-Buddhist Studies" in *SSL*, p. a, pp. 240c–241a.

15. Makita, "Sannei toso," p. 113.

16. Ibid., pp. 124–126.

17. *SSL*, p. b, p. 247a–b.

18. Ibid., p. a, p. 235a–b; Makita, "Sannei toso," pp. 114–115.

19. *SSL*, pp. 234c–235a.

20. *The Zen Teaching of Hui Hai on Sudden Illumination*, John Blofeld, trans. (New York: Samuel Weiser, 1962), p. 103.

21. Wang Yü-ch'eng, *Hsiao hsü chi, Kuo-hsüeh chi-pen ts'ung-shu szu-pai chung* vol. 277 (Taipei: 1968), *chüan* 20, p. 282 (hereafter *HHC*); Shih Tsung-chien, *Shih-men cheng-t'ung, HTC* 130, p. 450a (hereafter *SMCT*); Yüan-fu and Yüan-ching, *Wu-lin Hsi-hu Kao seng shih lüeh, HTC* 134, p. 239b (hereafter *WLHHKSSL*). There are other relevant sources, but for the most part this study concerns itself with Sung dynasty sources.

22. *HHC, chüan* 20, p. 282; *SMCT*, p. 450a; *WLHHKSSL*, p. 239b.

23. *HHC, chüan* 20, p. 282.

24. *HHC, chüan* 20, p. 282; *SMCT*, p. 450a.

25. Shih Wen-ying, *Hsiang-shan yeh-lu (Hsüeh-hai lei-pien*, p. 3714), 3.5b. *(HSYL)*; Ting Ch'uan-ching, ed., *Sung-jen i-shih hui-pien* (Peking: Shang-wu yin shu kuan, 1935), *chüan* 20, p. 1024 (hereafter *SJISHP*).

26. The *SJISHP* gives Wang Ch'u-na as his name; as such his biography can be found in the *Sung-shih (Szu-pu pei-yao), chüan* 461, p. 2a–b.

27. *HSYL*, 3.5–6; *SJISHP, chüan* 20, p. 1024. It should be noted that if Ch'ien Wen-mu did visit Tsan-ning's home at the time of his birth, A.D. 919, he was not yet "king of Wu-Yüeh," as his reign was from 932 to 947. See Edouard Chavannes, "La Royaume de Wou et de Yue," *T'oung pao* 17 (1916): 131.

28. I have, as yet, been unable to account for the difference in Wang's given name, Chia-na, as it appears in the *HSYL* and his given name of Ch'u-na as it appears in the *Sung-shih*.

29. There is some variation among the sources over Tsan-ning's birth date. See Ch'en Yüan, *Shih-shih i-nien lu* (Peking: Chung-hua shu chu, 1964), pp. 195–196, for an excellent discussion of Tsan-ning's birth and death dates. In both cases I have followed Ch'en conclusions (hereafter Ch'en, *SSINL*.) With regard to Tsan-ning's birthplace the Sung dynasty sources, *HHC, SMCT,* and *HLHHKSSL,* all agree on Hangchou's Te-ch'ing district. The later sources differ in specifying exactly where in Hangchou, but the majority give the Te-ch'ing district.

30. As I have noted in my article dealing with Tsan-ning's introduction to his *Biographies of Eminent Monks,* becoming a monk at such an early age was not unusual in traditional China. See Albert A. Dalia, "Tsan-ning's Lives of Eminent

Monks, Sung Dynasty Edition," *Journal of Buddhist Culture* (Taipei) 2 (June 1973): 31, n. 13.

31. Wang Yü-ch'eng, a contemporary of Tsan-ning, gives no place name. The other Sung dynasty sources all give Hangchou's Hsiang-fu monastery. When Tsan-ning became a novice, however, the Hsiang-fu monastery was named the Lung-hsing monastery; later, during the Hsiang-fu period (1008–1016) of the Sung dynasty, the emperor changed its name to correspond with that of the reign period. See *HHC, chüan,* 20, p. 282; *SMCT, chüan* 8, p. 450a; *WLHHKWSL,* p. 239b; *Hsien-shün Lin-an chih* (Rare Books, Peiping National Library, microfilm roll 304), *chüan* 70, p. 9a (hereafter *HSLAC*); *Lung-hsing szu chih* (*Wu-lin chuang ku ts'ung pien,* vol. 16) preface, p. 1a, *chüan* 7, pp. 4b–5a, and *chüan* 9, p. 1a (hereafter *LHSC*). The *LHSC* is a treasury of references to Tsan-ning. In *chüan* 6 alone, nineteen works are attributed to Tsan-ning; references for each work are given and in many cases they are commented upon.

32. *HHC, chüan* 20, p. 282.

33. Chou Yi-liang, "Tantrism in China," *HJAS* 8 (1944–1945): 248, n. 30. Jan, "Buddhist Historiography," pp. 362–363, seems to ignore this statement when he says: "During the year 934, he received full commandments at the T'ien-t'ai shan when he was fifteen."

34. The *HHC, WLHHKSSL,* and *HSLAC* say he was an expert in the Nan-shan (Southern Mountain) Vinaya school. *SMCT* mentions only that he was an expert in *vinaya* studies.

35. *HSLAC, chüan* 70, p. 9a. According to the *Chung-wen ta tz'u-tien* (Taipei, 1973), vol. 1, p. 1466, no. 627, the phrase *liu chi* has two meanings: (1) the six Confucian classics and (2) six particular Buddhist sutras. As used here, however, followed as it is by the reference to the "histories," there is no doubt that the first meaning is the proper one. (Hereafter *Chung-wen ta tz'u-tien* is referred to as *CWTTT.*)

36. *HHC, chüan* 20, p. 282; *SMCT,* p. 450a; *WLHHKSSL,* p. 239b; *HSLAC, chüan* 70, p. 9a; Fa-tao, "Chung-k'ai Seng shih lüeh hsu," *HTC* 150, p. 234b.

37. The Buddhist sources have always emphasized the pro-Buddhist bias of the Wu-Yüeh kingdom, and one could argue that they imply a direct relationship between that bias and the success at court of Buddhist monks. This emphasis contrasts with the "secular" histories. As Edouard Chavannes observes: "It remains finally to speak of Buddhism which, in the Chinese works, is generally passed over in silence." But this is more or less to be expected. See Chavannes, "Le Royaume," p. 140. What is rather odd is that of all the aspects of Tsan-ning's life his relationship with his teachers is the least developed by all the sources. Only six sources even indicate who his teachers were; and of these, three sources are merely genealogical charts.

38. Chavannes, "Le Royaume," p. 132. Chavannes's article, essentially a translation in French of the sections of the *Chiu wu-tai shih, Wu-tai shih,* and *Sung shih* relevant to the history of the Wu-Yüeh kingdom, gives ample illustrations of this point. Makita, "Sannei toso," p. 103, on the other hand, stresses both diplomatic and geographic reasons for the kingdom's success at remaining independent.

39. This survey represents a rather free translation of a portion of *Chung-kuo Fo-chiao shih kai-shuo,* Shih Sheng-yen trans., p. 106. While there were few great developments within the Buddhism of the Five Dynasties region, moreover, this is not to say that there were no great political developments. According to

Wang Gungwu's study, *The Structures of Power in North China During the Five Dynasties* (Stanford: Stanford University Press, 1967), it was within the Five Dynasties that the foundations of the Sung government were laid.

40. See Weinstein, "Imperial Patronage," pp. 265–306, for an examination of this trend in the Sui-T'ang period.

41. *Fo-tsu t'ung-chi, T* 49.206b–c. For information on both the *FTTC* and its compiler, Chih-p'an, see Jan, "Buddhist Historiography," pp. 371–372. For information on the archeological aspects of the Wu-Yüeh kingdom's Buddhist construction projects see Henri Maspéro, "Rapport Sommaire sur une Mission Archéologique au Tcho-Kiang," *Bulletin de l'École Française d'Extrême-Orient* 14 (1914): 1–70. Included in Maspéro's report are pictures of one of the 84,000 miniature stupas made in honor of King Aśoka. For information on King Chung-i's mission to Japan and Korea see *FTTC*, 206c.

42. Chavannes, "Le Royaume," p. 193; *Chiu wu-tai shih, chüan* 133, p. 8a–b.

43. Chavannes, "La Royaume," p. 170; *Hsin wu-tai shih (Erh-shih-szu shih), chüan* 67, p. 7b.

44. *HHC, chüan* 20, p. 282. With regard to Hui-cheng and the *wen-ke* style of literature, see Makita, "Sannei toso," n. 30, paraphrasing from Hui-cheng's biography in *Hsien chü pien, HTC* 101, *chüan* 10, pp. 412–413 (hereafter *HCP*). Makita says that Hui-cheng, during the confusion of the Five Dynasties period, maintained the traditional way of classical studies and developed the *wen-ke* style. I have been unable to discover a suitable definition of *wen-ke*. Although Wang Yü-ch'eng uses this term *(HHC)* it does not appear in the *HCP* or any other biography of Hui-cheng. In ordinary usage it would mean "to style literary compositions." The only other biography of Hui-cheng that I have found appears in a Ch'ing dynasty work by Wu Jen-ch'en: *Shih-kuo Ch'un-ch'iu* (Taipei: Kuo lao shu chu, 1962), *chüan* 89, p. 12b. It simply states that he was an expert in poetry and literature. The only mention of Kung Lin that I have found is the one made here by Wang Yü-ch'eng. For a detailed study of Hui-cheng's life and his relationship with Tsan-ning see Albert A. Dalia, "Tsan-ning (919–1001 A.D.): The 'Political Career' of a Buddhist Monk" (M.A. thesis, University of Hawaii, 1976), pp. 45–56.

45. Wang also states that Ch'i-ning was a master of *"shu i chih,"* which seems to be some form of literature, but I have been unable to identify it or find anything else about Ch'i-ning. Furthermore, Wang states that Ts'ung-i's essays were refined and clever. Wang gives Ts'ung-i's name as Ch'ang Ts'ung-i, while the *Lung-hsing szu chih, chüan* 6, p. 17a, gives it as Yung-ch'ang Ts'ung-i; but I have been unable to find any other references to him. Wang sums up this passage by saying that they were then known as the "Four Tigers." This seems to be a mistake as only three "tigers" are mentioned. Makita, "Sannei toso," p. 105, adds to the confusion when, obviously quoting from Wang, he gives Wu-en as the "Tiger of Meanings" and thus the fourth "tiger." Neither Wu-en nor the name Tiger of Meanings is mentioned in Wang's *HHC* preface to Tsan-ning's collected works. Moreover, Makita does not indicate his source of information for this "fourth tiger." Furthermore, he gives Ts'ung-i's name as I-ts'ung. A biography of Wu-en can be found in the *Ch'ih-hsiu che-chiang t'ung-chih*, vol. 17, *chüan* 198, p. 13a; there is no mention of a Tiger of Meaning.

46. Makita, "Sannei toso," p. 105. Kuan-hsiu died in 912, Ling-che (more commonly referred to as Seng-ch'e) died in 452, Ch'i-chi died near the end of the Later T'ang's Ch'ang-hsing period (930–933); see Ch'en, *SSINL*, pp. 165, 15,

and 174 respectively. None of my sources relates any of these monks directly with Tsan-ning. But it is interesting to note that Kuan-hsiu and Ch'i-chi both have biographies in the *Sung kao seng chuan,* which would indicate Tsan-ning's awareness of them. See *SKSC, chüan* 30, for both their biographies.

47. *HHC, chüan* 20, p. 282.

48. Weinstein, "Imperial Patronage," p. 277.

49. For a detailed study of Hsi-chüeh's life and his relationship with Tsan-ning see Dalia, "Tsan-ning," pp. 57–90.

50. Ibid., p. 57. The earliest biography of Hsi-chüeh appears in *SKSC, chüan* 16, p. 801b–c.

51. *Chiu wu-tai shih, chüan* 133, p. 8b; see also Chavannes, "Le Royaume," p. 198.

52. *SKSC, chüan* 16, p. 810c.

53. Ibid.

54. Ibid., *chüan* 7, p. 750a.

55. Ibid., *chüan* 13, p. 788a.

56. *FTTC, chüan* 10, p. 206c.

57. *SKCC, chüan* 89, p. 4b. See Chang Chung-yüan, *The Original Teachings of Ch'an Buddhism* (New York: Pantheon Books, 1969), pp. 251–252, for an excellent translation of Yen-shou's biography from the *Transmission of the Lamp.*

58. For the biographies of Ch'ien Chan, Ch'ien I, and Ch'ien Yen, see *Shih-kuo Ch'un-ch'iu,* vol. 3, *chüan* 83 (hereafter *SKCC*). The biography of King Chung-hsien's eldest son Ch'ien Yü is also in *SKCC, chüan* 83.

59. *SKSC, chüan* 13, p. 789b.

60. Both the *SKCC* and the *Wu-lin Ling-yin szu chih* relate this story. See *SKCC, chüan* 89, p. 7b, in Tsan-ning's biography; see *Wu-lin Ling-yin szu chih* (*Wu-lin chang ku ts'ung pien,* vol. 11), *chüan* c, p. 27a, in an essay titled "Treatise on Tide Control by the Ling-yin Monks." While neither the *SKSC* nor any of Yen-shou's other biographies that I have seen mention this story, both Tsan-ning, if only in his capacity as monk administrator, and Yen-shou undoubtedly were aware of each other through their relationship with King Chung-i.

61. See Dalia, "Tsan-ning," pp. 50–51.

62. *CTCTL, chüan* 26, p. 423b.

63. Weinstein, "Imperial Patronage"; this is a central theme that runs throughout his study.

64. *HHC, chüan* 20, p. 282.

65. *SMCT, chüan* 8, p. 450a.

66. For the four biographies in the *SKSC* that mention Tsan-ning's position, see *SKSC, chüan* 13, p. 789b; *chüan* 16, p. 810c; *chüan* 22, p. 852b; and *chüan* 27, p. 880c. See also Makita, "Sannei toso," p. 105. For the *Outline History of the Sangha* reference see *Seng shih lüeh, HTC* 150, p. 243c.

67. The most informative source dealing with the period under consideration here is the *SKSC.* Tsan-ning appears in five of its biographies, where he is found primarily engaged in the writing of epitaphs for the government or on his own initiative. See *SKSC, chüan* 13, p. 789b; *chüan* 16, pp. 809a and 810c; *chüan* 22, p. 852b; and *chüan* 27, p. 880c. See also Makita, "Sannei toso," pp. 105–106.

68. See *Hsin wu-tai shih, chüan* 67, p. 4b, which corresponds to Chavannes, "Le Royaume," p. 154. The title was *Chen-hai chen-tung chün chieh-tu shih.* For his other title see the *Sung shih, chüan* 480, p. 1a, which corresponds to

Chavannes, "Le Royaume," p. 209. The title was *Hang-yüeh liang-fan chieh chih* and was granted in conjunction with an appointment as commander of P'eng-ch'eng Chün (in present-day Chiangsu). Both positions were granted by the emperor of the T'ang dynasty, Chao-tsung (r. 888–904).

69. See *Sung shih, chüan* 480, p. 1a, for T'ai-tsu's granting of the title and pp. 1a–4a for Chung-i's relations with T'ai-tsu.

70. Ibid., *chüan* 480, p. 4a; Chavannes, "Le Royaume," pp. 224–225, translates this memorial.

71. In 975 King Chung-i (or Ch'ien Ch'u) sent his general-in-chief with troops to join with imperial forces in pacifying the Jun Chou area in present-day Chiangsu. The king was duly rewarded for his aid in pacifying the "Chiang-tso" region. See *Sung shih, chüan* 480, pp. 2a and 2b, respectively; see also Chavannes, "Le Royaume," pp. 215–217.

72. It does, however, mention an interesting incident between King Chung-i and a monk named Te-chao. Chung-i was prefect of T'ai Chou (in present-day Chekiang) before he ascended the Wu-Yüeh throne. At that time the monk Te-chao reportedly urged him to offer his submission to the Chin dynasty. See *Sung shih, chüan* 480, p. 1a; Chavannes, "Le Royaume," pp. 209–210.

73. J. J. M. De Groot, *Sectarianism and Religious Persecution in China* (reprint ed.; Taipei: Literature House, 1963), pp. 71–77, for the text of both the *Chiu wu-tai shih* and the *Hsin wu-tai shih* with De Groot's translations regarding the Later Chou "reformation" of Buddhism.

74. If this is the case, however, one must point out that this reaction was more complex than the impression given by the *FTTC*.

75. *FTTC, chüan* 43, p. 394c.

76. Ibid., *chüan* 42, p. 393a.

77. Kenneth K. S. Chen, *Buddhism in China* (Princeton: Princeton University Press, 1964), p. 400.

78. Wright, "The Formation," pp. 93–94.

79. *Chung-kuo fo-chiao shih kai-shuo,* trans. Shih Sheng-yen, pp. 115 and 122–124.

80. *FTTC, chüan* 42, p. 393a.

81. Wright, "T'ang T'ai-tsung and Buddhism," p. 263.

82. A. L. Basham, *The Wonder That Was India* (New York: Grove Press, 1954), pp. 54–56. Basham (p. 54) says that Aśoka "by no means gave up his imperial ambitions, but modified them in accordance with the humanitarian ethics of Buddhism." This is not to say that the rulers mentioned here had identical policies toward Buddhism; rather their concerns, as rulers, were of necessity similar.

83. *HHC,* p. 282.

84. *SMCT, chüan* 8, p. 450a; *FTTC, chüan* 43, p. 397c.

85. *Sung shih, chüan* 480, p. 4a.

86. *SKSC, chüan* 27, p. 880b–c; Makita, "Sannei toso," p. 106.

87. *HHC* does not mention this appointment. The earliest mention that I have seen appears in the *SMCT* (1237) biography of Tsan-ning.

88. *Taishō shinshū daizōkyō sakuin,* vol. 28. Reference was made to the entries listed under *Han-lin, Han-lin yüan,* and *Han-lin hsüeh shih.* Under the first category the reference to Yüan-cheng was found: *Shih chien chi ku lüeh hsü chi, T* 49, *chüan* 2, p. 927a.

89. *FTTC, chüan* 43, p. 397c; *SMCT, chüan* 8, p. 450a.

90. *FTTC, chüan* 43, p. 397c.

91. For Wang's works pertaining to Tsan-ning see *HHC* (Shanghai: *Szu-pu ts'ung-k'an chi pu,* Shang-wu yin shu kuan), *chüan* 7, pp. 11a and 13a–b. Other references to his admiration for Tsan-ning can be found in the prefaces to Tsan-ning's work the *Seng shih lüeh,* p. 234a–b, and also in *FTTC, chüan* 44, p. 402b–c. For Hsü Hsuan's poem see *Hsü-kung chi* (Shanghai: *Szu-pu pei-yao chi pu,* Chung-hua shu chu), *chüan* 22, p. 3a. See also Ts'ao, "Chung-kuo," p. 3, pp. 125–126, for more information on Wang's attitude toward Tsan-ning and Buddhism in general.

92. Ou-yang Hsiu, in his *Liu i shih hua,* p. 2b, relates an interesting incident that, even if true, I would not consider to be an example of further criticism of Tsan-ning by his contemporaries. The tone of the story is certainly that of a good-natured give-and-take between a scholarly monk and a ranking official. Ou-yang Hsiu himself does criticize Tsan-ning for being a "comedy actor"; this comment relates to Tsan-ning's advice to Sung T'ai-tsu about whether or not the Chinese emperor should bow to an image of Buddha. The problem here is that as far as we know Tsan-ning never met Sung T'ai-tsu. See Ou-yang Hsiu, *Kuei T'ien lu, chüan* 1, p. 1a. For the Buddhist reaction to this story see *FTTC, chüan* 44, p. 405a–b. Ts'ao, "Chung-kuo," p. 3, pp. 125–126, has some interesting comments on Ou-yang Hsiu's attitudes toward Buddhism.

93. *FTTC, chüan* 43, p. 398c. Both the *HHC* and the *SMCT* mention the same year. The *FTTC,* done in chronicle style, attempts a more precise dating through the indication of both month and year.

94. See Ts'ao, "Chung-kuo," p. 3, pp. 128–136, especially pp. 131–132, for this particular aspect of the *SKSC* and for a good treatment of the work in general. Unfortunately we cannot involve ourselves here in a discussion of the *SKSC,* for it would take a separate study to do justice to it.

95. *SSL,* p. 225a.

96. *FTTC, chüan* 43, p. 400a. The *HHC* (Taipei edition) and the *SMCT* mention these incidents without dating them. The latter quotes from a poem by Wan Yü-ch'eng written on the occasion of the completion of the *SKSC.* The emperor's memorial can be found in *T* 50.709b. Wang's poem is in the *HHC* (Shanghai edition), *chüan* 7, pp. 13a–b.

97. *SSL, chüan* a, p. 225a. Tsan-ning refers to the "eastern monastery," but since this was immediately after his presenting of the *SKSC* to T'ai-tsung (988) and the only monastery that he was appointed to in 988 was the T'ien-shou monastery, I assume that Tsan-ning was referring to the T'ien-shou monastery (possibly because it was situated in the eastern part of the capital). Furthermore, the first preface to the *SSL, chüan* a, p. 244a, states that after Tsan-ning was moved to the T'ien-shou monastery, he was ordered to write the *SSL.* Jan, "Buddhist Historiography," p. 363, says that the *SSL* was started in 989 and then revised in 991, but he gives no references for the latter date. See also Makita, "Sannei toso," p. 113.

98. *FTTC, chüan* 43, p. 400b; see also Jan, "Buddhist Historiography," p. 363. I have used his translation of the title of Tsan-ning's work here. The *HHC* (Taipei edition) places this work some time between Tsan-ning's being ordered to the T'ien-shou monastery (988) and his next appointment (990), but, as Ch'en Yüan points out, Wang mistook it as a separate book when it is actually a section of the *San-chiao sheng-hsien shih chi.* See Ch'en Yüan, *Chung-kuo Fo-chiao shih chi kai-lun,* pp. 35–36. The *SMCT* mentions Su I-chien and the compilation of this

work after Tsan-ning's appointment in 1000; however, Su I-chien died in 995. See Jan, "Buddhist Historiography," p. 363. The *SMCT* also follows the *HHC* in mistaking the *Chiu-ling shen-hsien lu* as a separate book. The *WLHHKSSL* (1256), p. 239b, adds further to the confusion by attributing the compilation of the *San-chiao sheng-hsien shih chi* solely to Tsan-ning. Of the extant Sung dynasty works of relevance here, only the *FTTC* seems to have stated the situation correctly.

99. *FTTC*, p. 400b. The *HHC* mentions the appointment but does not date it; the *SMCT* does not mention it; the *WLHHKSSL* follows the *HHC*. The positions of some high government officials were ranked in terms of the location of their offices on the left (lower rank) or right (higher rank) side of the imperial palace.

100. *FTTC, chüan* 43, p. 400c. The text literally reads: "Commanded to the Han-lin Academy, Tsan-ning filled the History Office post of compiler." However, the title *Shih-kuan pien-hsiu* can also mean "second-class Han-lin compiler." Neither *HHC* nor *WLHHKSSL* mentions this appointment. The *Hsien-shun Lin-an chih* (1268), *chüan* 70, p. 9a, records the appointment and gives the same date as the *FTTC;* the *SMCT* dates this appointment 991.

101. *FTTC, chüan* 43, p. 401b. Both *HHC* and *SMCT* give the date as 995. However, Tsan-ning in his postscript to the *SKSC* gives the date of this appointment as 996; see *SKSC, chüan* 30, p. 900a.

102. For Li Fang's biography see the *Sung shih, chüan* 265, pp. 1–6, and specifically pp. 5a–b for reference to the association. In the *CWTTT*, vol. 1, p. 495, no. 145, *Chiu-Lao Hui,* references are given to Po Chü-i's role in establishing the original association and to Li Fang's organization. The *Jung-chai sui-pi,* collection 4, *chüan* 12, pp. 10b–11a, has a section titled *Chih-tao Chiu-Lao.* For the monk Ju-man see *Chung-kuo Fo-hsüeh jen-ming tz'u-tien,* p. 108, no. 0843. The *HHC* contains an extensive reference to his association.

103. For Kenneth Ch'en's comments see *Buddhism in China,* p. 257. For Tsan-ning's appointment see *FTTC, chüan* 44, p. 402a. The *HHC, SMCT,* and *WLHHKSSL* all agree here with the *FTTC.* For Ennin's comments see *Ennin's Diary,* trans. E. O. Reischauer (New York: Ronald Press, 1955), p. 75. For Tsan-ning's own comments on the position of monk secretary, see *SSL, chüan* b, pp. 243c–244a.

104. The *HHC* makes no mention of this appointment. The *SMCT* and the *HSLAC* both date the appointment in 1000. I have used the *FTTC*'s date of 999 simply because that source has proved to be consistently careful in its use of source material; furthermore, the difference here is not that significant. See *FTTC, chüan* 44, p. 402a.

105. The *HHC* (Taipei edition), *chüan* 20, p. 283, says that at the age of eighty-two Tsan-ning's faculties had not deteriorated and then goes on to mention his long service to both the Wu-Yüeh and the Sung houses. The *SMCT* says that he died in the year after his appointment to the Left Street (1001). The *WLHHKSSL* gives the year 996. The best discussion of Tsan-ning's death dates is to be found in Ch'en Yüan, *SSINL,* pp. 195–196. Ch'en settles on the date 1001. I have relied upon both Ch'en and the *FTTC, chüan* 44, p. 402b. A eulogy of Tsan-ning can also be found after the notice of his death in the *FTTC.* Makita, "Sannei toso," p. 108, gives the date as 1002.

106. *Wu-lin chiu shih* (*Wu-lin chang ku ts'ung pien,* vol. 2), *chüan* 5, p. 9b; *Lung-ching chien wen lu* (*Wu-lin chang ku ts'ung pien,* vol. 13), *chüan* 3, pp.

10a–b. Makita, "Sannei toso," p. 108, gives the date 1029 but provides no reference. The *SMCT* notes the district where Tsan-ning was buried.

107. *SMCT, chüan* 8, p. 450b; *WLHHKSSL*, p. 239b. The *HSLAC*, p. 9b, gives the date 1104; see also Makita, "Sannei toso," p. 108. The *FTTC, chüan* 46, pp. 418–419, with regard to the Ch'ung-ning period (1102–1106), does not mention anything that relates to Tsan-ning. The first preface to the *SSL* gives the date 1105, as does the second preface, *SSL*, pp. 234a and 235a, respectively.

9

Ta-hui and Lay Buddhists:
Ch'an Sermons on Death

MIRIAM LEVERING

Ching-shan Ta-hui Tsung-kao P'u-chüeh Ch'an-shih, usually known as Ta-hui or Tsung-kao, was a teacher in the Yang-ch'i branch of the Lin-chi line of the Ch'an (or Zen) school.[1] He was born in 1089 to an Anwei family; his teaching career took place primarily in the southern part of China during the early Southern Sung period. During most of the latter part of his life he was one of the most influential Ch'an teachers of his time.[2] He had thousands of students, scores of dharma heirs, and many disciples among literati and officials.[3] His large following can be explained in part by the fact that he was the most prominent disciple of a famous teacher, Yüan-wu.[4] But more important were the vigor and accessibility of his personality and his teachings, as well as his success in bringing many students, both lay and monastic, to varying degrees of progress on the path to enlightenment.

Ta-hui made many contributions to the development of Ch'an theory and method: His teaching is best known for his contributions to the understanding of the *kung-an* (or *kōan*) as a means of concentrating and focusing doubt.[5] My purpose here is not to summarize his major contributions but to focus on one particular contribution: his development of the sermon form known as *p'u-shuo*. I have chosen this form and its use as the contribution of Ta-hui on which to focus attention because it illustrates Ta-hui's concern for the religious life and the enlightenment of laymen.

The fact that there were *p'u-shuo* sermons such as Ta-hui's in Ch'an monasteries suggests the existence of a new relationship between the laity and the Ch'an teacher. We can see five distinct steps in the development of these new relationships. First, laity could relate to teachers as "students outside the walls" on a one-to-one basis. We find this relationship of laity to Ch'an teachers throughout early Ch'an literature from the T'ang dynasty. Second, laity could be allowed to sponsor, for the sake of earning merits, events that would take place in the monastery whether they participated in them or not and which were unconnected with their own life in any specific way. This activity would include sponsoring talks on the dharma to the monks or offering meals. This relationship would reflect the view that the practice of laity, as distinct from that of a monk, consisted primarily in performing meritorious acts for the sake of their future happiness or that of their loved ones. Third, laity could ask that meritorious acts be performed on occasions other than the usual monastic occasions, as for example in a cycle of seven-day memorial offerings to earn merit for their deceased relatives or friends. The performing of the act was done specifically to meet their needs, but the content of the sermon or sutra reading need not do so. It appears that before Ta-hui's time and even afterward sermons on such occasions might mention directly neither the layperson, death, or grief. Fourth, a layman could join with other laity to form a society for performing acts of merit and for studying the dharma. The society would function under the aegis of the monastery and its teacher. Here laity might begin to require that their needs as people still living in the world be addressed by the monastic institution.

What we find with Ta-hui, however, is a fifth step—namely, addressing the needs of the lay sponsor not only in act or form but directly in the content of the sermon. This was clearly a sign of a new monastic concern for lay life, a new relationship sought out actively by Ta-hui himself. Thus Ta-hui's expansion of the *p'u-shuo* form and his new use for it can be seen as reflecting a new approach to the teaching of laity. Not only did Ta-hui reject the traditional approach that sought to distinguish between monks and laity by teaching monks practice and wisdom leading to enlightenment while teaching laity only about the truth of karma and the importance of merit; he also followed the Ch'an practice of teaching selected lay students about emptiness and enlightenment and initiating them in *kung-an* or *hua-t'ou* practice while continuing to assume that for the vast majority of laity the important teaching is karma and practices to accumulate merit. Ta-hui went as far as possible beyond the distinction between teaching and practice for laity and teaching and practice for monks. He encouraged all his lay hearers to understand the profound truth of emptiness and the Hua-yen doctrine of nonobstruction and to strive for enlightenment through *kung-an* or *hua-t'ou* practice.

I shall begin by focusing upon the *p'u-shuo* form itself, showing through a preliminary exploration of its history Ta-hui's original contribution to its development. Then we shall look closely at one *p'u-shuo* sermon to see how Ta-hui addressed the occasion of death and the emotions of bereavement on two levels in order to meet the immediate spiritual needs of grieving laity and to bring them to a higher understanding of the doctrine of emptiness and the path to enlightenment.

A SHORT HISTORY OF THE *P'u-shuo* FORM

The *p'u-shuo*, or "general preaching," was the last of three major sermon forms to be developed within the Ch'an monastery. Two earlier forms, the *shang-t'ang* and the *hsiao-ts'an*, are mentioned in the earliest recension of rules for Ch'an monasteries that remains to us, the *Ch'an-yüan ch'ing-kuei*, published in 1103.[6] The *p'u-shuo* clearly grew out of these forms and resembled them in many respects, especially until the influence of Ta-hui was generally felt.

For the *shang-t'ang*, the *Ch'an-yüan ch'ing-kuei* prescribed that the abbot of the Ch'an monastery should go to the dharma seat in the Dharma Hall six times a month and address the whole assembly of monks who would be seated formally before him. The fifth day of the month and all succeeding dates whose numbers were multiples of five were specified as the days for *shang-t'ang*.[7] For the *hsiao-ts'an* it was prescribed that preaching was to take place in the abbot's own quarters, the *fang-chang*, at least on the third, eighth, thirteenth, eighteenth, twenty-third, and twenty-eighth of the month.[8] Both forms of preaching were open to laity, who could attend them and also ask that they be given, perhaps in connection with a financial contribution. But the laity's part seems merely to have been to earn the merit of sponsoring a preaching of the law: Reference was rarely made in the abbot's remarks to the layperson himself or to anything specific in his situation or to laity in general.[9] Most commonly the abbot's remarks would be preceded by a question from monks and an ensuing exchange between monks and the abbot; alternatively the abbot himself would bring up a *kung-an* or make a remark of his own about the law and challenge his audience to understand, in the deepest sense, what he had said. For the most part these sermons were short, or so it seems from their recorded lengths; they were not vehicles for expanded discussion of a topic.[10] For the monk, or for the lay resident following the discipline of the monastery, every thought was already directed toward developing wisdom or clearing away ignorance. In the context of such concentrated practice extended sermons would almost certainly be unnecessary and might even be harmful, particularly if heard six or twelve times a month.

In the *Ch'an-yüan ch'ing-kuei* book of rules of 1103 the *p'u-shuo* form is not mentioned. Thus we may infer that the form was not in wide use prior to 1103. Short paragraphs describing the *p'u-shuo* form do appear in the next two extant rule books: the *Ch'an-lin pei-yüan ch'ing-kuei,* completed in 1311,[11] and the *Ts'ung-lin chiao-ting ch'ing-kuei tsung-yao,* published in 1274.[12] In the absence of contrary evidence this would seem to indicate that the form came into wide use between 1103 and 1274.

Did Ta-hui invent the *p'u-shuo* form? If not, what was the *p'u-shuo* like before his use of it? The accounts in these rule books written more than a hundred years after Ta-hui's death do not help us to answer these questions with any certainty, as they may tell us more about the *p'u-shuo* form as it developed after Ta-hui than about the form that Ta-hui invented or found and adapted as he began his own preaching. Nonetheless they do suggest the context in which the *p'u-shuo* preaching took place, and they make a historical remark. For the reader's convenience I quote here only the later and more complete of the two, that of the rule book of 1311, pointing out in the notes significant differences between the two similar texts:

> At all times when the *p'u-shuo* is given, an attendant orders the *k'o-t'ou* of the abbot's quarters [one whose duty it is to attend to guests][13] to hang up the sign of *p'u-shuo* in front of the Monks' Hall [the hall in which the monks lived] and the *Sangha* Hall [a hall in which the monks gathered to read sutras and eat and conduct other activities] and other halls, and also to arrange the seats in rows [for the *p'u-shuo*] in the Inner Hall or the Dharma Hall.[14] [The Inner Hall was apparently used for special ceremonies or lectures, the Dharma Hall for formal preaching of the law.] When the meal is finished, the *t'ang ssu hsing che* informs the attendant and then informs the abbot.[15] He strikes the drum five times. After the attendant leaves the Inner Hall he invites the assembly [of monks] to gather. He then goes in to invite the abbot to come out and take his seat.[16] The ceremonial for *p'u-shuo* is the same as that for *hsiao-ts'an.*[17] The teachers in the Ts'ao-tung line set up a seat in the *Sangha* Hall on the first and fifteenth of every month[18] and "speak generally" to the assembly. Only the monk Ta-hui, who had mastered both the essence of the teaching and the art of preaching, did not choose time or place [but gave *p'u-shuo* whenever or wherever it suited him].[19]

This account certainly suggests that although Ta-hui did use the form differently from his predecessors, he did not invent it.

A somewhat different historical account is given by Ta-hui himself:

> A hundred years ago there was no *p'u-shuo*. But in the period from Hsi-ning to Yüan-yu [between 1068 and 1094] when the monk Chen-ching lived at Tung-shan Kuei-tsung,[20] there began to be *p'u-shuo*. Chen-ching's great purpose was to bring students of the Way to enlightenment.[21]

This passage suggests that Chen-ching K'o-wen (1025–1102) was the originator of the *p'u-shuo* form in the Lin-chi school of Ch'an. Ta-hui's statement became the accepted view of the origin of the form in later tradition, as is evidenced by the following summary of the tradition on the subject by Muchaku Dōchū in Japan in 1716:

> *P'u-shuo* is a form of ascending the dharma seat [to preach]. *Shang-t'ang* is also [a form of] ascending the dharma seat. The difference is that in the *p'u-shuo* one does not burn incense or wear the dharma robe. The practice of *p'u-shuo* began with Chen-ching; the "three Buddhas" also practiced it. But only with Ta-hui did it begin to flourish. [22]

The historical accuracy of this traditional view is difficult to assess due to the nature of our sources. Chen-ching has left us a collection of "Recorded Sayings," but in them we find no record of a *p'u-shuo*. [23] The "three Buddhas" must refer to three disciples of the Lin-chi master Wu-tsu Fa-yen (?–1104) whose names or nicknames included the word "Buddha" (Fo): Yüan-wu K'o-ch'in in (1063–1135), known as Fo-kuo (Buddha Fruit); Fo-chien (Buddha Mirror) Hui-ch'in (1059–1117); and Fo-yen (Buddha Eye) Ch'ing-yüan (1067–1120). Of these three only two have left "Recorded Sayings" still extant, namely Yüan-wu and Fo-yen. [24] In both cases we do find *p'u-shuo*.

P'u-shuo by Ta-hui's Predecessors

What were *p'u-shuo* like before Ta-hui? How did they differ from *shang-t'ang* and *hsiao-ts'an*? To what extent were laity their sponsors? To what extent are the needs of laity reflected in their occasions, their form, or their content? The existence of *p'u-shuo* in the records of Yüan-wu and Fo-yen gives us some evidence with which to address these questions.

Yüan-wu (1063–1135) was perhaps the most eminent Ch'an teacher in the Lin-chi school during his lifetime. For this reason his "Recorded Sayings" are particularly extensive when compared to those of most of his contemporaries. Nevertheless we find in these records only one example of a *p'u-shuo*. This sermon in its recorded form runs some 1,400 words. [25] It is a straightforward discourse on the law and contains no specific reference to lay practice or to laity. A large part of it is an account of Yüan-wu's own search for the truth and his initial enlightenment experience. It is a lively and witty sermon describing certain fundamental truths of the dharma and the freedom that realization of them brings; it exhorts students to plunge in and realize these truths for themselves. It is, however, much longer than the average length of Yüan-wu's *shang-t'ang* or *hsiao-ts'an* as recorded; the former average 200 words and the latter 442 words.[26] It was also clearly given on a special occasion,[27] but there is no mention of lay sponsorship.

Yüan-wu's dharma-brother, Fo-yen (1067–1120), also left extensive "Recorded Sayings" that have survived to the present.[28] In them we find nine talks designated as *p'u-shuo* and thirty-nine talks recorded immediately after them under the heading of *shan-yü* (Good Words); these latter may or may not have been delivered as *p'u-shuo,* but since the format of the "Recorded Sayings" is ambiguous, and since they are identical in form and length to the nine that are clearly marked *p'u-shuo,* I shall consider them here tentatively as such. This impression is strengthened by the appearance immediately after them of a tenth clearly marked *p'u-shuo* that is further identified as having been given at the request of a layman.[29] The first nine *p'u-shuo* average 460 words each; the following thirty-nine average 420 words each. The final sermon for a layman is approximately 1,140 words; it is the second longest of the sermons.

In content none of Fo-yen's *p'u-shuo* (or *shan-yü*) make reference in the body of the sermon to a lay donor or to his situation, past history, or needs. The first of the nine *p'u-shuo,* for example, devotes most of its 320 words to types of Ch'an sickness, a subject of great interest to monks engaged in trying to "throw away body and mind" in the practice of *kung-an* inspection or silent concentration but of very little relevance to laity.[30] The forty-ninth sermon, the one designated as being given for a layman, seems to be similar in content and form to those that preceded it which were clearly addressed to "students of the Way," a term that in Fo-yen's sermons appears to refer only to those who had entered the monastery to study. More information about the layman or the context might reveal that the sermon was directed to the needs of the sponsoring layman, but no sign of such an intention appears in the text.

P'u-shuo by Ta-hui's Contemporaries

Hsü-t'ang Chih-yü (1185–1269) suggests that "since the 'three Buddhas' all [teachers] have had *p'u-shuo.*"[31] This remark raises the question whether Ta-hui's contemporaries also gave *p'u-shuo* sermons and, if so, whether their sermons differed in form, length, intended audience, or manner of address from those of Ta-hui's predecessors or from those of Ta-hui himself. To answer these questions I have made a preliminary survey of the surviving records of thirty-eight of Ta-hui's contemporaries and juniors in four different Ch'an schools.[32] The appendix presents the detailed results of this survey for the benefit of the reader who has greater curiosity about the history of the form. Here I offer only a summary of my findings in the following list and a few observations on the way in which the form was used during Ta-hui's lifetime:

I. *P'u-shuo* by Ta-hui's Predecessors in Existing Records:[33]
   1. Chen-ching K'o-wen (1025–1102): none
   2. Fo-chien Hui-ch'in (1059–1117): no record
   3. Fo-yen Ch'ing-yüan (1067–1120): nine (400 words average); thirty-nine (420 words average); one (1,140 words)
   4. Fo-kuo Yüan-wu K'o-ch'in (1063–1153): one (1,400 words)

II. *P'u-shuo* by Ta-hui's Approximate Contemporaries in Existing Records:[34]
   1. Hsüeh-t'ang Tao-hsing (1089–1151): two (280 words and 540 words)
   2. Shan-t'ang Seng-hsün (dates unknown): one (560 words)
   3. Hsüeh-feng Hui-k'ung (1096–1158): two (180 words and 400 words)
   4. Fo-hai Hui-yüan (1115–1169): three (1,280 words, 800 words, and 820 words)
   5. P'u-an Yin-su (1115–1169): one (1,120 words)
   6. Sung-yüan Ch'ung-yüeh (1132–1202): two (1,224 words and 700 words)

III. *P'u-shuo* by Ta-hui in Existing Records:[35]
   1. *P'u-shuo* in one *chüan:* fourteen (in some texts thirteen or fifteen) (2,503 words average)
   2. *P'u-shuo* in four *chüan:* sixty-six (2,294 words average)
   3. Total: eighty *p'u-shuo* (2,346 words average)

The first thing that may strike the reader on glancing at the list is that *p'u-shuo* sermons were recorded very infrequently: In most cases for a given teacher only one to three *p'u-shuo* were recorded. Were they in fact given so infrequently? It is possible that a much larger proportion of those given may not have been recorded than in the case of the *shang-t'ang* or *hsiao-ts'an* sermon forms. Thus one may presume that either *p'u-shuo* were infrequently given or else they were not regarded as a very serious occasion for teaching. This then raises the question of why so many more were recorded for Fo-yen and for Ta-hui than for any other teacher. Was it a matter of their skill with the form or their attitude toward it? Or was it simply that they gave *p'u-shuo* far more frequently than others did?

Second, *p'u-shuo* as recorded were generally short; the majority were recorded in well under a thousand words.

Third, *p'u-shuo* were not in wide use. In the records of thirty-eight of Ta-hui's contemporaries and juniors we have *p'u-shuo* by only six different teachers.

Fourth, the form for *p'u-shuo* was apparently identical to that of the *shang-t'ang* and *hsiao-ts'an:* All three most often began with a question and answer exchange between monk and teacher and then continued with comments by the teacher arising out of that exchange. Alternatively the teacher himself would bring up a *kung-an* or a remark on the law. It seems to be only in the ritual forms accompanying the *p'u-shuo* that it differs in structure from the *hsiao-ts'an* and *shang-t'ang*.

Fifth, the extant *p'u-shuo* were rarely recorded as having been sponsored by laity. Only the one sermon by Fo-yen refers to a lay sponsor.

Sixth, in the content of these *p'u-shuo* there is little indication that they were addressed to an audience that included laity. In some cases *p'u-shuo* may have been longer and more discursive than *shang-t'ang* by the same teacher, although not necessarily longer than the *hsiao-ts'an*. But the *p'u-shuo* do not refer in any way to the particular requirements of lay practice or lay life; even in the one case mentioning lay sponsorship we find no reference to the layman, to the occasion in his life that led him to sponsor the sermon, or to his intention in doing so. The strongest impression one receives on reading these sermons is that they were regarded primarily as devices for teaching monks, just as were the *shang-t'ang* and *hsiao-ts'an*.

Ta-hui's Use of the *P'u-shuo* Form

What we have seen of the use of the *p'u-shuo* form by predecessors and contemporaries of Ta-hui suggests that it was generally regarded as a sermon similar in form and purpose to the *shang-t'ang* and *hsiao-ts'an*, though perhaps less formal. Ta-hui's use of the *p'u-shuo* differs from his use of the *shang-t'ang* and *hsiao-ts'an* as well as from his colleagues' use of the *p'u-shuo*.[36] It is my contention here that these differences indicate a deliberate altering of the *p'u-shuo* form to enable it to serve the specific purpose of communication with lay or partly lay audiences.

First, many more of Ta-hui's *p'u-shuo* were recorded than had ever been the case before. We have approximately eighty *p'u-shuo* by Ta-hui in present records, including a volume of *p'u-shuo* in four *chüan* that circulated separately from his *Recorded Sayings*. As the reader has surely noted already, Fo-yen Ch'ing-yüan is the only other teacher among those surveyed who left a record of more than five *p'u-shuo*.

Second, Ta-hui's *p'u-shuo* average over 2,300 words in length—nearly double the length of the longest *p'u-shuo* prior to his time. In practice this means that Ta-hui allowed himself the scope to introduce a number of themes and develop a number of ideas. Whereas I have argued above that short sermons are more suited to the practice of monks, I am suggesting here that the lengthening of the form made the *p'u-shuo* more useful for addressing audiences that included laity.

Third, fifty-five of Ta-hui's eighty *p'u-shuo,* or 69 percent, are given at the request of laity.

Fourth, where a *p'u-shuo* is given at a layman's request, Ta-hui always acknowledges the lay sponsor by name and almost always refers also to the lay sponsor's intention to transfer the merit earned in sponsoring the *p'u-shuo* to another person or to use it to further the development of his own wisdom. This acknowledgment is not allowed to usurp the main function of teaching, but it is always made. When a monk or another teacher invites Ta-hui to preach, there is usually no reference to him in the *p'u-shuo* itself.

Fifth, and most important, Ta-hui departed from the usual practice in that he addressed the specific needs of the lay donor in the body of the sermon itself. Ta-hui almost always told his hearers more about the donor than his name; and when he saw that the occasion for the sponsorship reflected a personal need, as in sermons immediately following the death of a relative, he addressed the needs of the sponsor directly.

Ta-hui did not alter the outlines of the *p'u-shuo* form as he found it: His *p'u-shuo,* like those of his predecessors, begin with an exchange between himself and monks and then continue with a paragraph-long comment on some aspect of the questions or answers. His retention of these traditional openings shows that he was concerned to retain the meaning of the *p'u-shuo* as an occasion for the teaching of monks. But he simultaneously expanded the form, used it (or had it recorded) more frequently, and added remarks that made it a more direct means of addressing lay sponsors and lay needs.

How did Ta-hui himself conceive of the *p'u-shuo* form? Although it is tempting to read too much into it, one cannot help noting that Ta-hui's one recorded discussion of the *p'u-shuo* form itself pointed his listeners to the *Avataṃsaka Sutra:*

Now when the ancient [Chen-ching?] established this dharma-gate, he had a [scriptural] authority for doing so. How do we know? Do you not recall that in the *Avataṃsaka Sutra,* in the "Departing from the World" chapter, the bodhisattva P'u-hui raised like a cloud two hundred questions and the bodhisattva P'u-hsien poured forth two thousand answers? Among them there was the question: What is meant by the name *p'u-shuo san-chieh* [literally: to preach, universally, to the three worlds]? The answer was: Sons of the Buddha, bodhisattvas and mahāsattvas, there are ten kinds of preaching to the three worlds. What are the ten? In the world of the past to preach about the world of the past; in the world of the past to preach about the world of the future; in the world of the past to preach about the world of the present. In the world of the future to speak about the world of the past; in the world of the future to speak about the world of the present; in the world of the future to speak about the inexhaustible [the infinite]. In the present world to speak about the past; in the present world to speak about the future; in the present world to speak about equality. That makes nine worlds. In addition, if one sees one's own single thought as penetrating the nine worlds as if it were a string linking together a number of pearls, then this single thought binds all as the tenth world. Therefore it is said that in the present world one preaches to the three worlds, for this single thought makes them one.[37]

Let us restate the idea of this passage a little more concisely. One of the accomplishments of the bodhisattva—one that must at first seem mysterious, even miraculous—is to be able to preach to a variety of realms simultaneously, so that persons in different worlds all hear him at once. Here the separate worlds at issue are the worlds of the past, the present, and the future. P'u-hsien Bodhisattva explains that one thought in the present can contain and unite all the worlds of the past, present, and future, if that thought is the transcendent thought of the enlightened mind. To preach in the present through this one mind that unites them all is to preach in all nine modes at once.

We can connect this passage to a more immediate and mundane plane. If enlightened mind unites and communicates with all realms, and reveals their unity and interrelation within one indivisible totality, then it is possible to preach on different levels of understanding to mixed audiences and to transcend the distinction between monk and laity, between practice inside the monastery and practice beyond its walls. All the different audiences of monks and laity respond to preaching that comes from the one mind of enlightenment, for it is that one mind that penetrates and grounds their separate beings. Ta-hui grounded his understanding of his own mission in the world on the *Avataṃsaka's* stress on unity, generality, and totality: The title *"p'u-shuo"* and the scriptural authority that he cites are particularly suited to express his self-understanding and his intention in using the form.[38]

A SERMON FOR THE DEAD: THE OCCASION

Although many different occasions in the life of laity brought them to the monastery to sponsor *p'u-shuo,* and Ta-hui correspondingly addressed many different lay needs, among the most striking examples of *p'u-shuo* as "ministry" to laity are to be found in Ta-hui's sermons on the occasion of memorial offerings by laity on behalf of their dead relatives and friends.

Making offerings of wealth or of the law to earn merit for the dead is an ancient but controversial practice in Buddhism.[39] The idea that one can perform good acts and devote their good fruits to the future welfare of the dead is a development of the idea of merit as transferable, an idea that arose first in connection with the Buddha's offering gifts of his surplus merit to his disciples.[40] In the specific case of transfers to the dead, it was generally agreed that such transfers were most needed and most efficacious during the forty-nine days immediately after death when a dead person would be in an intermediate stage of existence *(chung-yin* or *chung-yu)* between his last birth and his next. In this period good karmic seeds sent to his aid might enable him to avoid the evil paths of existence and to be reborn in the human world or in one of the heavens.[41] It was customary during this period to offer a meal to monks and to sponsor a reading of sutras or a preaching of the law every seven days through the forty-ninth day after the person's death.[42] In Ta-hui's *P'u-shuo* we find three sermons recorded as given on the occasion of memorial offerings thirty-five, forty-two, and forty-nine days after the death of the donor's relative.

It was customary also to have a memorial service on the hundredth day after death; this was apparently a practice taken over from a similar Confucian custom and was generally known by its Confucian name, "the memorial of the end of weeping."[43] Confucians buried the body in its final resting place on this day, and on the following day they placed the memorial tablet of the deceased in the ancestral hall.[44] In the Confucian usage the service marked a transition from awareness of misfortune to hope for good fortune: On this day the deceased officially became an ancestor from whom his family could expect help.[45] Ta-hui followed the practice of conducting a service on the hundredth day, referring to the occasion by its Confucian name.[46] We also have records of sermons for the dead by Ta-hui that must have been offered well after the period of mourning had ended.[47]

The *p'u-shuo* sermon we shall examine was given by Ta-hui at the request of Sung official, T'ang Ssu-t'ui.[48] T'ang Ssu-t'ui held a number of important posts in the Sung government: At the time of Ta-hui's return from exile he held the positions of signatory official of the Bureau of Military Affairs and provisional executive of the Secretariat-Chancellery.[49] These high offices made him one of the four or five highest ranking officers of the state. T'ang's daughter, whom we know only as Lady T'ang, had recently died at age twenty-two. In the opening section of the sermon Ta-hui says that today's sermon is due to the intention of the minister to transfer merit to his deceased daughter Lady T'ang on the occasion of the forty-second day after her death. The purpose of this transfer is to contribute to her happiness in the world of the dead. To this end the minister has ordered Ta-hui to ascend the dharma-seat and propagate wisdom *(prajñā)*.

A Sermon for the Dead: The Teaching

What distinguished the way in which Ta-hui addressed laity on the subject of grief and death from the way he addressed monks? The first observation one can make is that the doctrines of karma, transmigration, and rebirth receive far more emphasis than one would expect in sermons addressed to monks.[50] In this sermon Ta-hui uses the doctrines of karma and transmigration as they apply to the case of Lady T'ang and others in order to comfort the bereaved. The deceased has led a good life and built up good karma toward enlightenment. The result has been a peaceful and clear mind at the time of death. This in turn is a definite sign of a desirable rebirth to come. Ta-hui says:

> I have heard that Lady T'ang's character was lofty and that she knew of the Buddha's teaching. She must in the past have planted the wisdom seeds of *prajñā* deeply, thereby being enabled in this life to believe in this great matter.[51] At the moment of abandoning consciousness she was clear in mind and died with her hands folded in the Amitābha *mudrā*. This is just what [Tsung-mi][52] talked about: "To do correct[53] things is awakened mind; awakened mind does not come from emotions. At death it can turn karma." He added a note to this: "Correctness is the correctness of principle *(i-li)*, not the correctness [righteousness] of benevolence and righteousness." If people follow correct principle in their actions, at the moment of death,[54] they will then be able to fold their hands and form a *mudrā* [and will feel] no pain or distress. If in life they follow correct principle, in death they will surely be able to turn the course of karma [for the better]. If so, then it is certain that they will be reborn in the Pure Land.[55] There is no possible doubt.

One need not grieve nor be apprehensive about the fate of one so protected by good karma. Death is no more than a transition, a taking off of old worn-out clothes and a donning a new ones:

> I have heard that your excellency has been in deep grief and that your excellency's pain and hurt have not yet ended. How can one use one's limited energy of spirit to weep for an insensible soul? For the dead lady, her death is like suddenly taking off worn-out garments she has been wearing for many years and then going to be reborn in a heaven or a Buddha-land or some other place. Since the dead and the living are separated, what is the use of crying?[56]

Turning to the reverse side of the coin, Ta-hui stresses in powerful images the terrors that death presents to one who has not prepared for it. Here his aim, of course, is not to comfort but to exhort his hearers to seek enlightenment:

> Tsung-mi went on to say: "That which does things with no correctness is crazed, confused mind. Crazed, disordered mind turns this way and that

according to feelings. At death it is entangled by karma." That is to say, when the four great elements part and scatter, and consciousness[57] becomes dark and confused, those who in their lifetimes were passionately attached to love are ensnared by love; those who were passionately attached to gold and precious jewels are ensnared by gold and jewels. At that time one's thoughts fly off like wild horses;[58] karmically determined consciousness rules one's mind, and ghosts and demons move in. This kind of person, because he has acted incorrectly and become entangled by karma, enters an evil rebirth. If there are no heavens, then that is that. If there are, then a superior man will be born there. If there are no hells, then that is that. If there are, then base men will enter them.

Here we find a subtle shift: No longer is it good karma which guarantees a safe and calm passage through the transition of death; it is the enlightened mind alone that can do so. Although good works lead to enlightenment, and thus are valuable, it is not enough to perform good works. One must actively seek enlightenment. Death comes quickly—if one does not haste to find enlightenment, one will be overcome by pain and confusion, fear and desire. Death is the moment of testing. However successfully one has maintained a façade of virtue and wisdom, it will fail one at the approach of death:

I often see men of the world loving pretense all their lives. When they come to the thirtieth day of the last month of the year [the day on which all accounts must be settled before the start of the new year, a metaphor for the day of death], all the sufferings of the five *skandhas* appear at once. At that time both their hands and their feet are revealed [that is, the reality behind the pretense becomes impossible to hide], for at times of drawing near to life and death, fortune and misfortune, pretense is both impossible and useless. Only the real thing will do.

What then is the "real thing" that can respond to the event of death? Ta-hui raises this question:

What is the "real thing"? For example, Lady T'ang was twenty-two years old this year. Tell me, twenty-two years ago, before she came to Minister T'ang's family to be born, where did she dwell?[59] If you do not know where she came from, then birth is a great matter. And did this great distress of her sudden death exist then or not? Her mind was clear and untroubled as if death were like throwing away old shoes—just where did this one moment [of her mind's activity] go? If you do not know where it went, then death is a great matter. Therefore it is said: "Impermanence [that is, death] is coming quickly; the question of life and death is a great matter."[60] A Confucian also said, "Death and life are great."[61]

Death is not only the moment of testing; it also poses the ultimate question, for death and birth are the ultimate riddles that confront the unenlightened mind. In one way, death for Ta-hui is perhaps the ultimate *hua-t'ou*. A person who does not know what will happen to him after death, not in the sense of where he will be reborn but in the sense of who he ultimately is, does not know the most important truth about himself. He is confused by his form, the worldly embodiment of his desires, and does not see into his true nature. The riddle of death is a form of the riddle of the meaning of existence that, if one is to be wise, he must confront and solve for himself. The fact of the inevitability of death and the shortness and unpredictability of our span in human form also determine the manner of our confrontation with the riddle of the meaning of existence. Death throws into high relief our ignorance and its consequences and imbues our search for wisdom with a sense of urgency. Thus the concern of death allows Ta-hui to arouse in his lay and clerical listeners the motivation to seek enlightenment.

Grief too is to be understood as an inevitable concomitant of the karmic bond between close relatives. It is one's karma from many births that causes one to be attached to one's child, for example:

> What parents love, how can they not long for? If this were so, then one's nature endowed by heaven could be destroyed. Moreover, body, hair, and skin are all inherited from our parents. When my body is in pain, then the body of my father and mother are also in pain. Since parents suffer pain this way, is it possible to talk about their not longing for and thinking [distractedly about departed children]?

Ta-hui's wisdom and compassion appear in his refusal to urge the bereaved not to grieve. Not to grieve, he says, would be unnatural. Instead, grieve with your whole mind, feel and express all of your feelings. When the feelings of grief exhaust themselves, in that still moment is your opportunity for reflection and enlightenment. The natural expression of grief leads to an occasion for the development of wisdom:

> Some teach people not to think [longingly and distractedly about the departed], but this understanding is one-sided.[62] If you want to overcome distress, then today you must feel distress. If you wish not to have your mind occupied with distracted thoughts [of your child], then today you must allow it to be so occupied. Go over and over it in your mind until the habit formations of love are eliminated and you will naturally reach the place of no thinking, the place of no distress. If today I were to urge you not to think, not to be distressed, that would be like pouring oil on a fire to put it out.[63]

In yet another sermon Ta-hui suggests:

> Therefore if you want to cry, just cry; if you want to think [distractedly], just think. When suddenly the moment arrives when you realize that you have cried

so much that thought and attachment are exhausted, then examine your thoughts.[64]

Ta-hui thus uses the belief in karma and transmigration, and the understanding of grief that they offer, to comfort, to explain, and to mobilize emotions that might motivate a serious search for enlightenment. It is the inexorability of karma that makes death a great matter on the provisional level of truth, the level on which the unenlightened live their lives. Karma is within its own sphere all-powerful. Even Śākyamuni, who can empty all forms and complete the wisdom of the ten thousand dharmas, cannot extinguish determined karma. How much less then can the ordinary person?

But Ta-hui does not neglect to offer his lay followers his ultimate understanding of death. This message, of course, is that death is empty, a nonevent, because there is no self—no one, that is, who can be said to have been born to die. To realize this is to realize the emptiness of karma and thereby transcend it; this is the only way out of the clutches of karmic retribution.

We find this theme woven throughout the sermon. For example, Ta-hui opens his sermon with this statement:

> If you clear a path in this direction [that is, toward knowing what it is that the Buddhas and patriarchs transmitted], you will know that although Lady T'ang was born years ago, she fundamentally was never born; her extinction today likewise fundamentally did not extinguish anything. Born and not born, like a reflection in a mirror; extinguished and yet not extinguished, like the moon in the water. The shape in the mirror, the moon in the water—both can be seen but not grasped.

At the climax of the sermon he poses this same truth in a more enigmatic form:

> The realm of sentient beings originally has no increase or extinction.
> Moreover not a single person can abide in its dharmas.
> To have dharmas and no abiding is called having no dharmas;
> Having no dharmas and having no abiding is called no-mind.
> According to my understanding the Buddha also has no magic powers,
> Yet he can by means of no-mind penetrate all dharmas.

Ta-hui comments:

> If you can understand "no dharmas and no abiding is called no-mind according to my understanding the Buddha also has no magic powers," then you will understand the saying of the ancient: "On one tip of a lion's hair a billion lion's hairs appear; to obtain a thousand, ten thousand, only know how to grasp one." What then is the one? Born and you do not know where you come

from, dying and you do not know where you will go. Make an effort, and in this lifetime you will grasp it.[65]

And again at the very close of the sermon, in his final *gāthā,* he says:

Today the minister has completed a cycle of Buddha-deeds
And has asked me to turn the wheel of the dharma [that is, to preach].
The wheel that I have turned has no movement,
The dharma that I have preached has no words.
You must know that the departed daughter was never born,
And now today has never been extinguished.
Since there is no birth and extinction, and no cycle of rebirth,
There is neither changing nor destroying of the diamond body.

The two major themes of Ta-hui's sermon—karmic retribution and the emptiness of birth and death—are reconcilable within one framework of thought, as Ta-hui elsewhere points out. Karmic causation is on one level a true and useful description of the world in which we live as unenlightened beings; if we prematurely take an "enlightened" standpoint and declare karma to be empty and therefore irrelevant, we shall find that we still suffer the unpleasant results of our evil actions, and the pains of our suffering will have their own experiential reality.[66] Karmic causation is also a true description of the path toward enlightenment: The greater our merits accumulated over many lifetimes, the greater our opportunities to hear the dharma and become enlightened. Thus meritorious acts may be considered a step toward enlightenment.

But from another point of view these two themes are difficult to reconcile. Enlightenment is after all the realization of the emptiness of karmic causality. So long as we continue to consider our deeds only in the framework of karmic retribution, we shall never be enlightened to the truth of emptiness. Furthermore, the orientation toward the proximate goals of happiness through merits seems to require a different religious approach than does the goal of an enlightenment that enables one to transcend the pleasures and pains of samsara.[67] One could imagine a number of logical and definitional moves to overcome this apparent divergence of goals; for example, one might say that it is the quality of enlightenment or selflessness (no-mind) in any act that makes it worthy of merits. But Ta-hui does not try to reconcile the two different goals. He suggests that Lady T'ang by virtue of her merits of wisdom will certainly be born in the Pure Land; he then suggests that a "correct thought" of enlightenment might free her from samsara altogether. He encourages the transfer of merits that she might avoid the three evil paths of existence in her next birth and then announces that she has never been born and has never died. Far from reconciling these two themes, he seems to play them off against one another, using the forceful emotions evoked by belief in karmic retribution both to offer comfort to the grieving and to spur monastic and lay listeners alike to confront the riddle of death and realize the ultimate truth of emptiness.

CONCLUSION

Ta-hui transformed the *p'u-shuo* into an instrument that would permit him to address the needs of laity directly while continuing to address the needs of monks. But to say what he wanted to say, Ta-hui needed a vastly expanded sermon form. And now that we have looked at a typical sermon for the dead, we can see one of the major reasons for the expansion: In these sermons sponsored by laity two levels of truth, and two levels of practice, had to be brought together and related to one another. If Ta-hui had been preaching only to monks, mention of the truth of emptiness or of the Hua-yen understanding of totality would have been sufficient. But many laity were used to thinking of themselves as limited in their Buddhist practice to the sphere of karmically significant good deeds, birth, and rebirth. Ta-hui could have chosen simply to preach to them on this level, believing as he did that karmic causality is a crucial dimension of reality and knowing also that it was what most laity expected to hear preached to them. But Ta-hui was not content with this, for he earnestly believed that laity could develop wisdom and become enlightened even while living ordinary lives in the world. Therefore his every invocation of the provisional truth of karma was made in order to bring laity as well as monks to see the need to find the ultimate truth that transcends the truth of karma without negating it.

In the sermon on death we see this interweaving of the two levels of truth particularly clearly. The sermon is given to create merits for the deceased, and death must be confronted on that level. Yet death is not fully understood until it is seen to be empty. Understanding on the one level must be combined with understanding on the other. Practice on the level of deeds and fruits must be combined with practice toward enlightenment. Comfort and reassurance based on the fairness and regularity of karmic retribution, bolstered by the sense of something still left to be done for the departed, must be combined with the aroused emotions connected with death to spur laity and monks alike to seek enlightenment. Either level of understanding without the other would be perniciously one-sided. Death is the ideal occasion that brings together both karmic faith and the doubt which, if focused wisely, can lead to enlightenment.

To meet the needs of the laity for reassurance and counsel in their immediate grief, to confirm their karmic understanding, while at the same time using this occasion to urge upon them the truth of emptiness as the only real solution to the riddle posed by death—such tasks require a skillful interweaving of themes in an extended talk. That Ta-hui apparently shaped the *p'u-shuo* to meet this need, and that he used it to compose sermons of the kind we have just examined, shows a constructive approach to the involvement of laity in the Ch'an school and its monastic institutions. In Ta-hui's case it specifically shows as well a commitment to the possibility of a path to enlightenment in daily life. Ta-hui's concern to show that Ch'an practice need not take place in separation from the world is a creative response to the new Ch'an lay constituency that begins to grow in the Sung dynasty.

It has been argued elsewhere that this increasing involvement of the laity in Ch'an life ruined the purity of Ch'an teaching and practice. Yet the sermon we have just examined, while certainly delivered in a new spirit, cannot be said to exemplify a watering down of the teaching or a neglect of the needs of monks in training: The teaching in both the preliminary exchanges and the body of the sermon itself may be seen to be still of a very high order. Whether Ta-hui's synthetic attempt to meet two disparate needs simultaneously brought unfortunate results for the Ch'an school in the hands of lesser followers is a subject for further study.

NOTES

The following abbreviations are used in the notes:

Manji zōkyō	*Nihon kōtei daizōkyō,* known also as the *Kyōtō Tripiṭaka,* printed during the years 1902–1905 by the Zōkyō Shoin of Kyoto.
P'u-shuo	*Ta-hui P'u-chüeh Ch'an-shih p'u-shuo,* five *chüan,* in *Manji zōkyō,* 31, 5, pp. 395a–509d.
Shuku zōkyō	*Dai-nihon kōtei daizōkyō,* known as the *Tōkyō Tripiṭaka,* printed during the years 1880–1885 by the Kokyo Shoin of Tokyo.
YCZESG	Kagamishima Genryū, Satō Tasugen, and Kosaka Kiyū, *Yaku-chū Zen-en shin-gi* (translated and annotated *Ch'an-yüan ch'ing-kuei*) (Tokyo: Sōtō Shū Shūmu Chō, 1972).
Zenrin shōkisen	Muchaku Dōchū, *Zenrin shōkisen* (completed 1716) (Tokyo: Seishin Shobo, 1963).

This study is based on research done for my Ph.D. dissertation, "Ch'an Enlightenment for Laymen: Ta-hui and the New Religious Culture of the Sung" (Harvard University, 1978).

1. Ching-shan was a mountain in Lin-an-fu in Chekiang province; Ta-hui taught there from 1137 to 1141 and from 1158 to 1161 at two different monasteries. "Ta-hui" was an honorary name given by the emperor just before his death.

"Tsung-kao" was Ta-hui's original dharma name taken when he first entered the *sangha*. "P'u-chüeh" was a posthumous honorary title given by the emperor just after Ta-hui's death. "Ch'an-shih" means Ch'an teacher, his title. See Tsu-yung, comp. and ed., *Ta-hui P'u-chüeh Ch'an-shih nien-p'u, Shukuzōkyō, teng* 8, pp. 1–16a.

2. After studying with a series of teachers from different schools of Ch'an, Ta-hui went to study with Yüan-wu K'o-chin in 1124. He had his first decisive enlightenment experience in 1125 and moved south with Yüan-wu in 1127. Until 1137 he lived in relative obscurity either with Yüan-wu or by himself in Kiangsi and Fukien. In 1137 he was invited to Ching-shan Neng-jen Ch'an-yüan where he attracted a considerable following. In his fourth year there he was banished to Heng-chou in Hunan province; after nine years there he was commanded to move his residence to Mei-chou in Kuangtung province. In 1155 he was pardoned and allowed to resume his status as a monk. After a slow progress north he was again invited to head a monastery on Ching-shan; at this time he was sixty-nine years old. He retired four years later and died two years after that. Despite the long period he spent far from the capital at the height of his career, his acclaim upon returning north was that of the most outstanding Ch'an teacher of his time. A glance at dharma lineage charts—as in Yanagida Seizan, ed., *Zenke Goroku* II (Tokyo: Chikuma Shobo, 1974), pp. 434–435 or elsewhere—will show how many of the prominent Ch'an teachers of the next generation were Ta-hui's students; Ta-hui's dharma descendants predominated in the Lin-chi school for several generations. Ta-hui's writings and *Recorded Sayings* entered the canon very soon after his death; that they were read both critically and appreciatively for a long time afterward is shown in the writings of Chu Hsi, Dōgen, and the Ming dynasty Ch'an teacher Han-shan Te-ching, among others.

3. Some sense of Ta-hui's following among literati and officials can be gained from reading his *P'u-shuo* and his *Letters*. For bibliographical information on his *P'u-shuo*, see note 35. Ta'hui's *Letters* can be found in his *Yü-lu;* they also circulated separately in many editions. For an annotated translation into Japanese see Araki Kengo, *Daie sho* (Tokyo: Chikuma Shobo, 1969).

4. Yüan-wu K'o-ch'in (1063–1135) was the most influential teacher of his time in the Yang-ch'i branch of the Lin-chi line. He is best known as the author of the final layer of commentary in the *Blue Cliff Records (Pi-yen lu)*.

5. The most interesting treatment of Ta-hui in connection with this development is by Yanagida Seizan, "Kanwa Zen ni okeru shin to gi no mondai," in *Bukkyō ni okeru shin no mondai*, edited by the Nihon Bukkyō Kyōkai (Kyoto: Heirakuji Shoten, 1963), pp. 141–163. In English, Suzuki Daisetz frequently mentions Ta-hui in connection with doubt and the function of the *kung-an (kōan)*. See for example his *Essays in Zen Buddhism*, 2nd series (London: Luzac and Co., 1933), pp. 10–18, 24, 75–78, 289–291, 303–305; *An Introduction to Zen Buddhism* (New York: Philosophical Library, 1949), pp. 90–91; and *Living by Zen* (Tokyo: Sanseido, 1949), pp. 171–173.

6. Kagamishima Genryū, Satō Tasugen, and Kosaka Kiyū, *Yaku-chū Zen-en shin-gi* [translated and annotated *Ch'an-yüan ch'ing-kuei*] (Tokyo: Sōtō Shū Shūmu Chō, 1972), pp. 1–28, give information on texts and history of this work, as well as a Japanese translation. (A text may be found also in *ZZ* 2.16. 5, pp. 438a–471c.)

7. *YCZESG*, pp. 71–75.

8. Ibid., pp. 78–85.

9. See my survey of Yüan-wu's *shang-t'ang* and *hsiao-ts'an* in note 36.

10. See note 36 below.

11. A text may be found in *ZZ* 2. 17. 1; a paragraph on *p'u-shuo* is on p. 36c. For the date of this work, see *YCZESG*, p. 2.

12. A text may be found in *ZZ* 2. 17. 1; a paragraph on *p'u-shuo* is on pp. 15b-c. For the date of this work, see *YCZESG*, p. 2.

13. See Muchaku Dōchū, *Zenrin shōkisen* (completed 1716) (Tokyo: Seishin Shobō, 1963), pp. 299–300.

14. *Ts'ung-lin chiao-ting ch'ing-kuei tsung-yao* mentions only the Inner Hall; *ZZ* 2.17. 1, *chüan hsia*, p. 15a.

15. The *t'ang ssu hsing che* was an assistant to the *wei no*, one of the chief administrative officers of the monastery; see *Zenrin shōkisen*, p. 299.

16. *Ts'ung-lin chiao-ting ch'ing-kuei tsung-yao* adds here: "Those in attendance and the two groups of officers of the monastery bow." For more information on the two groups of officers, see *Zenrin shōkisen*, pp. 219–221.

17. *Ts'ung-lin chiao-ting ch'ing-kuei tsung-yao* adds here: "[Earlier] books of rules do not mention [the *p'u-shuo*]."

18. *Ts'ung-lin chiao-ting ch'ing-kuei tsung-yao* adds: "When the *shang-tang* is over."

19. *Ts'ung-lin chiao-ting ch'ing-kuei tsung-yao* omits this last sentence about Ta-hui.

20. Kuei-tsung temple was on Lu-shan in Nank'ang prefecture in Kiangsi province. What the connection to Tung-shan was I have not been able to trace. Chen-ching K'o-wen was abbot of Lu-shan Kuei-tsung Ssu.

21. *Ta-hui P'u-chüeh Ch'an-shih p'u-shuo,* five *chüan,* in *Manji zōkyō,* 31, 5, p. 460a.

22. *Zenrin shōkisen,* p. 433.

23. This result of my own search is confirmed by Muchaku Dōchū; see *Zenrin shōkisen,* p. 436.

24. I base this statement on Yanagida Seizan, ed., *Zenke goroku* II, pp. 423–514, especially pp. 435 and 485–491. Yanagida does not know of a "Recorded Sayings" for Fo-chien Hui-ch'in.

25. Yüan-wu's *p'u-shuo* can be found in *Yüan-wu Fo-kuo Ch'an-shih yü-lu,* *chüan* 13, in *T* 47.774–775.

26. See note 36 below.

27. It was a *kao-hsiang p'u-shuo.* For differences between this and other kinds of *p'u-shuo,* see *Zenrin shōkisen,* p. 436.

28. Fo-yen Ch'ing-yüan's *p'u-shuo* can be found in *Fo-yen Ch'an-shih yü-lu,* *chüan* 5, in *Ku-tsun-su yü-lu, chüan* 31, *ZZ* 2.23. 4, pp. 280b–296a.

29. Ibid., pp. 295a–296a, *"Wei Li She-jen P'u-shuo."*

30. Of course a layman might desire to hear a sermon on this topic.

31. *Hsü-t'ang Chih-yü Ho-shang yü-lu,* *chüan* 4, *ZZ* 2. 26. 4, pp. 360d–366b.

32. See the appendix for a complete list.

33. See notes 24, 25, and 28 above.

34. See the appendix for references.

35. The most complete bibliographical work on Ta-hui to date is by Ishii Shūdō. See especially his *"Daie Goroku no kisoteki kenkyū (jo),"* *Komazawa Daigaku Bukkyōgakubu kenkyū kiyō* 31 (March 1973): 283–306, for his analysis of texts of Ta-hui's *P'u-shuo.* He concludes that there are basically two kinds of texts, *p'u-shuo* in four *chüan* and *p'u-shuo* in one *chüan.* The *p'u-shuo* in *Manji*

zōkyō used for this study is a combination of the two: first the one in four *chüan,* then the one in one *chüan.* The *p'u-shuo* included in *Ta-hui P'u-chüeh Ch'an-shih yü-lu (T* 47.811–942) is a version of the one-*chüan* text. One-*chüan* texts have thirteen to fifteen sermons.

36. For purposes of comparison I have made a study of Ta-hui's use of the more traditional *shang-t'ang* sermon form. Some 213 of Ta-hui's *shang-t'ang* are listed in his *Recorded Sayings.* Those that have no stated connection with laity or lay sponsorship are notably short in their recorded form, averaging about 130 words each. Only 15 of the 213 are sermons in which laity are either the sponsor or the occasion of the remarks. These 15 are a bit longer, averaging 358 words each. Of these 15, at least 4 can be clearly identified as meeting the needs of lay-men in connection with death. Thus if the sample of 213 may be taken as repre-sentative, Ta-hui in the *shang-t'ang* kept his remarks very short and only about 7 percent of the time used this form for addressing laymen.

As for Ta-hui's *hsiao-ts'an,* I find only one recorded in Ta-hui's *Recorded Say-ings.* It is approximately 175 words long and has no reference to laity. The copy of *Ta-hui P'u-chüeh Ch'an-shih yü-lu* that I used for this search is that in *Shukuzōkyō, t'eng* 8; the *hsiao-ts'an* is on p. 17b.

The reader may at this point perhaps wonder whether Ta-hui might merely have substituted one form for another, using the *p'u-shuo* form in the way that his predecessors used the *shang-t'ang* or the *hsiao-ts'an.* I have not had time to survey all the sermon forms used by all of Ta-hui's predecessors and contempora-ries in the Sung in order to test this hypothesis; in the absence of such a study my argument that Ta-hui created a new way of using a relatively new form must therefore remain tentative. As a beginning, however, I have looked at the *shang-t'ang* and *hsiao-ts'an* of Yüan-wu. I have chosen Yüan-wu because his lay follow-ing was very large, at least the equal of that of Ta-hui, and because his "Recorded Sayings" are extensive. Here are the results:

1. *Hsiao-ts'an*
Total: 81
Average length: 442 words
Total invited by laity: 11 (13.5%)
Number addressing laity or their needs directly: 0
2. *Shang-t'ang*
Total: 247
Average length: 200 words
Total invited by laity: ±39 (15%)
Number addressing laity or their needs directly: 1 (?)

If we compare these figures with the ones listed earlier for Ta-hui's *p'u-shuo,* we can see that Ta-hui was not merely doing under another name something Yüan-wu had done in the *shang-t'ang* or *hsiao-ts'an.* The fact that Yüan-wu was the teacher whose dharma Ta-hui inherited, and was therefore the person whose pat-terns of teaching Ta-hui was most likely to adopt, makes this difference in the fre-quency and the manner of their addressing laity in sermons stronger evidence of Ta-hui's originality than if Yüan-wu had been merely a famous predecessor.

37. *P'u-shuo,* p. 460a. Muchaku Dōchū points out that Ta-hui is not quoting exactly from the text of the *Avataṃsaka Sutra;* the question in the original pas-sage leaves out the word *p'u* ("generally"). But later in the passage one encoun-ters the phrase *p'u shuo* in this sentence: "Therefore the ten bodhisattvas by

means of this preach generally to the three worlds." See *Ta-fang-kuang-fo hua-yen ching, chüan* 53, in *T* 10.281b, beginning with *"yu shih chung shuo san chieh."*

38. Others discussing the form have found other scriptural sources. Muchaku Dōchū cites two, both from the *Avataṃsaka Sutra.* The first is from the "Vairocana" chapter and a commentary on it where the meaning of the word *p'u* is given. The second is from the "Ten *Samādhis*" chapter, where reference is made directly to *p'u-shuo*—"preaching universally all the teachings of the Buddha." Muchaku finds this the most convincing scriptural authority for the form; see *Zenrin shōkisen,* pp. 434 and 436.

39. For some indication of the controversy, see the *"Tsuizen"* paragraph in Muchaku Dōchū's *Zenrin shōkisen,* pp. 573–574.

40. See Mochizuki Shinkō, *Bukkyō daijiten,* 3rd ed. (Tokyo: Seikai Shoten Kangyō Kyokai, 1960), vol. 1, p. 270, for sutra references.

41. See Matsuura Shūkō, *Zenke no sōhō to tsuizen kuyō no kenkyū* (Tokyo: Sankibo Busshorin, 1969), pp. 239–242. See also Mochizuki, *Bukkyō daijiten* 4:3648–3650, *"Chuu,"* and 2:1809–1810, *"Shijūkunichi."* Compare *Ti-tsang P'u-sa pen-yüan ching* (translated into Chinese in A.D. 704), *chüan* 2, chap. 7: "If you can within forty-nine days after the death of their bodies create a large number of good deeds, then you will cause all the sentient beings to be able forever to depart from the evil paths [evil states of rebirth] and to be born in human or heavenly realms and enjoy supreme and marvelous delight" *T* 53.783, quoted in Matsuura, *Zenke no sōhō to tsuizen kuyō,* p. 239).

42. *Shih-shih yao-lan,* compiled by the Sung monk Tao-ch'eng in A.D. 1019: "As for the practice in the world of feasting for happiness on every seventh day, this is to 'follow to help with good' when the body is in the intermediate existence between death and birth and to make seeds for this intermediate stage, to cause him not to be reborn in an evil path" *T* 54.305.

43. Matsuura, *Zenke no sōhō to tsuizen kuyō,* p. 269.

44. Ibid. In the case of Chinese Buddhists, as soon as the offering on this day was finished, a tablet for the deceased was placed on the Buddhist altar where other tablets of ancestors were placed, and prayers and offerings took place there henceforth as with other ancestors.

45. Ibid.

46. By that time this practice was surely in general Buddhist use; see Matsuura, *Zenke no sōhō to tsuizen kuyō,* pp. 268–270. Ta-hui shows by his frequent references to graves in this sermon that he expects the body to be buried on or near that day. See *P'u-shuo,* pp. 469a–470b.

47. See for example *P'u-shuo,* pp. 450b–451b, where we find a sermon offered for a number of deceased relatives simultaneously. While it is conceivable that they might all have died at once, it is unlikely.

48. This sermon is found in *P'u-shuo,* pp. 468a–469a. Further references will not be given for passages quoted or summarized from these pages.

49. T'ang Ssu-t'ui, whose *tzu* was Chin-chih, held a number of important posts during the Sung dynasty. His biography appears in the *Sung shih, chüan* 371. Aside from two sermons in connection with his daughter's death, a copy of his invitation to Ta-hui to preach is included at the end of the *P'u-shuo,* and a letter to him is included in *Ta-hui shu, chüan hsia.* He is also mentioned in *Nien-p'u,* p. 92, where it says that he established a Wu-ai Hui. The translations of these

civil service titles in the Sung are taken from E. Kracke, *Translations of Sung Civil Service Titles* (Paris: École pratique des hautes études, 1957).

50. In what we shall call the karmic understanding, death is seen as an event in the broad context of the samsaric stream of repeated lives and deaths. In this understanding, the character of one's lives and deaths is determined by the quality of one's past deeds. Births may take place in ten planes of existence, of which the three "evil paths"—hells, the realm of hungry ghosts, and the animal realm—are the most frequent. More desirable are births in the human realm, the realm of *asuras,* and the realm of *devas* or heavenly beings. Most desirable of all, but not frequent, are births as a bodhisattva, a *pratyekabuddha,* a *śrāvaka,* and a Buddha. It is important in this context to do good deeds to ensure in future births one's own happiness or that of others.

51. *Tz'u tuan ta-shih yin-yüan;* more exactly, "this important karmic occasion," that is, enlightenment to the dharma.

52. The text has Kuei-feng Ch'an-shih, one of the names of the famous creator of a synthesis between Ch'an and Hua-yen philosophy Kuei-feng Tsung-mi (780–841). This passage is included in *Ching-te ch'uan-teng lu* (Taipei: Chen Shan Mei Ch'u-pan-she, second printing 1968), *chüan* 13, p. 67. Tsung-mi has supplied his own commentary on his verse.

53. *"Tso yu-i shih."*

54. Literally: "At the moment of one's repaying karmic ties and saying goodbye . . ." *(pao-yüan hsieh-shih).*

55. Literally: "the world of peace and nourishment," another name for the Pure Land.

56. *P'u-shuo,* pp. 461b–462a.

57. Literally: "spirit and consciousness" *(shen-shih).*

58. "*Ye ma*" also is used to mean "mist in the daytime" or "heat haze"; this would be another possible translation.

59. Literally: "make her person secure and establish her life" *(an-shen li-ming).*

60. This line is found in a different order in the *Platform Sutra of the Sixth Patriarch,* chap. 7. My translation follows that of Lu K'uan Yu (Charles Luk) in *Ch'an and Zen Teaching,* 3rd series (London: Rider and Co., 1962), p. 73.

61. This phrase appears in *Chuang-tzu,* chap. 5, "Te Ch'ung Fu": "*Chung Ni yüeh: ssu sheng i ta i, erh pu te yü chih pien.*" Chuang-tzu puts this statement in the mouth of Chung Ni (that is, Confucius); perhaps for that reason Ta-hui says that a Confucian said it. The second half of the sentence reminds one of *Doctrine of the Mean,* chap. 10, v. 5: "*Chih ssu pu pien.*"

62. Literally: "*to tsai i-pien.*" It is one-sided because it recognizes a distinction between thinking and not-thinking and, instead of saying that both are empty, identifies one as preferable.

63. *P'u-shuo,* p. 472a.

64. *P'u-shuo,* p. 422a.

65. That is, understand and obtain it.

66. Elsewhere Ta-hui says: "Although you can say that faults in their nature are originally empty, when it comes to the point of not being able to avoid suffering the retribution, there really is pain" (*P'u-shuo,* p. 458b).

67. See Winston L. King, *In the Hope of Nibbana* (LaSalle, Ill.: Open Court, 1964), for a discussion of this dichotomy as it affects ethics.

APPENDIX

P'u-shuo by Ta-hui's Contemporaries and Juniors

In *Hsüeh-t'ang Hsing Ho-shang yü,* a short record of the sayings of Hsüeh-t'ang Tao-hsing (1089–1151), we find two *p'u-shuo* recorded. In their recorded form both are very short, 280 and 540 words respectively; they have no identifiable connection with laymen. Nonetheless, the fact that Hsüeh-t'ang is an exact contemporary of Ta-hui makes the fact that he too used the *p'u-shuo* form significant.[1] Hsüeh-t'ang was a disciple of Fo-yen, who also used the *p'u-shuo.*

In *Shan-t'ang Hsün Ch'an-shih yü,* a short record of the sayings of Shan-t'ang Seng-hsün (dates unknown, but roughly contemporary with Ta-hui), we find one *p'u-shuo* of 560 words. In this *p'u-shuo* also there is no indication of lay sponsorship or lay hearers.[2] Shan-t'ang was in the Huang-lung line.

In *Fu-chou Hsüeh-feng Tung-shan Ho-shang yü-lu,* two *p'u-shuo* by Hsüeh-feng Hui-k'ung are recorded. Both are short; one is 180 words, the other 400. No reference is made to laymen. Hui-k'ung lived from 1096 to 1158;[3] he was in the Huang-lung line.

In *Fo-hai Hui-yüan Ch'an-shih kuang-lu, chüan* 3, there are three *p'u-shuo* by Fo-hai Hui-yüan (1103–1176). The longest is 1,280 words; the others are 800 and 820 words respectively. There is no identifiable connection with laymen. Fo-hai was a disciple of Yüan-wu (who also used the *p'u-shuo*) and a dharma-brother of Ta-hui.[4]

In *P'u-an Yin-su Ch'an-shih yü-lu* we find one *p'u-shuo* by P'u-an Yin-su (1115–1169), a man twenty-six years younger than Ta-hui but active during the latter part of Ta-hui's lifetime. This *p'u-shuo,* given for child novices, contains no direct reference to laymen. It is 1,120 words.[5] P'u-an was a dharma-grandson of Fo-yen.

At the end of *Ying-an T'an-hua yü-lu, chüan* 10, there is appended a *p'u-shuo* by Sung-yüan Ch'ung-yüeh (1132–1202). It is 700 words. Since it is a eulogy of the monk Ying-an T'an-hua (1103–1163), it must have been given around the time of Ta-hui's death or shortly thereafter.[6] Ying-an T'an-hua was a dharma-grandson of Yüan-wu. Sung-yüan Ch'ung-yüeh was a dharma-great-great-grandson of Yüan-wu and a dharma-grandson of Ying-an.

In *Sung-yüan Yüeh Ch'an-shih yü,* a short record of the sayings of Sung-yüan Ch'ung-yüeh (see the preceding entry), we find one *p'u-shuo* of 124 words.[7] Here also there is no expressed connection with laymen.

The first *p'u-shuo* that I have been able to find in the Ts'ao-tung school is in *Ju-ching Ch'an-shih yü-lu,* which records sayings of Ch'ang-weng Ju-ching (1163–1228). Ju-ching was born in the year Ta-hui died and was the mentor in China of the Japanese Sōtō teacher Dōgen. In his recorded sayings there is only one *p'u-shuo*.[8] Dōgen testifies that his teacher was accustomed to giving *p'u-shuo* frequently.[9]

Contemporaries for Whom There Were No Recorded *P'u-shuo*

Huang-lung line
 1. Huang-lung Hui-nan (1002–1069)
 2. Hui-t'ang Tsu-hsin (1025–1100)
 3. Chen-ching K'o-wen (1025–1102)
 4. Ch'ao-tsung Hui-fang (1073–1129)
 5. Chan-t'ang Wen-chün (1069–1115)
 6. Tou-shuai Ts'ung-yüeh (1044–1091)
 7. Chüeh-fan Hui-hung (1071–1128)
 8. Kuang-chien Hsing-ying (1071–1128)
 9. Ling-yüan Wei-ch'ing (?–1117)
10. Ssu-hsin Wu-hsin (1043–1114)
11. Ts'ao-t'ang Shan-ch'ing (1057–1142)
12. Ch'ang-ling Shou-cho (1065–1123)
13. Shang-feng Pen-ts'ai (no dates)
14. Pieh-feng Tsu-chen (no dates)
15. Wu-shih Chieh-shen (1080–1148)
16. Hsüeh-an Ts'ung-ch'in (1117–1200)

Yang-ch'i line
17. Pao-ning Jen-yūng (no dates)
18. K'ai-fu Tao-ning (1053–1113)
19. Yüeh-an Shan-kuo (1079–1152)
20. Fo-hsing Fa-t'ai (no dates)
21. Hsia-t'ang Hui-yüan (1103–1176)
22. Hu-chiu Shao-lung (1077–1136)
23. Ying-an T'an-hua (1103–1163)
24. Ta-sui Yuan-ching (1065–1135)
25. Chu-an Shih-kuei (1083–1146)

Ts'ao-tung line
26. Fu-jung Tao-k'ai (1043–1118)
27. Tan-hsia Tsu-ch'un (1064–1117)
28. Hung-chih Cheng-chüeh (1091–1157)
29. Chen-hsieh Ch'ing-liao (1090–1151)
30. Tzu-te Hui-hui (1097–1183)
31. Ku-yen Chien-pi (no dates)

Yün-men line

32. Wu-shan Ching-tuan (1030–1103)
33. Miao-chan Ssu-hui (1070–1145)
34. Tz'u-shou Huai-shen (1077–1132)

Notes to Appendix

1. *Hsüeh-t'ang Hsing Ho-shang yü* is in *Hsü-k'ai ku-tsun-su yü-yao, chüan* 4, *ZZ* 2.24.1, pp. 64c–68a; there are two *p'u-shuo* on pp. 66c–67a.

2. *Shan-t'ang Hsün Ch'an-shih yü* in *Hsü-k'ai ku-tsun-su yü-yao, chüan* 4, *ZZ* 2.24.1, pp. 3a–6b; there is a *p'u-shuo* on pp. 5d–6b.

3. In *Tung-shan Hui-k'ung Ch'an-shih yü-lu, ZZ* 2.25.2, we find two *p'u-shuo* on p. 140a–c.

4. *Fo-hai Hui-yüan Ch'an-shih kuang-lu, ZZ* 2.25.5; in *chüan* 3, pp. 475c–477b, we find three *p'u-shuo*.

5. *P'u-an Yin-su Ch'an-shih yü-lu, ZZ* 2.25.3, pp. 270c–271b, has a *p'u-shuo*.

6. *Ying-an T'an-hua yü-lu, ZZ* 2.25.5, *chüan* 10, p. 449a–c, has a *p'u-shuo*.

7. *Sung-yüan Yüeh Ch'an-shih yü*, in *Hsü-k'ai ku-tsun-su yü-yao, ZZ* 2.24.1, pp. 22b–23b, has a *p'u-shuo*.

8. *Ju-ching Ch'an-shih yü-lu*, also known as *T'ien-t'ung Ju-ching Ch'an-shih yü-lu, ZZ* 2.29.5, *chüan hsia*, p. 488a–c, has one *p'u-shuo*.

9. Dōgen Zenji, *Eihei kōroku*, chap. 2, as quoted in Mochizuki, *Bukkyō daijiten* 4:4422: "Sometimes in the middle of the night, sometimes in the evening or after meals, no matter what time of day, he would either strike the drum for entering his chamber and preach generally *(p'u-shuo)* or strike the drum for *hsiao-ts'an* and enter his chamber. Or else with his own hand he would hit the mallet in the Monks' Hall, and in the Illumination Hall he would preach generally *(p'u-shuo);* when the *p'u-shuo* was over he would enter his chamber. Or else he would hit the board outside the room of the head monk and preach generally in the head monk's room, and then when the preaching had finished enter his chamber." This sounds as if Ju-ching gave *p'u-shuo* not only frequently but also in total disregard of the usual forms.

Glossary

Ad libitum 隨自意
An-lo-chi 安樂集
An Lu-shan 安祿山
An-shen li-ming 安身立命
Araki Kengo 荒木見悟

Bhikṣu 比丘
Bodhisattva Chüeh-shou 覺首
Brahma Net Sutra 網經
Buddha-household 佛圖戶
Bukkyō daijiten 仏教大字典
Bukkyō-teki na dōshi 仏教的な道士
Bukkyōgaku-ronshū 仏教学論集

Ch'a-na ch'eng-fo 刹那成佛
Chai 齋
Chai-lang 齋郎
Ch'an 禪
Chan-jan 湛然
Ch'an-lin pei-yüng ch'ing-kuei 禪林
　備用清規
Ch'an-ting 禪定
Ch'an-yüan ch'ing-kuei 禪院清規
Chang Hsün 張巡
Chang-sheng 張生
Ch'ang Ts'ung-i 常從義
Chang Yüeh 張悅

Changja haengjang 長者行狀
Ch'ao-hsien 朝獻
Chao-mu 昭穆
Chen-hai chen-tung chün chieh-tu shih
　鎮海鎮東軍節度使
Chen-jen 眞人
Chen-yen 眞言
Ch'en Yuan 陳垣
Ch'eng-fa pen-chiao 稱法本教
Ch'eng (fo-) ming 稱（佛）名
Cheng-hsing 正行
Cheng-nien 正念
Ch'eng-nien 稱念
Cheng-ting-chih-yeh 正定之業
Cheng-tsung fen 正宗分
Ch'i (vessel, capacity) 器
Ch'i (breath, life-force) 氣
Ch'i-chi 齊己
Ch'i-ning 契凝
Chia-fu tso 跏趺坐
Chia-ts'ai 迦才
Chiang-tso 江左
Chiao-t'i 教體
Chieh 解
Chieh tu shih 節度使
Chieh-t'uo sheng-ssu 解脱生死
Chien 間

Ch'ien Chan 錢儹
Ch'ien-ch'iu chieh 千秋節
Chien-hsien 薦獻
Chien-hsin 薦新
Ch'ien Hua 錢鏵
Ch'ien I 錢億
Ch'ien Liu 錢鏐
Ch'ien-T'ang hsien chih 錢塘縣志
Ch'ien Wen-mu 錢文穆
Ch'ien Yen 錢儼
Ch'ien Yü 錢昱
Chih (calm, suppress) 止
Chih (wisdom) 智
Chih-chin shih-chiao 直進始教
Chih-hsiu Che chiang t'ung-chih
   勅修浙江通志
Chih-hui 智慧
Chih-i 智顗
Chih-jen 至人
Chih-kuan 止觀
Chih-p'an 志磐
Chih ssu pu pien 至死不變
Chih-tao Chiu-lao 至道九老
Chih-yen 智眼
Chin-chih 進之
Chin-chou 禁呪
Chin-lu chai 金錄齋
Ching-shan Neng-jen Ch'an-yüan
   徑山能仁禪院
Ching-te ch'uan-teng lu 景德傳燈錄
Ching-t'u Lun 淨土論
Chiu Lao Hui 九老會
Chiu-ling sheng-hsien lu 鷲嶺聖賢錄
Chiu wu-tai shih 舊五代史
Chou-ch'ih 盩厔
Chu 註
Chu-chi mo-chiao 逐機末教
Ch'u fa-hsin chu 初發心住
Chu-fa-wu-hsing-ching 諸法無行經
Chū-u 中有
Chu-yeh 助業
Ch'u yu, erh yu 出有而有
Chüan 卷
Chuang-tzu 莊子
Chüeh 覺
Chüeh-i san-mei 覺意三昧

Chūgoku kinsei bukkyōshi kenkyū
   中国近世佛教史研究
Ch'ung-hsüan hsüeh 崇玄學
Chung-i 忠懿
Chung-kuo Fo-chiao shih chi kai-lun
   中國佛教史籍概論
Chung-kuo Fo-chiao shih kai-shuo
   中國佛教史概說
Chung-kuo Fo-hsüeh jen-ming tz'u-
   tien 中國佛學人名辭典
Chung Ni 仲尼
Chung Ni yüeh: ssu sheng i ta i, erh pu
   te yü chih pien 仲尼曰：死生亦大
   矣，而不得與之變
Chung-shen 眾生
Chung-yin 中陰
Chung-yu 中有
Chung-yung 中庸
Constantly sitting *samādhi* 常坐三昧
Constantly walking *samādhi* 常行三昧

Dai-nihon kōtei daizōkyō 大日本校定
   大藏經
Dai-nihon zokuzōkyō 大日本續藏經
Daie goroku no kisoteki kenkyū (jo)
   大慧語錄の基礎的研究(上)
Daie sho 大慧書
Dōgen Zenji 道元禪師

Eihei kōroku 永平廣錄
Erh shih-chien 二世間

Fa 法
Fa-hsing yung-t'ung 法性融通
Fa-she 法社
Fa-shen 法身
Fa-shih Tsan 法事讚
Fa-tao 法道
Fan-fu ch'u-hsüeh 凡夫初學
Fan Tsu-yü 范祖禹
Fang-chang 方丈
Fang-pien 方便
Fen-tuan shen 分段身
Fo-chien Hui-ch'in 佛鑑慧懃
Fo-hai Hui-yüan Ch'an-shih kuang-lu
   佛海慧遠禪師廣錄

Fo-kuo 佛果
Fo-kuo Yüan-wu K'o-ch'in 佛果圓悟
　克勤
Fo-sheng T'ao-li-t'ien wei mu shuo-fa
　ching 佛昇忉利天爲母說法經
Fo-shuo fen-pieh san-o so-ch'i ching
　佛說分別善惡所起經
Fo-tsu t'ung-chi 佛祖統紀
Fo-yen Ch'ing-yuan 佛眼清遠
Four kinds of *samādhi* 四種三昧
Fu-ch'i 服氣
Fu-chou Hsüeh-feng Tung-shan
　Ho-shang yü-lu 福州雪峰東山和尚
　語錄
Fu-mu En Chung Ching 父母恩重經

Gensei rieki 現世利益
Great Treatise on the Perfection of
　Wisdom 大智度論

Half-walking-half-sitting *samādhi*
　半行半坐三昧
Han-lin hsüeh-shih 翰林學士
Han-shan Te-ch'ing 憨山德清
Han Te-shun 韓德純
Hang-yüeh Liang-fan chieh-chih
　杭越兩藩節制
Han'guk kosung chonjip 韓國高僧
　全集
Hao-tuan 皓端
Heng-chou 衡州
Ho-tse Shen-hui 荷澤神會
Honji 本師
Hsi-chüeh 希覺
Hsi-ning 熙寧
Hsi Wang Mu 西王母
Hsiang-shan yeh-lu 湘山野錄
Hsiao-ching (emperor of Eastern Wei)
　東魏孝靜帝
Hsiao hsü chi 小畜集
Hsiao-ts'an 小參
Hsiao Ts'ung-i 蕭從一
Hsien ching (fang) shih chüan 仙經
　(方)十卷
Hsin (mind) 心

Hsin chieh hsing cheng 信解行證
Hsin man ch'eng fu 信滿成佛
Hsin-ti li-nien 心體離念
Hsin wu-tai shih 新五代史
Hsin-ya hsüeh-pao 新亞學報
Hsing 行
Hsing-ch'ing kung 興慶宮
Hsü Hsüan 徐鉉
Hsü-k'ai ku-tsun-su yü-yao 續開古尊
　宿語要
Hsü Kao-seng-chuan 續高僧傳
Hsü-tang Chih-yü Ho-shang yü-lu
　虛堂智愚和尚語錄
Hsüan-chung Fa-shih 玄中法師
Hsüan-chung Ssu 玄中寺
Hsüan-tu kuan 玄都觀
Hsüan-yüan huang-ti 玄元皇帝
Hsüan-yüan huang-ti miao 玄元皇
　帝廟
Hsüeh-feng Hui-kung 雪峰慧空
Hsüeh-t'ang Hsing Ho-shang yü
　雪堂行和尚語
Hsüeh-t'ang Tao-hsing 雪堂道行
Hu-fa 護法
Hu-hsien 鄠縣
Hua-ch'ing kung 華清宮
Hua-shan 華山
Hua-t'ou 華頭
Hua-yen 華嚴
Hua-yen wen-ta 華嚴問答
Hua-yen yu-hsin fa-chiai chi 華嚴遊心
　法界記
Huang-lu chai 黃錄齋
Huang-lung 黃龍
Hui 慧
Hui-cheng 彙征
Hui-hsiang 廻向
Hui-neng 慧能
Hunan 湖南

I 義
I-hui 義會
I-i 義邑
I-ken 意根
I-ts'ung 義從
I-yu 乙酉

Ishida Mitsuyuki 石田充之
Ishii Shūdō 石井修道

Jen-t'ien-chiao 人天教
Jōdokyō Kyōrishi 淨土教教理史
Ju-ching Ch'an-shih yü-lu 如淨禪師
　語錄
Ju fa-chiai p'in 入法界品
Ju-lai hsing-chi p'in 如來性起品
Ju-man 如蒲
Jung-chai sui-pi 容齋隨筆

Kagamishima Genryū 鏡元隆
K'ai-yüan kuan ssu 開元觀寺
K'ai-yüan li 開元禮
K'an 看
K'an-ching 看淨
Kanwa Zen ni okeru shin to gi no
　mondai 看話禪に於る信と疑の
　問題
Kao 高
Keng-sang Tzu 庚桑子
Kiangsi 江西
Kleśas identical to bodhi 煩惱即菩提
K'o-t'ou 客頭
Kōan 公案
Kōrai Fushō Kokushi no kenkyū 高麗
　普照国師の研究
Kosaka Kiyū 小坂機融
K'ou-ch'eng 口稱
K'ou-ch'eng Mi-t'o ming-hao 口稱彌
　陀名號
K'ou-yeh tsan-t'an 口業讚歎
Kuan 觀
Kuan-ch'a 觀察
Kuan Ching 觀經
Kuan-fo 觀佛
Kuan-fo-ching (-shu) 觀佛經(疏)
Kuan-fo san-mei hai ching 觀佛三昧
　海經
Kuan-hsin 觀心
Kuan Hsü-k'ung-tsang p'u-sa ching
　觀虛空藏菩薩經
Kuan milo p'u-sa shang-shen tu-shi-
　t'ien ching 觀彌勒菩薩上生兜率
　天經

Kuan-nien fa-men 觀念法門
Kuang-ming 光明
Kuang-wen ta-shih 光文大師
Kuei-feng ch'an-shih 圭峯禪師
Kuei-feng Tsung-mi 圭峯宗密
Kuei t'ien lu 歸田錄
Kuei-tsung 歸宗
Kung 宮
Kung-an 公案
Kung Lin 龔霖
K'ung Tzu miao 孔子廟
Kuo-chi jih 國忌日
Kuo-fen 果分

Li (surname) 李
Li (principle) 理
Li (free from) 離
Li Fang 李昉
Li Lin-fu 李林甫
Li-nien 離念
Li-shan 驪山
Li T'ung-hsüan 李通玄
Liang-Che tu seng-cheng 兩浙都僧正
Liang-chou 涼州
Liang-kuo T'ien-tzu Hsiao-wang 梁國
　天子蕭王
Lien-she 蓮社
Lin-an-fu 臨安府
Lin-chi 臨濟
Ling 令
Ling-ch'e 靈徹
Liu chi 六籍
Liu i shih hua 六一詩話
Liu-tsu t'an-ching 六祖壇經
Liu-t'ung fen 流通分
Lo-yang 洛陽
Lo Yin 羅隱
Lou-kuan 樓觀
Lü 律
Lü hu 律虎
Lu Shan 盧山(白蓮社)
Lu-shan Kuei-tsung ssu 盧山歸宗寺
Lüeh-lun an-lo ching-t'u i 略論安樂淨
　土義
Lun-chu 論註
Lun hu 論虎

Lung-ching chien wen lu 龍井見聞錄
Lung-hsing 龍興
Lung-hsing (hsiang fu chieh t'an) szu chih 龍興祥符戒壇寺志

Manji zōkyō 卍藏經
Matsuura Shūkō 松浦秀光
Mei-chou 梅州
Men 門
Miao 廟
Michibata Ryōshū 道端良秀
Ming-chen chai 明眞齋
Ming chi fa 名即法
Ming i fa 名異法
Ming-i Tsung-wen 明義宗文
Mo 沒
Mo-ho chih-kuan 摩訶止觀
Mochizuki Shinkō 望月信享
Mu-kua tui huo yun 木瓜對火熨
Muchaku Dōchū 無著道忠

Nan-k'ang 南康
Nan-mo 南無
Nan-mo wu-liang-shou fo 南無無量壽佛
Nan-wu 南無
Nan-wu-fo 南無佛
Neither-walking-nor-sitting samādhi 非行非坐三昧
Nien 念
Nien-fo 念佛
Nien-men 念門
Nien mi-t'o ming-hao 念彌陀名號
Nien-p'u 年譜

Ōchō 橫超

Pa-chieh chai 八節齋
Pa-hsiang ch'eng-tao 八相成道
P'an-chiao 判教
Pan-chou San-mei Tsan 般舟三昧讚
P'an ku 盤古
Pao-chüan 宝卷
Pao P'u-tzu 抱朴子
Pao-sheng san-mei 報生三昧
Pao T'ien-tsu 報田祖

Pao-yüan hsieh-shih 報緣謝時
Pei-tsung 北宗
Pen-lai ch'eng-fo 本來成佛
P'eng chi-ch'eng 彭際清
Perfect and sudden 圓頓
Pi-yen lu 碧巖綠
Piao-fa shih 表法釋
Pien-yi shen 變易身
Po-chou 亳州
Pojo Chinul 普照知訥
P'u 普
P'u-an Yin-su Ch'an-shih yü-lu 普庵印肅禪師語錄
P'u-chüeh 普覺
P'u-hsien 普賢
P'u-hui 普慧
Pu-k'o ssu-i 不可思議
Pu-k'o ssu-i ching-chieh 不可思議境界
P'u-shuo 普説
P'u-shuo san-chieh 普説三界

Receiving the Ten Good (Precepts) Sutra 受十善戒經

Sai Pai-ti 賽白帝
Samādhi 三昧
San 散
San-chiao sheng-hsien shih chi 三教聖賢事迹
San-ch'ing ching 三清境
San-mei 三昧
San-sheng ch'eng-fo 三生成佛
San-yu 三有
San-yüan chai 三元齋
Sangha-household 僧戶
Sarva-rahasya-nama-tantra-raja 一切祕密最上名義大教王儀軌
Satō Tatsugen 佐藤達玄
Sekiguchi Shindai 關口眞大
Seng 僧
Seng-ch'e 僧徹
Seng-chia 僧伽
Seng hsien, Tao hou 僧先道後
Seng shih lüeh 僧史略
Seng t'ung 僧統
Sha-men-t'ung 沙門統

Shan-t'ang Hsün Ch'an-shih yü 山堂洵禪師語

Shan-t'ang Seng hsün　山堂僧洵

Shan-tao 善道

Shan-yü 善語

Shang-chieh 上界

Shang-t'ang 上堂

She (to unify) 攝

She (an association) 社

She-li-fei Hui-kuo Ching 舍利佛悔過經

She-ta-ch'eng-lun 攝大乘論

Shen-hsiu 神秀

Shen-hui 神會

Shen Luan 神鸞

Shen-shih 神識

Sheng-tsu 聖祖

Shih 事

Shih-ch'eng-cheng-chio 始成正覺

Shih-chien chi ku lüeh hsü-chi 釋鑑稽古略續集

Shih-chien kung chih 世間共知

Shih-chüeh 詩訣

Shih-hsiang shih 事相釋

Shih-kuo ch'un-ch'iu 十國春秋

Shih-men cheng-t'ung 釋門正統

Shih-shi wu-ai 釋氏無礙

Shih-shih i-nien lu 釋氏疑年錄

Shih-shih yao-lan 釋氏要覽

Shih-tzu 釋子

Shijūkunichi 四十九日

Shinran 親鸞

Shinshū Seikyō Zensho, Shūshi-bu 真宗聖教全書, 宗祖部

Shōshinge 正信偈

Shou 守

Shou-hsin 守心

Shu i chih 數一支

Shukuzōkyō 縮藏經

Shun-yu Lin-an chih 淳祐臨安志

Sīla Sutra 大乘戒經

Sui tzu-i san-mei 隨自意三昧

Sun T'ai-ch'ing 孫太清

Sung-jen i-shih hui-pien 宋人軼事彙編

Sung Kao seng chuan 宋高僧傳

Sung-shan 嵩山

Sung-shih 宋史

Sung-yüan Ch'ung-yüeh 松源崇岳

Sung-yüan Yüeh Ch'an-shih yü 松源岳禪師語

Synopsis 大意

Ta-chi ching 大集經

Ta-chih-tu-lun 大智度論

Ta-fang-kuang-fo hua-yen ching 大方廣佛華嚴經

Ta-hsien fang 大仙方

Ta-hui P'u-chüeh Ch'an-shih nien-p'u 大慧普覺禪師年譜

Ta-hui shu 大慧書

Ta-hui Tsung-kao 大慧宗杲

Ta-i-chu 大邑主

Ta-lo 大羅

Ta-ning 大寧

Ta-T'ang chung-hsing 大唐中興

Ta-t'ang liu-tien 大唐六典

Ta-tsu 大祖

Ta-t'ung tien 大同殿

Tai (a mountain) 岱

Tai (a generation, era) 代

T'ai-ch'ing kung 太清宮

T'ai-miao 太廟

T'ai-p'ing-ching 太平經

T'ai-shang hsüan-yüan huang-ti 太上玄元皇帝

T'ai-shang hsüan-yüan huang-ti miao 太上玄元皇帝廟

T'ai-wei kung 太微宮

Taishō Shinshū Daizōkyō 大正新修大藏經

T'an-ching 曇靜

T'an-hsüan-chi 探玄記

T'an-luan 曇鸞

T'an-luan Fa-shih Fu-ch'i Fa 曇鸞法師服氣法

T'an-yao 曇曜

T'ang ssu hsing che 堂司行者

T'ang Ssu-t'ui 湯思退

Tao-ch'eng 道誠

Tao-chieh 道誡

Tao-chü 道舉

Tao-hsüan 陶弘景

T'ao Hung-ching 道宣
Tao-sheng 道生
Tao Shih 道士
Te ch'ing-ching p'ing-teng wu-wei
　fa-shen 得清淨平等無爲法身
Te Ch'ung Fu 德充符
Te fa-shen 得法身
Te Tao 得道
Ten mental states (attitudes, modes)
　十乘觀法
Ten objects of contemplation 十境
Tendai Shikan no Kenkyū 天台止觀
　の研究
T'eng 藤
Ti chü 地居
Ti-hsia 禘祫
Ti-tsang P'u-sa pen yüan ching 地藏
　菩薩本願經
T'i-wei Po-li Ching 提謂波利經
T'ien-pao 天寶
T'ien-t'ai, Tendai 天台
T'ien-t'ung Ju-ching Ch'an-shih yü-lu
　天童如淨禪師語錄
Ting 定
Ting Ping 丁丙
To tzai i-pien 墮在一邊
Tongbang sasang nonch'ong 東方思
　想論叢
Tsa-hsing 雜行
Tsan A-mi-t'o fo chi 讚阿彌陀佛偈
Tsan-ning 贊寧
Tsao-chieh chiang-ching shou-tso
　左街講經首座
Ts'ao-tung 曹洞
Tso yu-i shih 作有義事
Tsu-yung 祖詠
Tsuizen 追善
Tsung-cheng ssu 宗正寺
Ts'ung-i 從義
Tsung-kao 宗杲
Ts'ung-lin chiao-ting ch'ing-kuei
　tsung-yao 叢林較定清規總要
Ts'ung-mi 宗密
Tu seng-cheng 都僧正
T'u-t'an chai 塗炭齋
Tui ping, shih yüan 對病識緣

Tung 動
T'ung-hui Ta-shih 通慧大師
Tung-shan Hui-k'ung Ch'an-shih
　yü-lu 東山慧空禪師語錄
Tung-shan Kuei-tsung 東山歸宗
Twenty-five expedients 二十五方便
Tzu 字
Tzu-chi kung 紫極宮
Tzu-jan chai 自然齋
Tz'u tuan ta-shih yin-yüan 此段大事
　因緣
Tzu-wei 紫微

Wang Chia-na 王家訥
Wang Ch'u-na 王處訥
Wang-sheng 往生
Wang-sheng-chuan 往生傳
Wang-sheng Li-tsan 往生禮讚
Wang-sheng-lun-chu 往生論註
Wang Yü-ch'eng 王禹稱
Wei 微
Wei-ching 僞經
Wei Hsüan-chieh Ta-shih 魏玄簡大士
Wei Li She-jen P'u-shuo 爲李舍人普説
Wei no 維那
Wen-hsüan-wang 文宣王
Wen-hu 文虎
Wen-i 文益
Wen-ke 文格
Wen Tzu 文子
Wu 物
Wu (emperor of Liang) 梁武帝
Wu-ai Hui 無礙會
Wu-chiao-chang 五教章
Wu-chieh pen-ch'i-ching 五戒本起經
Wu-chien 無間
Wu-en 晤恩
Wu-hsin 無心
Wu-i (no difference) 無異
Wu-i (inconceivable) 無意
Wu, K'ung, li, hsing 無空理性
Wu-liang chih 無量智
Wu-liang-shou Ching Yu-p'o-t'i-she
　Yüan-sheng chi-chu 無量壽經優
　波提舍願生偈註
Wu-liang-shou fo 無量壽佛

Wu-lin chiu shih 武林舊事
Wu-lin chuang ku ts'ung pien 武林掌
　故叢編
Wu-lin Hsi-hu kao seng shih lüeh
　武林西湖高僧事略
Wu-lin Ling-yin szu chih 武林靈隱
　寺誌
Wu-shih 無識
Wu-tsu Fa-yen 五祖法演
Wu-tung 無動
Wu-wei 無爲
Wu-Yüeh 吳越

Yaku-chū Zen-en shin-gi 訳註禅苑
　清規
Yanagida Seizan 柳田聖山
Yang ch'i 楊岐
Yang Kuo-chung 楊國忠
Ye ma 野馬
Yin 陰
Yin-fen 因分
Yin Hsi 尹喜
Yin-tz'u 音辭
Yin-yüan ti 因緣地
Ying-an T'an-hua 應安曇華
Yu-hsin 有心

Yü-lu 語錄
Yu shih chung shuo san chieh 有十種
　説三界
Yüan-cheng 願證
Yuan-chi-hsiang-yu 緣起相由
Yüan-chüeh-ching 圓覺經
Yüan-jen-lun 原人論
Yüan-ming 圓明
Yüan-shih t'ien-tsun 元始天尊
Yüan-wu Fo-kuo Ch'an-shih yu-lu
　圓悟佛果禪師語錄
Yüan-wu K'o-ch'in 圓悟克勤
Yüeh-ling 月令
Yün-chi Ch'i-ch'ien 雲笈七籤
Yün-men 雲門
Yung 用
Yung-ch'ang Ts'ung-i 永常從義
Yung-ch'iu 雍丘

Zenke Goroku 禅家語錄
Zenke no sōhō to tsuizen kuyō no
　kenkyū 禅家の葬法と追善供養の
　研究
Zenrin shōkisen 禅林象器箋
Zokuzōkyō 續藏經

Contributors

Charles Benn received his Ph.D. in Chinese history from the University of Michigan in 1977. His revised dissertation should soon be published by Asian Humanities Press. He is also engaged in translating the *Tao-chiao ling-yen chi,* a collection of records concerning Taoist miracles. His other projects include a study of a rare eighth-century account of a Taoist ordination for two royal princesses and research on the *Tso-wang lun,* a Taoist treatise on meditation by Ssu-ma Ch'eng-chen (647–735). He has taught at the University of Arizona, and is currently teaching at the University of Hawaii.

David W. Chappell, a professor of religion at the University of Hawaii, did his doctoral studies at Yale University on the Chinese Pure Land pioneer Tao-ch'o (562–645). He is founding editor of the annual journal *Buddhist-Christian Studies* and recently edited *T'ien-t'ai Buddhism: An Outline of the Fourfold Teachings.* Currently he is pursuing further T'ien-t'ai research.

Roger J. Corless is an associate professor of religion at Duke University. He holds a B.D. from King's College, University of London, and received his Ph.D. in Buddhist studies from the University of Wisconsin with, in lieu of an M.A., a minor in history of religions through the University of Chicago. He has published articles on Buddhism, especially Pure Land Buddhism, and on Buddhist-Christian studies, and two books intended to refresh the Christian contemplative tradition by the incorporation of Buddhist materials: *The Art of Christian Alchemy* and *I Am Food: The Mass in Planetary Perspective.*

Albert A. Dalia received his Ph.D. from the University of Hawaii in Chinese history. His research interests include Chinese Buddhist social history, regional history, religious geography, the biographical study of the Chinese Buddhist clergy and laity. He is completing a book-length manuscript on the Ch'an Ox-head Master Fa-jung (594–657).

Neal Donner received his Ph.D. from the University of British Columbia for a closely annotated translation of major portions of Chih-i's classic the *Mo-ho-chih-kuan* (Great concentration and insight). His translation (with S. Iida) of Yensho Kanakura's *Indo-tetsugaku-shi* has been published as *Hindu-Buddhist Thought in India.* Current interests center on the resemblances between the ideas of spontaneity and freedom in the modern Austrian (free market) school of economics, on the one hand, and in ancient Chinese Buddhism and Taoism, on the other.

Whalen W. Lai is an associate professor at the University of California, Davis, having received his doctorate on the *Awakening of Faith* at Harvard University in comparative religion. He has studied in Asia, America, and Europe, and published over forty articles on a wide variety of themes in Chinese Buddhism and comparative thought. Currently he is doing Buddhist-Christian research at Tubingen University and has a book-length manuscript on the rise of Chinese Buddhism (third to sixth centuries) as part of a projected trilogy.

Miriam Levering is associate professor of religious studies at the University of Tennessee. She is the editor of *Rethinking Scripture,* an effort to open up fresh perspectives on the global phenomenon of relating to texts as "sacred." Her research interests are in the fields of Chinese Ch'an Buddhism, Sung dynasty cultural history, and contemporary Buddhist practice. She is currently at work on a translation and interpretive study of the "Daily Office" rituals of Chinese convents and monasteries.

Julian Pas was born in Belgium and studied theology at the University of Louvain. He also studied Chinese language and culture in Taiwan and obtained his Ph.D. in Asian religions at McMaster University, Canada. Since 1969 he has been teaching at the University of Saskatchewan, where he is a professor of religious studies. He has published a dozen articles on Chinese religion and is now preparing several book manuscripts on Taoism and Chinese popular religion.

Jae-ryong Shim is an associate professor at Seoul National University. He received his Ph.D. from the University of Hawaii and has taught in the philosophy department at S.N.U. since 1979. His primary research interests center on Buddhist philosophy and the paradigmatic changes of Asian ideology in Korean history. He has published articles related to Asian philosophy in general, especially on Zen Buddhism in Korea.

Robert B. Zeuschner received his Ph.D. in Buddhist philosophy from the University of Hawaii. He served as director of Buddhist studies at the Institute for Transcultural Studies and has taught in the department of philosophy at the University of Southern California, at the University of California at Santa Barbara, and at Occidental College in Los Angeles. His primary research interests are Chinese Taoism and Buddhism, with special emphasis on the development of Buddhist thought as Buddhism moved from India to China to Japan. He is currently at work on a text on Taoism.

Index

Amitābha, 16–17, 192; as Bodhisattva
Dharmākara, 39; for Shan-tao, 67, 70–
81; for T'an-luan, 38–40
Amitāyus. *See* Amitābha
Antiperfections, 53, 55, 58
Avalokiteśvara (Kuan-yin), 38, 78
Avataṁsaka (Hua-yen) Sutra, 88, 95, 109–
122 passim; support for Ch'an preaching
to laity, 189–190
Awakening. *See* Enlightenment
*Awakening of Faith in the Mahāyāna (Ta-
ch'eng Ch'i-hsin lun or Ch'i-hsin lun),*
33n.8, 88–89

Bodhidharma, 86
Bodhiruci, 36–37, 42
Brahma Net Sutra, 18, 20
Buddhahood. *See* Enlightenment
Buddhism: Buddhist-Taoist synthesis, 23–
25, 30; relations with Taoism and Confu-
cianism, 148–153; teacher important in,
28. *See also* Ch'an; Enlightenment;
Faith; Hua-yen; Invocation of the Bud-
dha's name; Karma; Laity; Meditation;
Practice; Pure Land; Rituals; *Saṅgha;
Śīla;* State-*saṅgha* relations

Ch'an (Korean, Sŏn), 16–17, 109, 114, 119–
122; Lin-chi, 181; Northern Ch'an meditation, 97–105; Northern Ch'an texts,
65–97; Northern-Southern controversy,
85, 149; regulations *(Ch'an-yüan ch'ing-
kuei),* 183–184; sermon on death, 190–
198. *See also* Fo-yen Ch'ing-yuan; *Hua-*

t'ou; Kung-an; P'u-shuo sermons; Ta-hui
Tsung-kao; Yüan-wu
Chan-jan, 52–53, 56–58
Ch'an-yüan ch'ing-kuei (Ch'an regula-
tions), 183–184
Ch'en, Kenneth, 1, 11, 169
Chen-jen (Taoist Perfected One), 139–141
Ch'i (breath), 37; three primordial *ch'i,*
130
Chieh-ching (preceptual scriptures), 17–19
Chih-hui. See Wisdom
Chih-i, T'ien-t'ai (538–597), 3, 49–64, 72,
117; comprehensive writings, 146–148,
150; family ties to the elite, 159. *See also*
Three truths
*Ch'i-hsin lun. See Awakening of Faith in
the Mahāyāna*
Chinul, Pojo (1158–1210), 109, 121–122,
122–123n.2, 123n.3
Chung-i (Wu-Yüeh king), 157–161, 163,
166, 170
Confession (Buddhist), 20, 27, 76–78
Confucianism: Buddhist relations, 150–
151, 153, 167; funerals, 191; in Sung
times, 147. *See also* Five Confucian virtues

Death: Ch'an sermons on, 190–198; empti-
ness of birth and death, 195–196. *See also*
Immortality
Dharmadhātu, 116–118, 123n.3
Dharmakāya, 5, 41, 88, 95, 114
Dreams: about Lao Tzu, 127–128, 141n.1;
142n.2

219

Asian Studies at Hawaii

No. 1   *Bibliography of English Language Sources on Human Ecology, Eastern Malaysia and Brunei.* Compiled by Conrad P. Cotter with the assistance of Shiro Saito. September 1965. Two parts. (Available only from Paragon Book Gallery, New York.)

No. 2   *Economic Factors in Southeast Asian Social Change.* Edited by Robert Van Niel. May 1968. Out of print.

No. 3   *East Asian Occasional Papers (1).* Edited by Harry J. Lamley. May 1969.

No. 4   *East Asian Occasional Papers (2).* Edited by Harry J. Lamley. July 1970.

No. 5   *A Survey of Historical Source Materials in Java and Manila.* Robert Van Niel. February 1971.

No. 6   *Educational Theory in the People's Republic of China: The Report of Ch'ien Chung-Jui.* Translated by John N. Hawkins. May 1971. Out of print.

No. 7   *Hai Jui Dismissed from Office.* Wu Han. Translated by C. C. Huang. June 1972.

No. 8   *Aspects of Vietnamese History.* Edited by Walter F. Vella. March 1973.

No. 9   *Southeast Asian Literatures in Translation: A Preliminary Bibliography.* Philip N. Jenner. March 1973.

No. 10   *Textiles of the Indonesian Archipelago.* Garrett and Bronwen Solyom. October 1973. Out of print.

No. 11   *British Policy and the Nationlist Movement in Burma, 1917–1937.* Albert D. Moscotti. February 1974.

No. 12   *Aspects of Bengali History and Society.* Edited by Rachel Van M. Baumer. December 1975.

No. 13   *Nanyang Perspective: Chinese Students in Multiracial Singapore.* Andrew W. Lind. June 1974.

232

Orders for Asian Studies at Hawaii publications should be directed to the University of Hawaii Press, 2840 Kolowalu Street, Honolulu, Hawaii 96822. Present standing orders will continue to be filled without special notification.